The People's Government

The People's Government is premised on the idea that democracy is based on two fundamental rights: freedom and liberty. Many believe these rights are synonymous, but they are actually complementary opposites. Liberty is the right to be left alone, whereas freedom is the right to participate in a political community. How people view democracy depends on which of these two rights they think is more important. Liberal democrats place a higher value on liberty; free democrats see freedom as the primary right.

From this starting point, the author adds five dimensions to define and distinguish democratic societies: rights, participation and representation, inclusion, equality, and power. Liberal democracies tend to emphasize individualism, negative rights, representative government, inclusive citizenship, equal opportunity, and limited government. Free democracies stress community, positive rights, direct participation, exclusive citizenship, equal outcomes, and robust government.

Next, the book examines the most important arguments for and against democracy and explores the life cycle of democracies – how countries democratize, mature, and fail. Finally, the author uses the five dimensions established earlier to evaluate and grade American democracy.

Del Dickson is a professor of political science and international relations at the University of San Diego. He especially enjoys teaching Introduction to Political Science, Constitutional Law, Judicial Behavior, and Comparative Law. He has earned numerous teaching awards and was recently named one of the 300 best professors in the United States by Princeton Review. He received his BA in Political Science at Humboldt State, his JD at UCLA, and his PhD in Political Science at USC. He clerked for Chief Justice Robert Gardner of the California Court of Appeal and practiced law at Sherman and Howard in Denver, Colorado. His book, *The Supreme Court in Conference (1940–1985)*, earned the Association of American Publishers award as the best book in Government and Political Science in 2001.

For Ann

The People's Government

An Introduction to Democracy

DEL DICKSON

University of San Diego

CAMBRIDGE
UNIVERSITY PRESS

32 Avenue of the Americas, New York, NY 10013-2473, USA

Cambridge University Press is part of the University of Cambridge.

It furthers the University's mission by disseminating knowledge in the pursuit of education, learning, and research at the highest international levels of excellence.

www.cambridge.org
Information on this title: www.cambridge.org/9781107619555

© Del Dickson 2014

First published 2014

Printed in the United States of America

A catalog record for this publication is available from the British Library.

Library of Congress Cataloging in Publication data
Dickson, Del.
The people's government : an introduction to democracy / Del Dickson,
University of San Diego.
    pages cm
Includes bibliographical references and index.
ISBN 978-1-107-04387-9 (hardback) – ISBN 978-1-107-61955-5 (paperback)
1. Democracy.   2. Freedom.   3. Liberty.   4. Democracy – United States.
5. United States – Politics and government.   I. Title.
JC423.D624   2014
321.8–dc23   2014001778

ISBN 978-1-107-04387-9 Hardback
ISBN 978-1-107-61955-5 Paperback

Contents

Acknowledgments

Thanks to Noelle Norton and Mike Williams of the University of San Diego for their support, ideas, and good-natured abuse. I am grateful to the USD College of Arts and Sciences for its continuing commitment to undergraduate liberal arts education. Thanks to my students, who make teaching a joy. Thanks to my parents, Bill and Margie; my sister Jackie; my brother Kevin; and my sister Janice, because they are great. My biggest thanks go to my wife, Ann, for her help and encouragement, but mostly for her willingness to put up with me. Thanks to JoJo and Sam for their unwavering enthusiasm and moral support. I owe a debt to Mark Kann and Robin Romans for planting the seeds for this book long ago. Finally, thanks to Ian Zell for his original illustrations.

Prologue

The premise of this book is that liberty and freedom are the two source rights from which other political rights are derived, and democracy is the only form of government that gives both of these rights their due. But what sort of democracy best promotes liberty, freedom, and other associated rights? That is an interesting question, and it has more than one good answer.

I

Liberty and Freedom

Americans do not need to be convinced that democracy is a good thing. There has been a national consensus about the virtues of self-government since 1620, when the Mayflower Compact became the Plymouth Colony's founding social contract. The birth of American democracy goes even farther back, to the Iroquois, who established a sophisticated democratic confederacy a hundred years before the Europeans arrived.

If America's long-standing attachment to democracy has a downside, it is that too many people take it for granted. Most Americans never give democracy a thought, beyond dragging themselves to the polls every few years and trying to get out of jury duty.

Over the last century, democracy has become a global phenomenon. It is now fashionable for politicians everywhere to promote democracy in glowing, even messianic terms. Almost every country in the world claims to be democratic, although most must be thankful that their claims are not subject to truth-in-advertising laws.[1]

These are heady times for political leaders who claim to love democracy, but perilous for ordinary people who actually believe in it. In many countries, those who take democracy seriously run the risk of official harassment, persecution, prison, and worse.

---

[1] Saudi Arabia, an autocratic monarchy controlled by the Al-Saud dynasty, is the major exception. A few other smaller states, such as Brunei, remain unapologetically undemocratic. In 2005, Saudi Arabia took its first tentative steps toward democratization when the regime held unprecedented nonpartisan municipal elections. The elections were largely for show. Suffrage and contestation were strictly limited to Muslim men, elected officials had no real power, and no political parties were allowed to organize or contest elections. A second round of municipal elections, originally scheduled for 2009, was repeatedly postponed until September 2011. The third round of municipal elections is currently scheduled for 2015, and the Saudi government has hinted that women might be allowed to vote this time.

Even in developed democracies, public officials routinely disregard basic democratic principles in the name of security, order, efficiency, and expediency. Politicians praise democracy to the skies in public while working quietly in private to subvert it. Like termites, the damage that they do is largely unseen, but if left unchecked, all that eventually remains is a hollow democracy, with a thin veneer of formal public accountability that barely conceals the rot underneath.

Despite these challenges, American identity and ego are inseparably wrapped up in democracy. This has led to two fundamental misperceptions about republican government: that Americans invented it, and that American democracy is the only model worthy of serious consideration.

Most Americans would agree with Pericles that "[o]ur system of government does not copy the systems of our neighbors; we are a model to them, not they to us."[2] Such pride is understandable but counterproductive.

We need to think critically about democracy and consider alternative approaches to popular government. By understanding how democracy works, and seeing the different forms that it takes, we can reexamine our own system to strengthen what works, fix what is broken, and improve what we can. The American tree of liberty might not need to be regularly refreshed with the blood of tyrants and patriots, but it still requires care if it is to continue to shelter future generations.

KEY TERMS

Liberty and Freedom

Ask any American to define liberty, and chances are they will give you a pretty good definition of liberty. Ask any American to define freedom, and chances are they will give you a pretty good definition of liberty. Like most people who live in a liberal democracy, Americans tend to conflate these two distinct rights.

Liberty is the right to think and speak one's mind, to follow one's conscience, and to make independent decisions about one's own life without undue external interference. It is the right to be an autonomous individual, whose thoughts and beliefs are unrestricted, and whose actions are limited by reason, conscience, consent, and the rule of law.

Freedom is the right to participate in politics. It is the right to deliberate, decide, and act with others as part of a political community.

Liberty is a natural right, in that it exists apart from state and society. States can recognize, respect, limit, or destroy liberty, but they do not grant it in the

---

[2] Thucydides, *Pericles' Funeral Oration*.

first instance. All one needs to do to secure liberty is to move away from other people and beyond the reach of government.

Hermits and wild animals have liberty, but only people who live in a well-ordered political community can have freedom. Freedom is a human invention that cannot exist apart from society and government. Freedom is a right people grant to each other when they join together to form a political commonwealth.

Liberty and freedom are the two great pillars of democracy. They are the metarights from which other political rights are derived. They are discrete concepts, yet complement and complete each other. Liberty is the right to be left alone; freedom is the right to be included. Liberty is an individual right; freedom is about community. Liberty finds its purest form in the realm of thought; freedom belongs to the realm of action. It is common to have liberty without freedom, and possible to have freedom without liberty, but the official democracy owner's manual does not recommend either option.

Power, Politics, and State

Power is the ability to get people to do something they would not have done otherwise. Most forms of power are at least implicitly coercive: obedience is based on fear of the perceived consequences of noncompliance.

There are some exceptions to the rule of coercive power.[3] The most important form of noncoercive power is *authority*, which is legitimate power.[4] People comply with an authoritative order because they have internalized the source and content of the order and subjectively accept that it *should* be obeyed. They yield voluntarily, though not necessarily happily.

In the motion picture *The Wizard of Oz*, the Gale family surrenders Toto to the malevolent Miss Gulch, not out of fear, but because she has a signed a legal document authorizing her to take the plucky terrier. The Gales obey the law because they believe that it is the right thing to do, even though it goes against their interests – and Toto's, too.

[3] In his essay, "Of The First Principles of Government," Scottish Enlightenment theorist David Hume identified five forms of political power and obedience: (1) interest, (2) opinion of utility and necessity (that is, the apparent interests and necessities of human society), (3) habitual sense of obligation (i.e., authority), (4) force, and (5) influence (e.g., the state offers rewards for obedience). Hume, David, *Essays, Moral, Political, and Literary*. Machiavelli might have added a sixth category: trick or deception.

[4] Max Weber, *Economy and Society* (2 vols., University of California Press 1978). Weber identified three distinct types of political authority: *traditional* (voluntary compliance based on customary power relationships among individuals, such as the mutual sense of duty between a feudal lord and vassal), *charismatic* (voluntary obedience based on a leader's personality), and *legal-rational* (voluntary obedience based on the internalization and subjective acceptance of established norms and principles).

Sidebar 1: The Politics of Oz

Some scholars see L. Frank Baum's *The Wonderful Wizard of Oz* as an allegory of American democracy.[5] Baum himself insisted that his book was just a fairy tale, but his protests did not stop speculation about possible hidden meanings in his classic story. Here are some of the more interesting theories:

DOROTHY GALE: An ordinary American, "simple, sweet, and true," and a stranger in a strange land. In Dorothy, Baum – the son-in-law of early feminist Matilda Joslyn Gage – created a new archetype of all-American heroine and the direct precursor of modern icons like Ellen Ripley and Buffy Summers.

YELLOW BRICK ROAD: The Gold Standard, presidential candidate William McKinley's monetary policy.

SILVER SHOES: The Silver Standard, favored by Populist Party presidential candidate William Jennings Bryan. The silver shoes can take Dorothy anywhere she wants to go, once she learns how to use them. The 1939 movie substituted ruby slippers, to show off MGM's new Technicolor film process.

THE COWARDLY LION: Presidential candidate and populist William Jennings Bryan.

THE TIN MAN: American labor – once fully human, turned piece by piece into a machine.

THE SCARECROW: American farmers.

THE WIZARD OF OZ AND GLENDA THE GOOD WITCH OF THE NORTH: charismatic and manipulative rulers who seek to use Dorothy for their own purposes.

THE EMERALD CITY: The golden road leads to the illusory paradise of paper money, or greenbacks.

FLYING MONKEYS: American Indians – primitive spirits, once free, but now captive and exploited. Baum's mother-in-law was an activist on Indian issues and an adopted member of the Mohawk Wolf Clan.

THE WICKED WITCHES OF THE EAST AND WEST: Eastern bankers and Western railroad companies.

TOTO: No one has come up with a plausible theory about the dog's political significance – feel free to make up your own.

---

[5] Henry Littlefield, "The Wizard of Oz: Parable on Populism," 16 *American Quarterly* 47 (1964); Gretchen Ritter, "Silver Slippers and a Golden Cap: L. Frank Baum's The Wonderful Wizard of Oz and Historical Memory in American Politics," 31 *Journal of American Studies* 171 (1997); Bradley A. Hansen, "The Fable of the Allegory: The Wizard of Oz in Economics," 33 *Journal of Economic Education* 254 (2002).

Authority is the Holy Grail, the Maltese Falcon, the melange, and the Precious of politics, all wrapped into one. It is so highly prized because governing is much easier when people comply voluntarily, rather than being compelled to submit through force or fear.[6]

Politics is the theory and practice of power. One standard definition is who gets what, when, how, and why. But this is only half of the equation. Politics also has a behavioral dimension: who *does* what, when, how, and why. Combining these approaches, one material and one behavioral, politics is how power is organized and used to allocate resources and regulate human activity.

The ultimate form of organized political power is the *state*. A state consists of an ordered hierarchical society, with a clear geographical border that separates it from all other societies, where leaders are distinguished from ordinary people or citizens, and with a government that has a monopoly on the authoritative use of violence.[7] States are not the only source of political power, but they are the strongest and most pervasive form of institutionalized power.

WHO SHOULD RULE?

The Tyranny of Scarce Resources

For the foreseeable future, our lives will remain subject to the power of states. Accordingly, one of the most important questions to consider is, who should be in charge of the state – who should rule? The best answer to this question depends on many variables, but the most important single factor involves a basic assumption about resources – the essential goods that makes life possible.

Conventional political wisdom assumes that these resources are scarce; that there are not enough essential goods and services to go around. Politics is how societies determine who wins and who loses in the competition for scarce resources, knowing that some people *have* to lose.

This conception of politics is closely related to economics, but the two are not synonymous. Both begin with the assumption of scarce resources, but differ in how the competition for resources plays out.

Economists look to market forces to allocate scarce resources. They use cost-benefit analysis to understand how the process works, and either assume or advocate rational and efficient resource allocation through markets. An efficient system allocates scarce goods according to their "highest use," meaning that resources go (and *should* go) to those who are willing to pay the highest price in a free market exchange. You might notice a subtle bias there.

---

[6] Another example of noncoercive power is money. One of the most effective ways to get people to do something they would not otherwise do is to pay them.
[7] Max Weber, *Economy and Society*.

Political scientists study resource allocation through the prism of power. They look first to elite decision making, rather than to market forces, to understand how this works. Who gets what, when, and how is based primarily on power differentials among competing individuals and groups. Political scientists expect this to be a messy process. Reason and rationality have their place, but so do will, desire, passion, greed, hypocrisy, and corruption. Most political scientists assume that the authoritative allocation of resources is, and always will be, at least somewhat irrational, contradictory, volatile, inefficient, unfair, exploitative, corrupt, and brutal.

The Merry-Go-Round of Politics

If we accept for now the assumption that politics is about how communities organize the struggle for scarce resources, then there are three broad answers to the question of who rules: the one, the few, or the many. Each of these has two iterations: a moderate form and a corrupt form. The one can rule as a monarch or a tyrant, the few can rule as an aristocracy or an oligarchy, and the many can rule either as a democracy or a mob.

Aristotle's Ring Cycle[8]

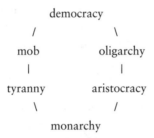

More than two millennia ago, the ancient Greeks understood politics to be a no-holds-barred competition for scarce resources, where the stakes are literally life or death. This makes political power inherently unstable, as different groups struggle for control and survival. States, governments, and rulers come and go as power flows from one group to another. Yet while instability and change are inevitable, the options concerning who is in charge remain perpetually limited to the six choices listed here.

Governments, states, and civilizations come and go, yet nothing truly new can happen. All societies are trapped in the same repeating loop of power, privilege, and privation, where the winners rule and enjoy the spoils while the losers suffer in poverty and want. When the one or the few are in charge, the

---

[8] Borrowed from composer Richard Wagner's epic "Ring Cycle," *The Ring of the Nibelung*. Both ring cycles seem endless, their plots do not always make sense, and lots of people die for no good reason.

many are inevitably oppressed. When the many rule, the few must suffer. It is the world's worst merry-go-round.

Democracies are not exempt from the tyranny of scarce resources or the resulting competition, oppression, and instability. In a world with too little for everyone to share, the many must exploit the few in order to secure enough resources for themselves. Ancient Attica purchased its male citizens' unprecedented liberty and freedom with slavery and the exclusion of women from public life.

Two thousand years later, America's Founders likewise assumed that in order to enjoy their rights, someone else had to pay the price. Thomas Jefferson knew perfectly well that slavery was morally reprehensible and fundamentally irreconcilable with the spirit of his Declaration of Independence. Yet like the Athenians he so deeply admired, Jefferson believed that in order to have the time and resources he needed to be free, others, regrettably but inevitably, had to be kept in chains.

Getting off the Merry-Go-Round

As it turns out, the universal assumption that scarcity is the limiting constant of politics was wrong, or at least exaggerated. With the discovery of the New World and its vast store of natural resources, a new conception of politics developed that revolutionized modern politics, just as the leap from Aristotelian to Newtonian physics transformed the natural sciences. It gradually became apparent that essential goods might not be in critically short supply after all, and that long-standing assumptions about resource scarcity need not define or limit politics. This marked the liberation of politics from economics.

First in the New World, then in Europe, a new view of politics slowly emerged. If old assumptions about material scarcity can be overcome, or at least dealt with creatively, then poverty, deprivation, and endless class warfare are not inevitable. Politics can become an inclusive, civilized, and even cooperative enterprise – an administrative puzzle to solve, rather than an existential struggle with no exit. In a world with enough essential resources to go around, politics can be a game that everyone can play, and if not everyone can win equally, at least no one has to lose everything.

With this revolutionary redefinition of politics, two new possibilities emerged to answer the question of who should rule: *everyone* should rule, or *no one* should rule. The former led to modern democratic theory, whereas the latter inspired social anarchism[9] and communism.[10] All of these theories were premised on the radical new idea that there are enough essential resources for everyone, if politics can just be made to work properly.

---

[9] Most notably Mikhail Bakunin, Peter Kropotkin, and P. J. Proudhon.
[10] Including Karl Marx, Friedrich Engels, V. I. Lenin, Rosa Luxemburg, Eduard Bernstein, and Karl Kautsky.

Equal Rights as a Birthright

The catalyst for this radical reconception of politics was the Enlightenment and the systematic, semi-scientific study of history. The brightest light of the Scottish Enlightenment, David Hume, concluded that human experience had at last provided enough examples of different political systems to understand empirically the political life cycle – how governments worked, and more importantly, how they failed. In the United States, Alexander Hamilton called this the science of politics.[11]

Rather than naively dreaming of utopia or glumly assuming that class warfare is inevitable, Americans sought to use the new science of politics to distill objective principles of good government, in order to establish the world's first stable federal republic – a *novus ordo seclorum*.[12] America was the first democratic state founded on the promise that equal political and legal rights are a birthright, and American history has been the story of trying to live up to that promise.

Beautiful Choices

The liberation of politics from economics means that, at least in relatively prosperous countries, politics can transcend the grim task of sorting out society's winners and losers. Political decisions are no longer strictly limited by scarcity and necessity, but can include what Aristotle called "beautiful" or "free" choices.

Beautiful choices are the options that people have once their survival needs are met. By definition, beautiful choices are not necessary to sustain life; they make life more pleasant, enjoyable, and rewarding.

New horizons open when communities can make beautiful choices. Once everyone's basic needs are secure, what should we do with our spare time and treasure? Establish new parks and wilderness lands? Build public schools? Promote the arts? Add bike lanes to local streets? Provide health and child care for working families? Build rockets to explore the universe? Cut taxes and give money back to taxpayers? These are all beautiful choices.

---

[11] Alexander Hamilton, *The Federalist Papers*, No. 9. Hamilton closely followed Hume's essay, "That Politics May Be Reduced to a Science." Both favored the quasi-empirical, "scientific" study of history as the best way to discover why previous regimes failed, and the best way to establish rigorous principles of good government. This was a novel approach at the time, and they claimed that their approach yielded wisdom unavailable to the ancients. Hume and Hamilton believed that the science of politics would allow governments to be designed like an engineering or architectural project, and that these new, scientific principles would provide long-term stability and avoid the "perpetual vibration" between tyranny and anarchy that had long plagued previous governments, especially democracies.

[12] "A new order of the ages." The quote, often attributed to Virgil, was first included on the reverse of the Great Seal of the United States in 1782. More than a century later, in 1935, Franklin D. Roosevelt resurrected the motto and placed it on the back of the dollar bill as a symbol of the New Deal.

All of this allows for a new, post-materialist dimension of politics that extends, and perhaps transcends, Harold Lasswell's conventional definition. Post-materialist politics deals with how communities deliberate, decide, and act once the necessities of life are assured and people have spare time and resources to do as they please. Economics will always be the dismal science, but politics can be beautiful.

Democracy

Democracy means rule by the people. Political power originates with individuals, and is either exercised directly by them or is held in trust by their representatives in a responsive and accountable government. At a minimum, democracy means government by consent, where government officials must seek public approval at regular intervals to remain in power. There must be regular opportunities for public political participation, including the right to take part in the periodic, free, fair, and transparent selection of most important government officials.

In a democracy there are no permanent classes of rulers and subjects. Citizens take turns ruling and being ruled.[13] This is what Abraham Lincoln meant when he wrote, "As I would not be a slave, so I would not be a master. This expresses my idea of democracy. Whatever differs from this, to the extent of the difference, is no democracy."[14]

Lincoln later articulated a more elegant definition of democracy as *government of the people, by the people, and for the people.* This is hardly the last word on what democracy is, but it is a good place to begin.

This book proposes different ways to think about democracy. Ideas vary widely, but can include any combination of the following characteristics: direct popular decision making, representative government, random selection of major public officials, direct or indirect elections, limited or near-universal adult suffrage, limited or open contestation rights for offices, powerful or limited government, unitary or federal government, accountable government, government by consent, transparent government, responsive government, a government responsible for safeguarding popular rights and liberties, government based on the rule of law, and government premised on the routine peaceful transfer of power among competing factions according to popular will.

[13] Hannah Arendt, *On Revolution.*
[14] Abraham Lincoln, "On Slavery and Democracy." Lincoln scribbled these words on a scrap of paper in August 1858, apparently in response to the Kansas-Nebraska Act, which he had opposed. Mary Todd Lincoln saved the fragment and later gave it to the pioneering lawyer Myra Bradwell, after Bradwell helped secure Mrs. Lincoln's discharge from a sanatorium in 1875.

2

Freedom or Liberty?

Like beer, ice cream, and people, democracy comes in two basic types but an infinite variety of flavors. Which type one prefers depends on the answer to a deceptively simple question: which right is more important, freedom or liberty? Are people better off being an active part of a community, or making individual decisions on the basis of enlightened self-interest? *Free democracy* emphasizes freedom and community; *liberal democracy* stresses liberty and individualism. Free democrats long to belong; liberal democrats mostly just want to be left alone.

FREE DEMOCRACY

Free democracy begins with Aristotle's view that people are political animals. Our social nature leads us to seek the company of others, and to organize ourselves into communities on the basis of shared political, social, and economic interests. It is the same impulse that leads people to enjoy going to movie theaters, ball games, shopping malls, and using social media. If Aristotle was right, then freedom is not only essential to democracy; it is a central aspect of human nature.

In a free democracy, government is not merely accountable to the people; it *is* the people. Every eligible citizen is a legislator engaged in, and responsible for, collective decision making. With habitual popular participation in government, the gap between ruler and citizen virtually disappears.

Free democracy is catholic in spirit, centered on community and public life. Free democrats believe that it is only as an integral part of a good and just society that people can realize their individual and collective potential. Whereas some communities take pleasure in being together, a free community takes pleasure in doing things together. Politics in this context is a cooperative enterprise, a team sport where ultimately everyone is on the same team. Accordingly, free democracies sometimes go to great lengths to try to avoid factional infighting and partisanship, in favor of unity and communal harmony (Figure 2.1).

Curtis is slow to grasp the concept of community.

FIGURE 2.1 By permission of Jerry Van Amerongen and Creators Syndicate, Inc.

Despite emphasizing the virtues of community, most free democrats are equally committed to individual rights and liberties. They believe, however, that it takes a village for individuals to grow and flourish. Or put another way, a free community is like a forest where everything is interconnected, and only by tending to the overall health of the woodland will the individual trees be able to fully develop and prosper.

In a free democracy, liberty usually plays an important, but subordinate, role as freedom's sidekick. As the junior partner, liberty provides individuals with the privacy and quiet space they need to think, before they join with others to discuss, deliberate, and act. Although most free democracies value liberty, in the final analysis it is a means to a greater end.

The Athenians valued freedom over all other political rights. They had a word for people who are not interested in politics and public affairs – they called these people *idiotes*.

Pericles proclaimed the virtues of free democracy in his funeral oration in 430 BC.[1] At the ceremonial public funeral for Athens's war dead during the first year of the Peloponnesian War, Pericles spoke about what made Athens great:

---

[1] Athens held public funerals annually to honor its war dead. Pericles himself died the following year, during a devastating plague. Thucydides, *Pericles' Funeral Oration*.

We differ from other states in regarding the man who keeps aloof from public life not as 'private' but as useless. We decide or debate, carefully and in person, all matters of policy, and we hold, not that words and deeds go ill together, but that acts are foredoomed to failure when undertaken undiscussed.

In America, the spirit of free democracy animated the Mayflower Compact of 1620. The Pilgrims, following the democratic principles of Congregationalism, founded their new political community on a social contract drawn among equals:

> Having undertaken ... a Voyage to plant the First Colony in the Northern Parts of Virginia, (we) do ... mutually in the presence of God and one of another, Covenant and Combine ourselves together into a Civil Body Politic, for our better ordering and preservation ... (to) enact, constitute and frame such just and equal Laws, Ordinances, Acts, Constitutions and Offices, from time to time, as shall be thought most meet and convenient for the general good of the Colony: unto which we promise all due submission and obedience.[2]

Freedom spread throughout colonial New England in hundreds of townships, where all free male citizens had the right to participate in town meetings. Every man was a citizen-legislator and expected to be an active, informed, and responsible community member. But the township system did not spread far beyond New England, and after the American Revolution it gradually withered away there, so that, for the most part, only weak echoes of the old town meeting system remain today.

With the decline of the township system in the first half of the nineteenth century, the American res publica shrank, but never entirely disappeared. Direct democracy made something of a comeback during the Progressive era of the early twentieth century, when twenty-two states and the District of Columbia established new avenues for direct citizen participation through voter initiatives, propositions, and referenda. These reforms were – and remain – especially popular in the upper Midwest and far West. Some states adopted more limited versions of these new freedoms; Illinois, for example, permits only advisory citizen initiatives. All fifty states allow lawmakers to place issues on the ballot for voter approval.

The federal government never joined in these reforms, and there has never been a national mechanism for voter initiatives, propositions, or referenda. As a result, at the federal level, Americans have much liberty but little freedom.

Other modern examples of free democracy include the *gram panchayats* (grassroots village councils) of India, the *Landsgemeinde*[3] cantons in Switzerland (discussed below), the Scandinavian custom of seeking social consensus on important public policy decisions, African village meetings, and the Dutch polder model of democracy – the consensual decision-making process that originated with the Netherlands's need to coordinate complex public projects to reclaim land from the sea.

---

[2] (http://ia600202.us.archive.org/6/items/mayflowercompact00bow/mayflowercompact00bow.pdf)
[3] Landsgemeinde assemblies are open-air political gatherings, where all citizens of the canton (the Swiss equivalent of a state) have the right to attend in order to discuss and decide political questions affecting the canton, including constitutional amendments, laws, and the selection of cantonal officials. Eight of Switzerland's cantons originally had Landsgemeinde assemblies,

Sidebar 2: Polder Politics: The Democracy of Dry Feet[4]

In Holland they say that "God made the world, but the Dutch made the Netherlands." Polder democracy originated in the Netherlands during the Middle Ages, a product of the country's eternal fight against the sea. A *polder* is formerly submerged land that has been drained through a network of dikes, canals, and pumps (Holland's famous windmills powered the pumps for centuries). With more than a quarter of the country below sea level, creating and maintaining new polders has required extraordinary cooperation for more than 600 years. During the Middle Ages, even when rival cities went to war, they continued to cooperate to maintain their shared polders.

The necessity of close cooperation to maintain the polder system led the Dutch to develop strong, consensual democratic habits. Local residents share responsibility to make sure that their communities are safe from floods. Elected local water boards (*Waterschappen/Hoogheemraadschapp en*) are the oldest democratic institutions in the Netherlands, dating from the thirteenth century. They are charged with land reclamation, waterway maintenance, and sewage disposal. Local water boards supervise polder construction and maintenance, enforce water laws, and levy the taxes needed to keep the system going.

As Dutch historian Herman Pleij put it, "The Netherlands owes its existence to the democracy of dry feet. We need each other literally in order not to drown."

Free democracy is inherently optimistic about the possibilities of people power. It seeks to harness freedom to release a people's individual and collective will, so that they can realize their full potential. Some of the noteworthy political theorists most closely associated with freedom and free democracy are Pericles, Niccolo Machiavelli, Jean-Jacques Rousseau, Alexis de Tocqueville, Thomas Jefferson, and Hannah Arendt.

but one by one they dropped the practice, because of population growth and alleged concerns about citizen privacy (votes are traditionally by a public show of hands, rather than by secret ballot). Today, the Landsgemeinde system survives in just two small, rural cantons: Appenzell-Innerrhoden and Glarus. The Appenzell-Innerrhoden assembly is discussed in the next chapter. Although most of Switzerland's cantons have abandoned their assemblies, many municipalities still hold periodic town meetings, especially in the French- (*assemblee communale*) and German- (*gemeindeversammlung*) speaking regions.

[4] Herman Pleij, *Hollands Welbehagen* (*The Well-being of Holland*) (Ooievaar 1998); Yda Schreuder, "The Polder Model in Dutch Economic and Environmental Planning," 21 *Bulletin of Science, Technology & Society* 237 (2001); Frank Hendriks and Th. A. J. Toonen, *Polder Politics: The Re-invention of Consensus Democracy in the Netherlands* (Ashgate Press 2001).

Some problems commonly identified with free democracy include:

1. *General Will and Compelled Consensus.* Rousseau's idea of autonomous free communities ruled by consensus, or general will, is attractive in theory but problematic in practice.

   The desire to maintain social harmony and avoid factional infighting is perfectly understandable. After the American Revolution, George Washington and other Founders sought to establish a nonpartisan, consensus-driven political system without any organized political parties. Their hopes did not survive Washington's first term, as Hamilton and Jefferson quickly squared off to found the rival Federalist and Democratic-Republican parties, ending the brief American idyll of nonpartisan cooperation.

   In a few places the idea of a nonpartisan political system lives on – barely. Nebraska and the Swiss Canton of Appenzell-Innerrhoden are among the last remaining examples of nominally nonpartisan legislatures among developed democracies.[5]

   To critics, the dream of a consensus-based political system is worse than a hollow hope; it is a dangerous delusion. As Madison explained, factions are a natural condition of human society. They are an unavoidable consequence of liberty and individualism, and can be eliminated only by removing one or both of these root causes. The problem, as Madison pointed out, is that eradicating either liberty or individualism would defeat the whole point of republican government.

   It is relatively easy to eliminate faction by destroying liberty. This is what tyrants always do, so that they can rule without fear of challenge or dissent.

   Eliminating individualism is more difficult, because it requires changing human nature to make everyone the same. Utilitarian theory holds that this is impossible, because human nature is immutable. But utilitarianism did not anticipate modern "scientific" totalitarian efforts by Stalin and Hitler to degrade and reconstruct human nature to match a desired ideal. Even though these attempts to create a homogeneous utopia failed, the consequences were horrific.

   Totalitarian dictators who seek to reshape human nature worship at the altar of Procrustes, the patron saint of conformity. They are not content merely to silence dissenters; they want to make them fit a common mold. As Winston Smith discovered in George Orwell's *1984*, ordinary dictators are usually satisfied when people are willing to say that two plus two equals five, when ordered to do so. Totalitarian leaders, however, demand that their subjects *believe* that two plus two equals five. The result is an extraordinarily oppressive society, in which the nail that sticks up is ruthlessly pounded down.

   It might seem unfair to blame Rousseau for later perversions of his ideas about community and general will – akin to blaming the Lumière brothers

---

[5] Several small South Pacific states have formally nonpartisan governments, including Nauru, Tuvalu, Micronesia, and Palau.

for *Plan Nine from Outer Space*. But Rousseau implicitly advocated the absorption of autonomous individual will into the collective consciousness of the community, so the criticism is not entirely unjustified.

2. *Homogeneity and Xenophobia.* Because free democracies place such a high value on community and social solidarity, they are inclined to favor cultural homogeneity. If the Procrustean method outlined above is off limits, two alternatives are to restrict immigration and/or citizenship rights in the hope that familiarity breeds content.

In part because of their strong communitarian impulses, free democracies tend to draw a bright line between citizens and everyone else. Think of a closely knit ethnic neighborhood, or a small resort town, where the locals know and treat each other like family, but view outsiders with suspicion and disdain.

Athenian citizenship laws were specifically designed to build and maintain an exclusive, homogeneous community. To be an Athenian citizen, both parents had to be citizens. There were no provisions for naturalization, and no alternative path to citizenship. This limited political rights to a small number of free men who were all drawn from the same limited gene pool.[6] Athens and the other Greek democracies were closed and insular societies; they constantly fought with each other, united only by their shared view that all non-Greeks were barbarians.

In modern Switzerland, free democracy survives in part because of the country's longstanding isolation, and because most Swiss cantons have historically had relatively small, stable, and homogeneous populations. Switzerland today is more populous and pluralistic than it used to be, but it remains instinctively insular, and is sensitive to perceived threats posed by outsiders. There is a widely shared perception that immigrants can never be truly Swiss, and that they threaten to undermine Swiss identity, social cohesion, and stability. This suspicion is not limited to foreigners; within Switzerland, most of the French-speaking, Italian-speaking, and German-speaking cantons retain their distinct linguistic and cultural identities, even after hundreds of years of confederation. All of this results in a residual nativism – a latent desire to secure "Fortress Switzerland" as a closed and exclusive preserve. Switzerland's reflexive isolationism recently bubbled to the surface in 2009, when 58 percent of Swiss citizens approved a national referendum banning the construction of minarets, even though there were only four in the entire country.

There are some hopeful signs of change. Over the past half-century, Switzerland has gone from 5 percent of the population being foreign residents in the 1950s to more than 27 percent today.[7] Five cantons, including Neuchatel, Jura, and Geneva, have granted some foreign

---

[6] Athenian men were assigned to one of ten different "tribes," or *phylai*. These divisions were for administrative convenience only, and were not based on genealogical or ethnic differences.

[7] Most foreign residents are from Southern Europe, including large expatriate populations from Portugal, Italy, Greece, Spain, and Turkey.

residents local voting rights, and several other cantons have authorized
local authorities to do so if they wish.[8] These changes, however, have
sparked considerable public controversy.

3. *Demographic Mobility and Social Stability.* Like international immigration, internal migration and social fluidity can also undermine social
cohesion. As citizens become more mobile, once-stable communities tend
to fall apart as residents come and go with greater frequency. Transitory
populations mean neighborhoods of relative strangers, with few local
attachments and little stake in the community's long-term well-being. To
address these problems, some countries seek to control internal migration, either by limiting travel rights or compelling populations to settle in
specified locations. Russia, China, Tanzania, Burma, and Cambodia are
among the countries that have limited rural migration to urban centers,
and forced the relocation of urban populations to depopulated rural
zones, in quixotic attempts to stabilize urban and rural communities.

4. *Forced to Be Free.* Rousseau believed in the total commitment of the
individual to the community. The active participation of every citizen is
necessary to establish social consensus and the general will. This sort of
all-in commitment is so critical to Rousseau's vision that apathetic, alienated, and disaffected residents can be compelled to participate against
their will. This is what Rousseau meant when he said that people can be
forced to be free. To Rousseau's critics, this is a contradiction in terms –
or more precisely, it betrays a troubling willingness to sacrifice individual
liberty in favor of an overtly coercive political process.

5. *Loss of Liberty and Privacy.* A singular focus on freedom means that liberty
and privacy are, at best, secondary considerations. Because free democracies often grant government broad powers to promote the common good,
and almost anything anyone thinks or does affects the community in some
way, there is no clear limit to state power, and no bright line dividing the
public and private realms. Some free democrats are coolly indifferent to
individual liberty; others are overtly hostile to the idea that individuals
have private lives and interests that lie beyond the community's reach.[9]

[8] Liberal democracies are, in theory, less concerned about immigrants than free democracies. In
practice, liberal democracies are not immune to fits of xenophobia. California voters, for example, overwhelmingly passed Proposition 187 in 1994, limiting the rights of illegal immigrants to
state services, including education and medical care. A federal district court, however, struck it
down on constitutional grounds in 1997, and Governor Gray Davis refused to appeal the judge's
decision, effectively killing the law.
[9] Some communitarians consider liberty and privacy to be destructive of social solidarity. One
theory is that these rights reinforce patriarchal domination, by placing family and other "private" activities beyond the reach of the community.
    The conscious rejection of liberty and privacy in favor of a total commitment to communal
life can be seen in utopian housing projects popular among Christian and socialist communities during the nineteenth and twentieth centuries. Purposefully designed to require residents
to adopt a communal lifestyle, homes lacked private kitchens and other facilities, which forced
residents to cook, eat, and live as a community. Some leading examples include the Amana
Colonies in Iowa, Brook Farm in Massachusetts, and dozens of similar communes in Indiana,

LIBERAL DEMOCRACY

I am not in favor of abolishing the government. I just want to shrink it down to the size that we can drown it in the bathtub.

– Grover Norquist[10]

Liberal democracy begins with the dictum that the government that governs best governs least.[11] Consistent with the broader political philosophy of liberalism,[12] it rests on the idea that liberty is the prime political right. Liberal democrats value the private realm and individual autonomy, and are skeptical about the claimed virtues of public life. They believe that the best way to maximize human happiness and achievement is to leave people alone to make their own choices and take responsibility for the consequences of their own actions.

Liberty, privacy, individual initiative and responsibility, contract, and voluntary associations are the key elements of a vigorous, creative, productive, and prosperous liberal society. Autonomous individuals, motivated by enlightened self-interest, work alone or with others to achieve self-selected goals, largely independent of government.

Sidebar 3: Liberty, Community, and Limited Government in College (A Letter to "Dear Abby")[13]

Dear Abby: You have had many letters in your column about the lack of moral supervision in college dorms. I hope you won't mind one more.

Nine years ago, I entered one of the top universities in the country. I will never forget the morning all the new residents of my freshman dorm were gathered together to learn how to live harmoniously in our coed dorm.

For openers, the resident adviser said, "You may drink whatever you wish, smoke whatever you like, and sleep with whomever you desire, but PLEASE DO NOT PLAY WITH THE FIRE EXTINGUISHERS."

– Disillusioned

Michigan, Illinois, and Wisconsin. Internationally, similar communal housing projects include the famous Narkomfin Building in Moscow. Many university dorms follow this model, whether consciously or not. Traditional Japanese housing – wood-framed houses with paper walls – reinforced communal living in a slightly different way, by offering only symbolic privacy.

[10] Grover Norquist interview with Mara Liasson, *Morning Edition*, NPR, May 25, 2001. Former Republican Senator Alan Simpson of Wyoming responded, "I hope he slips in there with it." *Hardball with Chris Matthews*, November 27, 2012.

[11] This saying is often – and wrongly – attributed to Thomas Jefferson. Although the proper attribution is unknown, it is highly doubtful that Jefferson said it, because it is so at odds with his personal political philosophy.

[12] "Liberalism" and "liberal democracy" are often used interchangeably, but they are not synonymous. All liberal democrats are liberals, but not all liberals are democrats. The best measure of the difference is the philosophical distance between Thomas Hobbes, the godfather of liberalism, and John Locke, the patron saint of liberal democracy.

[13] *Dear Abby*, January 25, 1988.

Government in a liberal democracy has as few as five responsibilities: (1) to protect individual liberties; (2) to prevent or remedy fraud, duress, coercion, and violence; (3) to enforce contracts; (4) to establish the rule of law; and (5) to conduct international relations, including national defense. Government is based on popular consent; state power is limited, and government must be accountable to the people. Individuals have presumptive rights against the state, including the right of revolution if the government proves oppressive, unjust, or unresponsive.[14]

Liberals are ambivalent about the state, and usually regard it as a necessary evil. States are necessary because people cannot live in peace and security without a higher power to keep the lid on bad behavior. In a state of nature (that is, without government), life is brutally Darwinian – the strong and wicked prosper; the meek and honest perish. Absent a state, society inevitably degenerates into a war of all against all, where there is no justice and no peace.

Although liberals concede the necessity of a state, they mistrust all forms of institutionalized power, and state power most of all. Ronald Reagan summed up this skepticism when he warned that government is not the solution to the problem, it *is* the problem. He once claimed that the nine most feared words in the English language are, "I'm from the government, and I'm here to help."

Limited government does not mean weak government. Liberal democracy requires a vigorous state that is powerful enough to execute fully its core responsibilities. But that power is limited by law, and channeled through a system of checks and balances, so that it does not become tyrannical.

All liberals agree with the primacy of liberty and the necessity of limiting state power. They disagree, however, about the proper limits of government power and responsibility.

Dry liberals, including Robert Nozick, Ayn Rand, and Tea Party Republicans, would strictly limit government's role to the five essential responsibilities outlined previously. These five tasks define Nozick's ideal minimal state, and constitute the alpha and omega of government. Anything less is inadequate; anything more is tyrannical.

Wet liberals, including John Stuart Mill and John Rawls, envision a broader potential role for government. Government has the duty to promote the public good, and the responsibility to ensure that everyone receives essential goods and services, including food, shelter, and education. Government also has a crucial role to play in improving society, by crafting progressive social and economic policies that promote the greatest good for the greatest number.

[14] Democracies accommodate peaceful civil disobedience in various ways, such as recognizing the right to dissent as a core component of liberty. It is noteworthy that in many democracies, those who refuse to obey what they consider to be unjust laws often come to be regarded as public heroes. A short list of persecuted dissidents who became famous for their individual acts of resistance would include Henry David Thoreau, Eugene Debs, Rosa Parks, and Mohammed Ali. Many victims of Senator Joseph McCarthy's notorious Army-McCarthy hearings eventually emerged with their reputations restored, if not enhanced. The same cannot be said of Senator McCarthy.

Like other liberals, Mill considered government a necessary evil and natural enemy of liberty. Government exists to promote the general welfare, and states must have the authority to limit and regulate liberty, in order to protect people from each other and from themselves. But Mill warned that governments make poor nannies. When states curtail individual liberty out of paternal concern for public safety and morality, they often act with the best of intentions but are inherently clumsy and incompetent, and always prone to do more harm than good. Mill argued that the private sector is more nimble and competent at providing public goods and services, and government usually does best when it steps back and stays out of the way. Nonetheless, the government must be ready to serve as the ultimate social safety net when the private sector fails to provide adequately for the young, old, poor, weak, sick, and others in need.

John Rawls went further, to insist that government must actively promote broad social and economic equality. Rawls sought to reconcile traditional liberalism with the modern welfare state. He favored a state with broad redistributive powers to help disadvantaged groups in order to create and maintain a more egalitarian society.

Liberal democrats tend to see politics as a tough competition played under Marquis of Queensbury rules. Society is made up of countless individuals and factions, whose interests routinely clash as they compete for resources and seek to influence public policy. To avoid the destructive instability caused by uncontrolled factional infighting, government should use its political and legal institutions to ritualize and pacify social conflict.

Government should be a neutral referee, to promulgate and enforce the rules with an even hand to ensure fairness and keep the peace. Otherwise, the state has no inherent virtue or moral authority, and should allow individuals to determine their own interests and chart their own course in life, as long as their actions do not significantly infringe on the equal rights of others.

Liberal democracy is premised on vigorous but orderly competition through debate, negotiation, accommodation, and compromise. This is based on the principle that "it is better to jaw-jaw than to war-war."[15] Most problems are resolved more or less amicably, through negotiated compromises that allow both sides to claim some measure of success. In liberal democracies, there are few absolute winners or losers. Unlike some other systems, in which the losers are taken out back and shot, defeated factions in liberal democracies can return to the fight tomorrow and try their luck again.

In a stable democracy, most factions continue to play by the rules, even when they consistently lose and seem to have little hope of future success. Why? For the same reasons that the Chicago Cubs return every year for spring training. As long as they see the process as fair, feel that they have a stake in the

---

[15] Winston Churchill, quoted by attendees at a private White House luncheon on June 26, 1954. *New York Times*, June 27, 1954, p.1.

system, and believe that they have a chance to win someday, they are likely to accept today's results and play on.

It helps that most people belong to multiple interest groups, which allows them to offset a loss in one area with success in another. If things do not go your way with government health care policy, you might take comfort when your side gains ground on government-subsidized student loans.

Finally, liberal democracy allows – and sometimes encourages – people to disengage from politics to tend exclusively to their own private affairs. Low participation rates are not necessarily a fundamental concern in liberal democracies, as they are in free democracies.

Low participation rates are often interpreted as implicit support for the status quo. People who do not vote are presumably happy with how things are going, or they would vote for change. Second, low participation rates means fewer demands and less stress on the political system, which allows government to stretch its resources and concentrate on the most pressing public needs. There are, of course, alternative explanations for low participation rates that are less rosy, and we will consider some of these later.

If free democracy is catholic in spirit, liberal democracy is literally Protestant in origin. The Reformation posited the idea that individuals are responsible for their own souls, rather than having to depend on clerical intercession for salvation. From this insight, new theories emerged about individual responsibility (to save one's own soul), education (necessary to read and understand God's word), reason (necessary to determine divine will), liberty (necessary to think, study, reflect, and pray), and equality (because God loves everyone equally). These were the ideas that sparked the Enlightenment, which in turn led to liberalism and ultimately liberal democracy.

The core of Enlightenment thought is that individuals are responsible for their own lives – and afterlives – so the burden falls on each person to read, think, and learn in order to develop their individual powers of reasoned judgment in the pursuit of truth. To do this, individuals need liberty to study, learn, and believe as they wish, as well as the right to make their own decisions about their own lives, as long as their actions do not significantly infringe on others' equal rights to do the same.

As John Locke explained, no one knows the true path to salvation until the final judgment, so it makes sense to keep an open mind, and to be slow to judge those who make different choices. This approach teaches tolerance as a by-product of enlightened self-interest.

In that spirit, here are five reasons to be tolerant of others. First, if each individual is responsible for her or his own life, then everyone should have the liberty to pursue their own path; just as others should tolerate your choices, you should tolerate theirs.

Second, a person's thoughts and beliefs, no matter how bizarre or radical, are of no real concern to anyone else – least of all to the government. Mere thoughts do not threaten anyone else's rights in any way. The only possible risk of erroneous belief is to the life and soul of the believer, so there is no social price to pay for unlimited tolerance of thoughts and beliefs.

Problems arise when the right of unencumbered thought and belief becomes a claimed right to act on one's beliefs. Whereas thought and belief are purely internal processes that cannot significantly affect others' rights, acting on one's beliefs can significantly affect others, and so raises a different set of questions. The state must retain the right to limit or prohibit harmful actions, even those based on sincere belief, if they infringe significantly on others' rights.

The third reason to tolerate unconventional beliefs is that even views well outside the mainstream might still be reasonable. Reasonable minds often disagree, and reasonable people should not be quick to condemn or proscribe what other reasonable people profess.

Fourth, tolerance – even tolerance of others' mistakes – is an act of charity and forgiveness, which are important social virtues.

Finally, tolerance is often the smartest course in terms of self-interest. By being tolerant and observant, we can learn from others and perhaps find a better way for ourselves, whether the lesson on offer is a good example or a terrible warning. Tolerance does not necessarily imply endorsement or approval; it just means a willingness to mind one's own business and live and let live.

Enlightenment ideas about faith, salvation, individualism, liberty, reason, education, responsibility, equality, and toleration formed the founding principles of liberal democracy. In the seventeenth century, Congregationalists were among the first to apply these principles to church governance,[16] and they later applied the same principles to secular politics with faith-based social contracts such as the Mayflower Compact.

The Pilgrims, along with other religious dissenters who fled to the New World to escape persecution at home, were not always paragons of tolerance themselves.[17] Tolerance has always been an essential part of liberal theory, however, and liberal democracies are more inclined than other political

---

[16] Anglican theologian Richard Hooker (1554–1600) published the first volume of his eight-volume treatise, *Of the Laws of Ecclesiastical Polity*, in 1593. Hooker dealt with, among other things, church governance and church-state relations. He believed in the primacy of reason and toleration in religion and politics, favored a broadly ecclesiastic approach, and saw no reason to fight over minor doctrinal disagreements. Hooker maintained that God was indifferent about how churches or political communities should be organized, but Hooker himself preferred democratic governance, because it was consistent with Martin Luther's view that each congregation is a common priesthood of all believers. He believed, however, that each individual, and each congregation, should follow their conscience in matters of faith, and that the same principle applies to civil society. Hooker's views directly inspired John Locke, who acknowledged his intellectual debt by habitually referring to him as "the judicious Hooker."

[17] The Pilgrims left England because religious intolerance made life there untenable. They initially went to The Netherlands and settled in Leiden. They found, however, that Dutch society was too open and tolerant for their tastes, and they worried about the effects that Dutch liberalism was having on their congregation, especially their children. They decided to relocate to the New World, where they could exercise complete control over their community.

systems to accept diversity, pluralism, nonconformity, and dissent as normal and nonthreatening.

Liberalism's Polaris – its navigational star – is liberty. But liberals take pains to note that liberty is not license, and individuals cannot do whatever they please. Liberty is limited by, among other things, reason, law, and others' rights. These limits include prohibitions against fraud, duress, coercion, and violence.

Liberty's thoughtful champion, John Stuart Mill, wrestled with how to balance individual liberty against a community's right of self-defense against unreasonable, dangerous, destructive, or immoral behavior.[18] Mill thought that government's ultimate responsibility for the health, safety, and morals of its citizens could justify reasonable limits on individual liberty. His three cardinal rules for regulating individual liberty are:

1. If a person's actions do not significantly interfere with another person's rights, the state has no legitimate reason to limit liberty.
2. If a person's actions significantly interfere with another person's rights, the state may place reasonable limits on liberty to protect or vindicate those rights.
3. If in doubt about whether a person's actions significantly interfere with another person's rights, apply Rule #1.

In Mill's view, government should always be reluctant to restrict liberty. Governments should measure any potential regulations carefully, should not impose more burdensome restrictions than necessary, and all reasonable doubts should be resolved in favor of liberty and private choice.

One corollary to Mill's three rules is that regulation is almost always preferable to prohibition. This applies even to dangerous, destructive, or immoral products and behaviors, such as drugs, guns, or prostitution. Acceptable regulations might include reasonable time, place, and manner restrictions, indirect restrictions such as sin taxes, or other reasonable regulations that limit dangerous products or activities without proscribing them outright.

Mill believed that anyone, including the government, may at any time present factual information to educate people, and may use reasoned persuasion to channel or discourage undesirable behavior. He did not consider such tactics to be coercive or destructive of liberty; he considered them to be educational and informative, empowering individuals to make more fully informed choices. Mill strongly believed that one of government's most important responsibilities was to serve as a central repository of reliable information and advice.[19]

---

[18] John Stuart Mill, *On Liberty*.

[19] Mill thought that providing factual information and issuing warnings about potential dangers was noncoercive, and did not restrict liberty so much as it empowered individuals to use liberty wisely and responsibly. He thought that government should serve as a central clearinghouse

Liberals love liberty more than freedom, and more than democracy for that matter. Liberal democrats are half-hearted democrats, who consider free democracy a threat to liberty. Contrasting American democracy to Athenian democracy, James Madison argued that the true wisdom of American democracy "lies in the total exclusion of the people in their collective capacity."[20]

Liberals trust the many no more than they trust the few or the one, and consider majoritarian democracy to be, potentially, the worst form of tyranny. Popular majorities are inherently powerful, with more political muscle than the few or the one, because of their sheer weight of numbers. This makes majorities uniquely dangerous. John Stuart Mill worried about the tendency of ordinary people to become unthinking bullies when in the majority. He dismissed the middle and lower classes as instinctively parochial, narrow-minded, and neophobic. They are, he argued, reflexively intolerant of nonconformists and progressive ideas, and they cannot be trusted to protect liberty or make good policy decisions when the chips are down.

Despite liberal democrats' skepticism about the claimed virtues of people power, they fear unaccountable power even more, and so accept the principle of government by consent. There must be regular opportunities for popular political participation, although these opportunities are usually limited to periodic elections. The people are the ultimate fountain of sovereign power, but the fountain is turned on only on Election Day. Citizens are free while in a voting booth, but afterward return to their private lives, leaving politics – and freedom – to their elected representatives.

Most liberal democrats are indifferent to the charms of freedom, and see no inherent link between liberty and freedom. Liberty is not necessarily a means to an end, but can be an end in itself. Liberal democrats have nothing against freedom; they just do not value it as highly as do free democrats. Mill and some other liberal democrats, however, are beguiled by freedom, because they see educational benefits in political participation.

for reliable information, by providing an easily accessible source of information that is readily available to everyone. Mill believed in centralized information, but decentralized power. Two examples of Mill's conception of government as a one-stop source of information are the Library of Congress and British Library. Of course, Mill lived and died long before the Internet age, when companies such as Google demonstrated how the private sector can make vast amounts of information available to everyone, making centralized government repositories less important, although not obsolete. Mill would worry if the government used its information to coerce or trick people, rather than informing everyone of the facts and the risks and then allowing individuals to make up their own minds. Some seemingly neutral uses of "official" information might be coercive. For example, requiring pregnant women to view officially selected pictures of a developing fetus before obtaining an abortion might be considered purely informative, or it might be considered manipulative and coercive, depending on context and perspective.

[20] James Madison, *The Federalist Papers*, No. 63, pg. 387.

Finally, liberal democrats value individuals over community.[21] In a liberal society, the whole is rarely worth more than the sum of its parts. Returning to an earlier metaphor, carefully tending to each individual tree is the best way to care for the forest. If the government vigorously protects every individual's rights, the community as a whole will prosper.

Among the most notable liberal democrats are John Locke, James Madison, John Stuart Mill, Robert Nozick, and John Rawls. Some problems peculiar to liberal democracy include:

1. *Ambivalence about Democracy.* Liberal democrats are conflicted about democracy, and many liberals are not democrats at all. Democracy is not necessary for liberty; enlightened authoritarian regimes can be quite liberal, and democracies can be brutally illiberal. Liberal democrats worry about tyranny of the majority, and believe that "too much" democracy is dangerous and destabilizing. They do not trust ordinary people to protect liberty or respect minority rights. Free democrats dismiss liberal skepticism about democracy as elitist, condescending, and implicitly authoritarian.

2. *Ambivalence about Freedom.* Liberal democrats have similarly mixed feelings about freedom. They like elections, but do not necessarily care for other direct forms of popular participation. Moreover, because liberals favor the private realm, and generally hold politics and government in low regard, they are relatively sanguine about low voting rates. This indifference about political participation can sour public opinion about politics, turning apathy into ennui and ambivalence about government into antipathy.

3. *Creeping Authoritarianism.* Liberal democracies are vulnerable to a constellation of problems that, individually and collectively, push government to become more authoritarian over time. Governments in liberal democracies are, by design, insulated from popular will and majority rule. There is an intentional distance between the people and government that encourages popular skepticism, disaffection, and alienation. Ordinary people tend to turn inward to look after their own private interests and disengage from politics. Declining voting rates allow elected representatives to grow increasingly autonomous and indifferent to public opinion. Elections become less competitive, and incumbents stay in office longer. As electoral turnover slows, power becomes entrenched and unaccountable. In extreme cases, incumbents begin to pass their offices on to spouses and family members, in the manner of aristocracies. A ruling political class eventually emerges, as democracy degenerates into a formal abstraction and the political system slouches toward authoritarianism.

---

[21] Both liberal and free democrats believe in the primacy of the individual. The essential difference is that liberal democrats believe that individuals are better off when they are left to act on their own, and free democrats believe that individuals are at their best when they are an integral part of a larger community. In contrast, fascism promotes the good of the collective, without regard for individual well-being.

4. *Selfishness, Loss of Community, and Collapse of Civil Society.* By promoting individualism and self-interest over community and the common good, liberal societies risk becoming selfish, narcissistic, atomized, and Darwinian. The single-minded pursuit of self-interest aggravates social and economic inequalities, allowing the strong to prosper while the weak and poor fall further behind. This can result in class conflict, loss of social cohesion, and ultimately the collapse of civil society.

5. *Illiberal Democracy.* Illiberal democracy is not so much a liberal democracy gone bad as an illusory democracy; an authoritarian regime with symbolic trappings of democracy, but without the substance. It has pseudo-liberal architecture and institutions, but lacks the underlying commitment to core liberal ideas such as limited and accountable government and the rule of law. It lacks the rules, procedures, practices, and habits that make democracy come to life. Illiberal democracy is a form of demfauxcracy, in which leaders use the appearance of democracy to entrap and oppress their people, rather than liberate them. Illiberal democracies are especially common in the Middle East and Africa, and are part of the legacy of colonialism and postcolonial pressures to democratize along traditional Western lines.[22] These pressures led traditional authoritarian regimes to reinvent themselves as Potemkin democracies; Hollywood sets that might pass a cursory inspection from a safe distance, but on closer scrutiny are revealed to be shabby and perverse imitations of the real thing. Instead of protecting popular liberties, illiberal regimes suppress human rights, use intimidation and oppression to eliminate dissent, assert state control over the media and civil society, and rig elections to favor the ruling party. Examples of modern illiberal democracies include Cuba, Iran, and Zimbabwe.

Sidebar 4: Free Democracy versus Liberal Democracy

Free Democracy	*Liberal Democracy*
Freedom	Liberty
Public	Private
Community	Individual
Villagers	Islanders[23]
Common good	Self-interest
Cooperation	Competition
Good Results	Fair Procedures
Equitable Outcomes	Equal Opportunities

[22] Fareed Zakaria, "The Rise of Illiberal Democracy."
[23] *Contra* poet John Donne, who wrote, "No man is an island."

REPRISE: FREEDOM OR LIBERTY?

Which is more important, freedom or liberty? Communities or individuals? Companionship or elbow room? Do you favor mass transit or driving alone? Would you rather go to a movie with friends, or stay at home and watch TV? Do you prefer shopping malls or shopping online? Do you spend your free time visiting social media sites or quietly reading a book? Would you choose to walk in a big charity event or sneak off to take a quiet hike in the woods alone? There is no objectively correct answer to any of these questions, but your answers might say something about what kind of democracy you prefer.

On the one hand, human beings are inherently individualistic. Because of innate and learned differences in personality, genetic variations, how people are born and raised, free will, and our ability to shape our own nature, we are not just uniquely individualistic – each individual is unique. Individualism is an essential part of what it means to be human, and it leads people to value individual identity, autonomy, and liberty.

On the other hand, we are also social creatures, by nature and choice. We seek out and enjoy the company of others, and we quickly develop strong social attachments – strong enough that people sometimes willingly sacrifice their own lives to save others. These factors lead people to value human interaction, community, and freedom.

Human beings, along with canines and a handful of other species, possess two distinct kinds of intelligence: individual and social. Individual intelligence makes us self-reliant and able to figure things out for ourselves. We are excellent individual problem solvers, capable of rapid and sophisticated situational analysis. Our capacity for complex thought allows us to develop our individual powers of reason, which is a cornerstone of liberalism.

We also have the social intelligence of highly evolved pack animals. Most people thrive on social interaction and play well with others. Even if people speak different languages and come from radically different cultures, they can still communicate on a sophisticated level. We depend on other people for all manner of needs, wants, and desires. We find sympathy, comfort, love, support, stimulation, help, and happiness in other people's company.

Some forms of pack behavior and social intelligence are common in the animal world, but empathy is not. We are one of just two known species (bonobos are the other) who will voluntarily share essential resources with strangers, even when we desperately need them for ourselves. Human beings seem to be unique in terms of our capacity for deep empathy – the ability to imagine ourselves in other people's skins, see the world from alternative perspectives, and modify our own behavior accordingly. Our extraordinary ability to intuit a sympathetic understanding of others was the genesis of the golden rule, and it is what makes civil society possible.

Human beings readily cooperate with others to accomplish things that we cannot do alone. This is how we solve the most complex problems and reach our most ambitious goals. The great things we have achieved as a species have, of necessity, been done in cooperation or in competition with others.[24] We learn from each other, help each other, and push each other. We seem to thrive on cooperation and competition in equal measure, and both are essential social behaviors.

It is said that the person who wants to travel fastest should travel alone, but the person who wants to travel farthest should travel with others. There is more than one good answer to the question of whether people are naturally individualistic or community oriented, and there is more than one good answer to the question of whether liberty or freedom is the more important right. The best answers to these questions ultimately depend on subjective preferences and historical circumstances.

Sidebar 5: Individualism versus Community[25]

If you show Americans an image of a fish tank, they will usually describe the biggest fish in the tank and what it is doing. If you show a group of Chinese or Japanese the same image, they will usually describe the context in which the fish swim.

When psychologist Richard Nisbett showed Americans pictures of a chicken, cow, and hay, then asked them to pick the two images that went together, most chose the chicken and the cow, because they are both animals. Most Asians chose the cow and the hay, because cows depend on hay. Americans are more likely to see categories; Asians see relationships.

Individualistic countries place a higher value on individual rights and initiative. People in these societies tend to overvalue their own skills and overestimate their own importance in any group effort. People in collective societies, such as China and Japan, value harmony and duty. They tend to underestimate their own skills and are self-effacing when describing their individual contributions to group efforts.

---

[24] Our greatest achievements are often the result of both cooperation and competition, as was the case with the great space race of the 1960s, between the United States and USSR.

[25] Excerpted and adapted from Brooks, David, "Harmony and the Dream," *New York Times*, August 12, 2008; cf., Nisbett, Richard E., *The Geography of Thought: How Asians and Westerners Think Differently… And Why* (Free Press 2003).

TWO STYLES BUT MANY FLAVORS

Given the two basic categories of free and liberal democracy, we can now add five new dimensions to create a simple typology of democratic systems:

Rights
Participation and Representation
Inclusion
Equality
Power

Free and liberal democrats tend to see these five dimensions differently, and there is some degree of theoretical consistency in their distinct perspectives. As we will see, free democrats tend to prefer positivism, positive rights, group rights, direct participation, exclusive political systems, socioeconomic equality, robust government, and majoritarian or consensual decision making. Liberal democrats are more likely to emphasize natural rights, individual rights, negative rights, representative government, inclusive political systems, political-legal equality, limited government, and isocracy. Theoretical consistency, however, does not count for much in the real world. In practice, democratic societies freely mix and match preferences, which helps explain the rich variety among democratic states.

3

Rights

Rights are what the state and others owe you. Duties are what you owe to the state and others. In a democracy, rights are acknowledged by government assent; duties are justly imposed only with popular consent. Because different societies disagree about the proper balance of rights and duties, this is an especially interesting area for comparative study.

Some rights are tied primarily to liberty; other rights are tied primarily to freedom. Some rights have significant aspects of both liberty and freedom. Four issues help illuminate the complex relationship between rights and duties, and between individual and state: (1) where rights come from; (2) how different societies balance rights and duties; (3) negative versus positive rights; and (4) individual versus group rights.

WHERE DO RIGHTS COME FROM?

Where do rights come from? There are two basic answers to this question: they come either from a source superior to humans (*natural rights*), or they come from the same place as soylent green – the people themselves (*positivism*).

Most Americans believe in natural rights. According to this theory, God, Nature, or some other higher power endows human beings with their rights. People have rights simply because they were fortunate enough to be born human, and no earthly authority can justly limit or revoke these rights absent consent, or at least without good cause and due process. Natural rights exist apart from and above state, society, and positive (i.e., man-made) law.

Thomas Hobbes popularized the idea of natural rights in the mid-seventeenth century. He theorized that individuals are born with a full range of natural rights, including life, liberty, and the pursuit of self-interest. All legitimate political power flows from these individual rights (Hobbes vigorously rejected the

Stuart monarchs' claim to rule by divine right), meaning that the people are the ultimate source of sovereign authority.

Unfortunately, Hobbes believed that in order to escape the hellish state of nature – where life is solitary, poor, nasty, brutish, and short – and live in relative peace and safety, people must surrender all but one of their rights to the state. The state pledges, in return, to secure the one essential and inalienable right – the right to life. This wholesale transfer of individual rights to the state results in an all-powerful government – the Leviathan – to rule over a virtually powerless citizenry. Although Hobbes's Leviathan was monstrous, his conception of natural rights was revolutionary, and the fact that under his system people retained even one fundamental right against the state was a profound moment in political history.

John Locke began with Hobbes's theory of natural rights, but came to radically different conclusions about individual rights and the state. Locke believed that everyone is born to equal rights, among them life, liberty, and property. To live in relative peace and security, however, people need only surrender two relatively unimportant rights to the state: the right to judge one's own case, and the right of self-help. This relatively modest exchange gives the government limited, although still considerable, delegated powers to create and execute laws, and do justice according to law. Individuals retain all of their other natural rights, and it is government's sworn duty to protect them.

Hobbes, Locke, and others developed and popularized natural rights theory, but Thomas Jefferson gave the idea its clearest voice. In the Declaration of Independence, Jefferson wrote, "All men are created equal and endowed by their Creator with certain inalienable rights, among them life, liberty, and the pursuit of happiness."[1] A decade later, French revolutionaries distilled Jefferson's declaration to the elegant phrase, "liberté, egalité, fraternité."

The idea that everyone is born to equal rights eventually led to the proposition that all people are naturally morally, legally, and politically equal. This bolsters the case for democracy, and takes the wind out of the sails of those who would claim the right to rule as our betters.

One problem with natural rights and natural law theory is that these concepts are usually tied to religious belief, and different religions have strikingly different ideas about the content and scope of these rights. Whereas some religions support broad rights consistent with democratic values, other faith-based claims about rights and law are distinctly illiberal and undemocratic. Iran is the poster child for states that use natural rights and law as a reactionary and oppressive force, to enforce authoritarian rule, oppress nonconforming beliefs, and keep women confined behind closed doors and chadors. One extreme interpretations of Islam gives believers the divine right to slaughter infidels, blasphemers, and apostates on sight.

---

[1] Jefferson changed Locke's original list of "life, liberty, and estate," because he and Benjamin Franklin, who edited Jefferson's draft, agreed that private property was a human invention and not a natural right.

The leading alternative theory about rights is that they derive not from nature, but from the exercise of sovereign power. This is positivism, which became fashionable in Europe in the nineteenth and twentieth centuries,[2] and has subsequently influenced modern U.S. legal and political thought.[3] Positivism leaves gods, nature, and other hypothetical higher powers out of the equation. Rights and duties are explicitly human constructs – gifts that the state gives to the people, or that the people give themselves, in the form of duly enacted laws.

Positivism is strictly agnostic when it comes to democracy. It can be used to justify rights and duties in any kind of political system, from anarcho-syndicalist communes to fascist hive collectives. The only formal requirement is that rights and duties must be properly enacted and promulgated through authoritative rules and procedures. There is no requirement that these institutions, rules, and procedures be democratic, liberal, conservative, progressive, or benign.

Another problem with positivism is its tautological position that whatever the sovereign says is lawful and just is lawful and just, as long as the government followed its own rules. With positivism, there is no higher power to appeal to beyond the state. By establishing the state as the ultimate source of rights and duties, positivism negates the idea that people have inalienable rights against the government, except for those rights that the state itself chooses to recognize.

This leads critics to charge that positivism creates privileges rather than rights, because what the state grants it can just as easily take away. For our purposes, however, so long as positivist norms impose effective limits on state power, and these limits cannot be revised or revoked without popular consent or without good cause and due process, they are secure enough to be considered rights.

BALANCING RIGHTS AND DUTIES

Striking the proper balance between rights and duties is crucial for any society. Historically, most states have focused almost exclusively on duties. In Plato's *Republic*, individuals had no rights at all – only privileges that the state could change or revoke at will.[4] Even in democratic Athens, most "rights" were

---

[2] The leading German work on positivism is Hans Kelsen's *Pure Theory of Law (Reine Rechtslehre)*, first published in Vienna in 1934. In 1960, Kelsen published a revised and expanded second edition, translated into English in 1967 by the University of California Press. In the UK, the leading proponents of legal positivism include John Austin, *Lectures on Jurisprudence, or, The Philosophy of Positive Law* (1869); and H. L. A. Hart, *The Concept of Law* (1961).

[3] A leading American critic of legal positivism is Ronald Dworkin, whose best-known works include *Taking Rights Seriously* (Harvard University Press, 1977), and *Law's Empire* (Harvard University Press, 1986).

[4] According to Plato, the only "right" that ordinary citizens have is the right of obedience. Plato considered obedience to be a right, because it results in a happy, harmonious, and just society in which everyone benefits.

privileges that the majority could freely alter or eliminate. Things did not improve much during the Roman Empire, Middle Ages, or Renaissance, when all-powerful states were the rule and ordinary people helpless subjects of sovereign whim and caprice.

Magna Carta was the birth certificate of rights against sovereign authority, but the American Revolution marked the moment that the world's attention shifted decisively from what the citizen owed the state to what the state owed the citizen, and government came to be regarded as the people's servant rather than their master. Although most modern democracies follow the American example of emphasizing rights over duties, this trend is not universal, inevitable, or irreversible. How to balance popular rights and duties remains an open question, and different societies approach the issue differently.

In his 1960 inaugural address, President John F. Kennedy challenged Americans to, "Ask not what your country can do for you – ask what you can do for your country." Kennedy stressed duty and service, and not only in the routine duties of citizenship – paying taxes, registering for the draft, jury duty, and the like. He wanted Americans to assume broad responsibilities to make the country and the world a better place. Others would argue that Kennedy had the rights-duty equation exactly backward. If states exist primarily to protect individual rights and liberties, then we *should* ask what our country can do for us, because that is the point of government.

NEGATIVE AND POSITIVE RIGHTS

Rights can be negative or positive. Negative rights are liberties – they limit external intrusions into people's lives by government or private parties. Important negative rights include privacy, thought, belief, conscience, speech, press, association, and travel.[5] Most of the rights embedded in the American Constitution are negative rights, limiting government power in the name of liberty.

Positive rights are entitlements that give government (and sometimes private groups and individuals) an affirmative duty to provide specified goods or services. There are two types of positive rights: positive political-legal rights, and positive socioeconomic rights.

Most positive political-legal rights are freedoms, in that they oblige the government to facilitate or accommodate rights of individual and collective action. Positive political rights include rights to petition the government, vote, and run

---

[5] Some rights, including speech, press, and religion, have roots in both liberty and freedom. Speech and press rights are primarily tied to liberty, and are negative rights in the sense that the main point is that governments cannot unduly interfere with the right to speak or publish. But these rights, especially when combined with rights of association and assembly, include the freedom to join with others to create political communities and to take public action. Similarly, the free exercise of religion is primarily a liberty to prevent government interference with private religious beliefs, but the right implicitly includes the freedom to join with others to create all manner of religious associations.

for public office. They are positive rights because the government is responsible for organizing free and fair elections, ensuring the public's right to know, accepting and considering all manner of public petitions, input, comment, and debate, and seeking public consent for important government decisions and policies. Governments also have positive duties to provide for public safety and security, including protecting people from fraud, duress, coercion and violence, and defending the country from all enemies foreign and domestic. Positive legal rights might include such things as the right of indigents to free legal representation in criminal cases, and the right to trial by jury.

The second category of positive rights involves socioeconomic rights. These rights are more controversial, especially among liberal democrats. Positive socioeconomic rights might include entitlements to education, public assistance (welfare), social security, unemployment benefits, and health care. Some social democrats define positive socioeconomic rights more broadly, to include rights to work, minimum income, housing, and personal development.[6]

The United Nations International Covenant on Economic, Social, and Cultural Rights enumerates a comprehensive list of positive rights, including the right to work under just and favorable conditions, receive social security and social insurance payments, and maintain a certain standard of family life, including paid parental leave and special protections for children. It guarantees an adequate standard of living, including food, clothing, and housing, as well as rights to "continuous improvement of living conditions" and "the highest attainable standards of physical and mental health." It guarantees the right to education, including free primary education, generally available secondary education, and equally accessible higher education. This litany of rights leads to a comprehensive right to "the full development of the human personality and the sense of its dignity." This includes the right to participate effectively in society, cultural life, benefits of scientific progress, and a share of intellectual property rights in any scientific or artistic works that one helps create.

INDIVIDUAL RIGHTS

The source spring of individual rights was the *Magna Carta Libertatum* (Great Charter of Liberty) of 1215. It guaranteed, among other things, the fundamental rights of habeas corpus and trial by jury. In signing Magna Carta, King John reluctantly accepted the radical proposition that sovereign will can be limited by contract and law.

Five centuries later, the American Constitution and Bill of Rights became the essential modern expression of individual rights. Enumerated rights include life, liberty, property, speech, press, religion, assembly, petition, due process, speedy trial, fair trial, the privilege against self-incrimination, and trial by jury.

---

[6] Positive rights now reach into cyberspace. In 2010, Finland became the first country to make broadband Internet access a legal entitlement.

The Constitution also contains numerous implied rights, including free association, privacy, domestic travel, protection against coerced confessions, and the right to effective counsel in criminal cases.

America was built on the rock of individual liberty, and unsurprisingly the Constitution strongly favors individual rights over group rights. Even rights that seem at first glance to be communal rights – including the free exercise of religion, free press, and assembly – are actually individual rights, in part because individuals must sue to vindicate them. Groups and organizations may file lawsuits, but only on behalf of their individual members. In American law, groups are rarely worth more than the sum of their parts.

The most important international documents enumerating individual rights are the Universal Declaration of Human Rights (UDHR), and UN International Covenant on Civil and Political Rights (ICCPR). The UN General Assembly approved The UDHR in December 1948. It was the first global declaration of human rights.[7] Although it has no binding force, it has been influential in shaping national constitutions around the world. Among the rights it enumerates are the rights of life, liberty, and security of person. It prohibits slavery, torture, and inhuman or degrading treatment or punishment, and recognizes fair trial rights, including the presumption of innocence, right of privacy, and right of free movement within state borders. It also enumerates a few positive rights, including the right to social security and education and work. The General Assembly approved the ICCPR in 1966, and it came into force in 1976. It protects the sanctity of life and guarantees speech, assembly, religion, electoral, due process, and fair trial rights.

GROUP RIGHTS AND RESPONSIBILITIES

Although Magna Carta represents the genesis of individual rights, many of the rights articulated in the Great Charter were actually group rights – or more precisely, class rights. This is not surprising, given that thirteenth-century Britain was a feudal society, where class status governed almost every aspect of life.

The right to trial by a jury of one's peers, for example, was not originally an individual right, but a guarantee that each class would be able to judge its own. It meant that knights would judge knights, earls would judge earls, barons would judge barons, and no juror would be drawn from a class inferior to the defendant's social rank.[8] The idea of group rights and duties remains firmly entrenched in Europe, where the feudal spirit endured well into the modern era.

---

[7] No countries voted against the Declaration, but eight nations abstained: Byelorussia, Czechoslovakia, Poland, Saudi Arabia, South Africa, Soviet Union, Ukraine, and Yugoslavia.

[8] A similar principle applies in American military trials. The Uniform Code of Military Justice, 10 USC §825, Art. 25(d)(1) states, "When it can be avoided, no member of an armed force may be tried by a court-martial any member of which is junior to him in rank or grade."

During the first half of the twentieth century, group rights and duties became more controversial, thanks to the Bolsheviks and Nazis, whose ideas on the subject were not widely admired. World War II, however, led all of the major powers, including the United States, to wrestle anew with the idea of group rights and responsibilities. Toward the end of the war, the three great Allied leaders, Roosevelt, Churchill, and Stalin, debated whether mere membership in Nazi organizations such as the SS would be sufficient to justify summary punishment – including execution – without trial or proof of individual guilt. All three men initially favored the summary execution of several hundred to several thousand Nazi leaders as soon as they could be captured and their identities verified. They eventually changed their minds, and established special war crimes tribunals in Nuremburg and Tokyo, along with regional tribunals in China, Russia, France, and the Philippines. Even so, mere membership in some Nazi and Axis groups was enough to justify punishment in some cases, even absent evidence of individual criminal behavior.

Group rights have never been favored in American law, in part because America was never a feudal society and so lacks a cultural attachment to class-based rights or obligations. Although American law has been reluctant to embrace group rights, the American labor movement of the late nineteenth and early twentieth centuries promoted group rights through unionization and collective bargaining.

The organized labor movement served as a template for the women's and civil rights movements, which combined the quest for individual rights with a growing awareness that, just as governments could deny rights based on group identity, governments might be compelled to recognize rights on the same basis. Although both the women's and civil rights movements initially focused on traditional individual rights such as voting and jury service, their demands eventually broadened to include group rights to equal access to public services, education, jobs, transportation, and housing, equal pay, and other remedial rights.

The second wave of the civil rights movement, which began in the 1960's, pushed for broad, class-based affirmative action programs to remedy past discrimination, rather than limiting redress to individuals who could prove that they were actual victims of discrimination.

The concept of group rights gained momentum in the second half of the twentieth century, bolstered by emerging ideas about social justice. This new approach resonated most strongly among community-oriented social democracies, but also influenced staunchly individualistic societies, including the United States.

In 2007, the UN Declaration on the Rights of Indigenous Peoples proclaimed that native populations have inalienable collective rights to the ownership, use, and control of land and natural resources, maintain and develop their own political, religious, cultural, and education institutions, and protect their own

cultural and intellectual property. The declaration is not legally binding, but
has aspirational weight.[9]

International law has always been more concerned about group rights than
individual rights. States created international law specifically to vindicate their
collective rights and duties, and international law has traditionally been reluctant to recognize or protect individual rights absent state intercession. It is
still rare for individuals to be able to file private complaints with international
tribunals; states or other qualified organizations must intervene on their behalf
as the true rights-holders.

Group rights are not always benign or progressive. In America, Jim Crow
laws recognized group rights to segregated facilities that were deemed separate but equal. In practice, of course, the focus was always on separation, not
equality.[10]

Perhaps the most infamous modern example of repressive group rights was
the apartheid regime in South Africa. Apartheid laws created a complex web of
group political, economic, and social rights based solely on race and ethnicity.
Although the white minority government claimed that apartheid laws benefit-
ted everyone, these laws were designed to quarantine nonwhite groups and
consolidate white political and economic power, while giving the South African
government a useful façade of legal and political respectability.

South Africa is still trying to overcome the toxic residuum of the apartheid era. The current government, dominated by the black majority African
National Congress (ANC), continues to use group rights to make amends for
the previous regime's bigotry.

The ANC's Black Economic Empowerment program (BEE) is a leading
example of a postapartheid program designed to give black, Asian, and mixed-
race groups compensatory social, political, and economic opportunities that
were systematically denied under apartheid. The BEE program is controversial,
however, because it continues the apartheid-era practice of recognizing group
rights and privileges based solely on race.

A similar program has been a disaster in neighboring Zimbabwe, where the
government routinely confiscates white-owned farms and transfers the land to
well-connected blacks with close ties to President Robert Mugabe and his ruling ZANU-PF Party. State-sanctioned racism and corruption in Zimbabwe have
fueled racial hatred, economic chaos, and violence, and there are growing concerns
that South Africa's remedial programs might degenerate along similar lines.

At the United Nations, a more recent effort to establish a new group right began
in 2010, when a coalition of Muslim nations pushed to outlaw "defamation of

[9] The United States, along with Canada, Australia, and New Zealand, voted against the Declaration
on the Rights of Indigenous Peoples, and many African countries abstained. The Declaration has
proved especially popular in Latin America.
[10] In much of the American South through the 1950s, white schools were stone, brick, and glass
buildings, whereas black schools were often shacks, hastily built from scrap wood and tar
paper.

religion." The UN Human Rights Council resolution on Combating Defamation of Religions was a thinly disguised attempt to criminalize any speech that questioned, criticized, satirized, or insulted Islam. It authorized Islamic governments worldwide to punish any form of religious dissent or unorthodoxy on behalf of the faithful. Critics rightly condemned the Council's actions as a transparent attempt to forge a new instrument of faith-based oppression.

Moving from the appalling to the absurd, high school students in Bangladesh claim a collective right to cheat on their college entrance exams. When government officials tried to stop the organized cheating in 1988, riots broke out and more than 500 people were injured. Since then, violent conflicts over students' right to cheat have become semiannual events.

The United States, with its highly individualistic culture, has shown little sustained interest in recognizing or promoting group rights, with four notable exceptions. First, U.S. courts give considerable leeway to the federal and state governments, as well as foreign governments, to sue on behalf of their citizens. Second, the federal government treats officially recognized American Indian tribes as semi-sovereign entities, and grants them special group rights concerning collective land ownership, timber and mineral rights, fishing, and casino operations.

Third, since the early 1970s, the United States has maintained an uncomfortable commitment to racial, ethnic, and sex-based affirmative action programs. The original focus of these laws was to remedy past discrimination by offering compensatory relief to recognized groups, regardless of whether specific individuals had personally suffered from unlawful discrimination. More recently, however, most remaining affirmative action laws have reverted to reflect traditional individual rights, by requiring prospective beneficiaries to demonstrate that they were actual victims of past discrimination.[11]

Finally, the most significant exception to the American preference for individual rights involves corporations. In two obscure nineteenth-century decisions, the Supreme Court declared that corporations were "persons" for some purposes under the 14th Amendment.[12] In 2010, the Roberts Court exhumed

---

[11] Because of a quirk in American constitutional law, affirmative action laws involving gender or sex discrimination are more likely to pass constitutional muster than affirmative action laws aimed at remedying racial discrimination. In order to justify any form of racial discrimination, even if it is compensatory and "benign," the state must prove that the law promotes a compelling state interest, and that there are no less discriminatory alternatives available. This is the strict scrutiny test, and it is an extremely difficult test to pass. In cases of gender or sex discrimination, however, the state needs only to demonstrate an important state interest, and that the means are reasonably related to that end. This is the intermediate scrutiny test, and it gives lawmakers greater flexibility in dealing with sex and gender issues.

[12] *Dartmouth College v. Woodward*, 17 U.S. (4 Wheat.) 518 (1819), ruled that corporations have the constitutional right to enter into contracts. In *Santa Clara County v. Southern Pacific Railroad*, 118 U.S. 394 (1886), the Court held that corporations are persons for some purposes under the 14th Amendment. In *First National Bank of Boston v. Bellotti*, 435 U.S. 765 (1978), the Supreme Court ruled for the first time that corporations have a First Amendment right to contribute money to influence the political process.

and reanimated these precedents to grant corporations broad new First Amendment rights, including the right to spend unlimited amounts of money on political advertising.[13] These decisions granted corporations, with their collective wealth and legal immortality, significant advantages over natural-born persons in their ability to influence the political process. With the *Citizens United* case, the Court effectively transmogrified corporations into persons, and individual rights into group rights, for corporations only.[14]

---

[13] In *Citizens United v. Federal Election Commission*, 558 U.S. 50 (2010), the Court ruled that corporations have broad First Amendment speech rights, including the right to spend unlimited amounts of money to broadcast independent political messages intended to influence elections, as long as they do not coordinate their activities with candidates or their campaign organizations.

[14] Ironically, conservative justices who formed the majority in *Citizens United* insisted in earlier affirmative action cases that U.S. law recognizes and protects only individual rights, not group rights.

4

Participation and Representation

Should democracies rely on direct citizen participation, or should governance be left to representatives? Is government a do-it-yourself job, or is it best contracted out to professionals, subject to some degree of public accountability and consent?

Free democrats prefer participatory democracy; liberal democrats favor representative democracy. Free democrats see value in political participation, whereas liberal democrats are skeptical of direct democracy and worry about the consequences of having "too much" democracy.

PARTICIPATION AND DIRECT DEMOCRACY

In participatory democracies, citizens are encouraged, expected, and sometimes required to engage in politics and government. Participatory democracy depends on an active and informed citizenry to make important policy decisions, rather than leaving them to representatives or civil servants.

It might seem that free and participatory democracies are the same thing, but they are not quite synonymous. All free democrats are participatory democrats in theory, but in practice they invariably must rely, to some degree, on representatives and civil servants – a necessity in the era of large nation-states. Conversely, some liberal democrats, notably John Stuart Mill, value the educative benefits of political participation. As a rule, however, free democrats place a much higher value on political participation than do liberal democrats. Participation in liberal democracies usually ends where participation in free democracies begins: voting in periodic elections.

Direct political participation provides a practical, experiential education on how to balance, and ideally align, self-interest and the common good. Being an active member of a political community serves as a useful check on selfishness, and helps build a cohesive civil society on the basis of shared interests, common goals, and mutual support.

People are naturally quick to look after their own interests. Children learn to do this at an early age. Toddlers vigorously defend their rights against any perceived threat, which is why the second year of life is known as "the terrible twos." Participatory democracy teaches the adult version of self-interest: that for one's own rights to be respected, one must first be prepared to respect others' rights. Understanding the mutuality of rights and responsibilities is the mark of political maturity, and participatory democracy is especially effective at teaching this lesson.

Participatory democracy offers other practical lessons about the interdependence of self and society. It is only by interacting with others that people can truly learn about themselves – what they have in common with others, and what makes them different. In this sense, political participation is a voyage of self-discovery. By talking and acting with others, people learn to make a place for themselves in society, as they develop their own unique personalities. Participatory democracy leads to self-awareness, self-actualization, and enlightened self-interest.

How It Works

In a participatory democracy there is no bright line separating rulers from citizens. Ordinary people take turns ruling and being ruled. Citizens are directly involved in all aspects of government, including legislative, executive, and judicial decision-making, although they usually have help executing their duties. Even Rousseau, who otherwise disdained representatives and civil servants, provided a Lawgiver to guide the general will and make sure that everyone follows the rules. In Colonial New England, citizens made the most important decisions, but relied on selectmen and other administrators to implement the people's will. In the administration of justice, judges and other legal professionals routinely advise juries and lay judges,[1] and their verdicts can usually be appealed to professional judges.

Switzerland
Direct democracy is alive and well in Switzerland, although even there it is not all that it once was. Switzerland is famous for its Landsgemeinde system of cantonal assemblies, where citizens gather in the capital city's town square

---

[1] In common law jurisdictions, judges offer jurors instruction on the law before the jury retires alone to deliberate and decide the case. British judges are generally more inclined to comment on evidence and witness testimony than are U.S. judges.

England and Wales also have a system of lay judges in magistrates' courts. Lay magistrates routinely rely on legally trained clerks to advise them on legal issues. Russia and other former socialist countries use mixed panels of lay and professional judges that jointly decide cases.

to elect officials, discuss important political issues, air grievances, and vote on proposed laws and constitutional amendments. Of the twenty-six Swiss cantons, however, the Landsgemeinde system survives today in just the two smallest, most rural cantons of Glarus and Appenzell-Innerrhoden, and their assemblies meet only once a year.

Appenzell-Innerrhoden is a sparsely populated, predominately Catholic canton in the German-speaking northeast corner of the country. It is rural, insular, and staunchly conservative. Women did not gain the right to vote there until 1991, and then only on order of the Swiss supreme court. Its Landsgemeinde dates officially from 1403, although now-lost historical documents indicated that it was already well established by 1378. Appenzell-Innerrhoden abandoned its Landsgemeinde system during the seventeenth and eighteenth centuries, but restored it with a new constitution in 1872. The Landsgemeinde assembly is the canton's highest legislative authority, with broad powers to amend the cantonal constitution and pass laws on virtually any subject.

The annual meeting takes place on the last Sunday of April,[2] in Appenzell's Landsgemeindeplatz, a large public square near the center of town. Hotels, cafes, and shops line the plaza, with a public fountain near the southwest corner that provides the best ground-level view. The square slopes gently downward from south to north, like an amphitheater. On assembly day, half of the square is roped off and only eligible citizens are allowed to enter. At the north end is a temporary platform for local officials, and on the eastern side are bleachers for visiting VIP's. Other visitors must stand along the perimeter, well outside the rope barrier.

Every adult citizen has the right to attend the assembly.[3] Before women gained the right to participate, men carried ceremonial rapiers as their sole means of identification. After women gained the right to vote in 1991, every citizen received a yellow voting card. Today, men may bring either their rapier or voting card. If a man carries a rapier, he cannot be asked for any other form of identification. Women do not have rapiers, and must show their yellow cards.

At the 2011 assembly, rain was in the forecast. The men carried rapiers; the women carried umbrellas. They began to gather noisily in the Landsgemeindeplatz at 11 AM. For leading canton officials, the meeting began an hour earlier and several blocks away from the town square, at the Rathaus (Town Hall), with a special religious service, followed by a parade to the square. The procession consisted of a band, colorful flags, local police and military officers, and officials in traditional dress. The word "parade" might be a misnomer, because the music and the pace were funereal.

---

[2] If the last Sunday in April falls on Easter Sunday, the meeting is postponed until the first Sunday in May.

[3] Until 1993, the Landsgemeinde also had the power to confer cantonal citizenship. This is now left to the governing council.

FIGURE 4.1 Voting at the Appenzell-Innerrhoden Landsgemeinde assembly.

After the local notables marched into the square and took their places on the dais, the meeting commenced at a few minutes after noon. Everyone took the cantonal oath and listened to official reports. The assembly then quickly elected the seven-member governing council, the chief magistrate, chief judge, other members of the cantonal court, members of the canton's Ethics Committee, and finally the canton's representative to the Swiss Council of States.

A free comment period followed, during which citizens were allowed to address the crowd. The unofficial theme this year was the waning influence of rural cantons in Swiss politics. Although any citizen may speak on any topic, the process was surprisingly low key and passive; there was no crowd reaction to any of the speeches, whether by public officials or private citizens.

In contrast with the processional dirge, the meeting moved along at a brisk pace. Proposed laws were announced and voted on without discussion or debate. The assembly listened quietly, and then voted by a show of hands (Figure 4.1). There were no secret ballots; everyone could see how everyone else voted. The results were proclaimed by general assent – no one counted the yeas or nays. Not that it would have mattered, because none of the votes were close.

There were no landmark issues this year, certainly nothing to compare to 2009, when citizens voted to ban nude hiking in the local Alps. This year, the assembly voted on one minor constitutional amendment, several laws concerning inter-cantonal cooperation, public funding for a nursing center, and plans for a proposed underground parking garage.

At the close of business, the officials recessed at the same deliberate pace that they used to enter the square. This time they accepted polite applause from the assembly, and some smiled and waved as they trudged back to the Rathaus. Immediately after the last official left the square, the meeting broke up and everyone quickly scattered to attend rallies in the various small public squares around town. Back in the Landsgemeindeplatz, two administrators announced the official election results to the handful of citizens and tourists who stayed to listen.

Landsgemeinde assemblies are not as common or important as they once were. They nonetheless offer useful insights into the practice and potential of people power. Free democracy in Switzerland promotes community building and civic education; helps ensure official transparency, accessibility, and accountability; and directly engages citizens in the day-to-day business of government.

These virtues do not imply, however, that direct democracy is trouble free, or superior to other forms of democracy. Among the problems commonly associated with participatory democracy:

1. *Size.* Participatory democracies historically have been limited to small, compact rural communities, towns, and city-states. If every citizen is a legislator, everyone needs to be able to gather at the same time and place to deliberate and vote. This means that only small places with large public spaces need apply. As states grow larger and more diverse, direct citizen command and control becomes impracticable, and day-to-day responsibility for decision-making inexorably passes from the people to representatives and administrators.

   In the Roman Republic, all male citizens had the right to participate in public assemblies. Elites – consuls, praetors, or tribunes – usually convened these meetings, controlled the agenda, and determined the questions for public discussion and vote. Throughout the republican era, the assembly had considerable freedom to debate and decide a broad range of public issues.

   The catch was that citizens had to be physically present in Rome to exercise their rights. As Roman rule spread, the republic grew larger but more tenuous, as far-flung expatriates could no longer remain engaged citizens. The political system, designed to serve a small city-state, faltered as it expanded beyond its functional capacity to operate as a participatory republic. As more and more nominally free citizens effectively forfeited their political rights, the Republic became an empire in fact long before it became one in name.

   With the fall of the Republic, the idea of participatory democracy faded, but never entirely disappeared. Even during the bleakest days of the Dark Ages, local democratic folk traditions survived in isolated villages and towns, and in the handful of small democratic city-states in Switzerland, Iceland, and the Italian peninsula. These islands of democracy were weak and unstable, and with the exception of the Swiss confederacy (which the Holy Roman Emperor Charles IV tolerated as a useful buffer against the rival Hapsburgs), larger authoritarian states eventually swallowed them up.

   The sixteenth century saw the dawn of modernity, with the emergence of the first great nation-states. City-states gradually went the way of the dinosaurs, as Spain, France, and other coalescing superstates centralized political power and asserted authoritarian rule on an unprecedented scale. Participatory democracy by now was largely confined to a few political lost worlds in the Alps and colonial New England. Elsewhere, princes, popes, and potentates dismissed democratic beliefs as absurd and treasonous, if not blasphemous.

By the seventeenth century, the oppressive spirit of political and religious absolutism began to subside. The Enlightenment resurrected classical ideas about democracy and updated them to suit modern circumstances. New theories about political power, individual rights, and accountable government emerged. In the eighteenth century, Montesquieu and Madison's revolutionary ideas about federalism made democratic government possible on a large scale. Liberal democracy fit the new political zeitgeist, and American colonists eagerly sought to put these new theories into practice.

At about the same time, misfit philosophe Jean-Jacques Rousseau broke with mainstream Enlightenment thought, and proposed a radical, back-to-the-future revival of small participatory city-states. Rousseau's ideas profoundly influenced the subsequent course of Western politics, sparking Europe's longstanding romance with revolutionary democracy. His ideas directly inspired the 48 Communes of the French Revolution, and later animated Marx, Lenin, and other scientific socialists, as well as social anarchists such as Bakunin, Kropotkin, and Proudhon.

During the 1960's, Rousseau's small, simple, self-contained democratic communes became fashionable among the American counterculture. His ideas echo today in progressive social movements that advocate democratic localism, sustainable development, local sourcing, the slow-food movement, and the Occupy protests.

Recent technological advances hint at exciting new possibilities for participatory democracy in the twenty-first century. Interactive social technologies now allow for effective two-way communications among massive populations, making virtual town meetings and participatory decision making possible for the first time in modern nation-states. Such innovations might one day allow free democracy to transcend conventional size limitations.

2. *Declining Participation.* Participatory democracies need citizens to pay close attention to public affairs and take an active role in government decision making. This takes considerable time and effort, which can cause participation rates to decline as people grow frustrated, bored, distracted, alienated, or disaffected. People might not have the time or resources to participate, or they might simply prefer to mind their own business and let others deal with politics. Whereas liberal democrats can afford to be relatively sanguine about modest participation rates, citizen apathy poses an existential threat to participatory democracies.

3. *Coercion.* Participation is so important that some countries compel citizens to take part in political decision making. Forced participation is troubling, but perhaps not surprising given the stakes.

Many countries require citizens to vote, and impose fines or other sanctions if they fail to do their duty.[4] Some countries take a different approach, marking voters' fingers with election ink or employing some other visible sign of participation. This is done to prevent multiple voting, but it also makes it easy to identify non-voters.[5]

The United States does not require citizens to vote, but does compel eligible persons to serve as jurors, with stiff penalties for those who fail to respond to a jury summons. De Tocqueville approved, writing that, "By obliging men to turn their attention to other affairs than their own, it rubs off that private selfishness which is the rust of society." All jurisdictions compensate jurors for their involuntary servitude, but it is usually only a token amount – often not enough to buy lunch or pay for downtown parking.

4. *Instability*. Participatory democracies have a poor track record when it comes to system stability and long-term survival. They burn brightly but quickly, as the simple elegance of direct democracy is betrayed by a lack of adequate checks and balances necessary to control the corrosive effects of faction and majoritarian tyranny. As Madison argued in *The Federalist* No. 55, "Had every Athenian citizen been a Socrates, every Athenian assembly would still have been a mob."

Sidebar 6: Freedom Is Not Free: Mandatory Community Service[6]

In the Southern Mexican state of Oaxaca (*wa-háwk-ah*), more than 400 *municipios* (local governments) run by Zapotec Indians follow the indigenous *usos y costumbres* (uses and customs) system to select local government officials. Public assemblies elect all municipal officers, including mayors, councilors, water officials, school caretakers, police, and other government workers, with terms ranging from one to three years. All male citizens are expected to serve the community in some capacity, without pay, for at least fifteen years before reaching age sixty, although they may pay others to serve in their place. The *usos y costumbres* system is designed to keep men involved in public affairs, reinforce communal solidarity, and ensure that everyone gets essential services at the lowest possible cost.

---

[4] Among the countries where compulsory voting laws are enforced: Argentina, Australia, Brazil, Chile, Congo, Ecuador, Fiji, Lebanon (men only), Liechtenstein, Nauru, Peru, Singapore, and Uruguay.
  Among the countries where compulsory voting laws are on the books but not actively enforced: Belgium, Bolivia, Costa Rica, Dominican Republic, Egypt (men only), El Salvador, France (Senate elections only), Gabon, Greece, Guatemala, Honduras, India, Indonesia, Luxembourg, Mexico, Panama, Paraguay, Philippines, Thailand, Turkey, and Venezuela.

[5] Among the countries that use election ink to mark voters' fingers: Afghanistan, Benin, Burkina Faso, Congo, Gambia, India, Indonesia, Iraq, Lebanon, Mauritania, Philippines, South Africa, Sri Lanka, Surname, Uganda, and Zimbabwe. In Zimbabwe's 2008 elections, government-sponsored thugs attacked adults caught in public without election ink on their fingers.

[6] Adapted from Sam Quinones, "Bonds of Tradition Are a Financial Bind for Oaxacan Migrants," *Los Angeles Times*, November 21, 2012.

One complication is that more than 300,000 Zapotec men have left over the past few decades to seek work in the United States. Migrants are expected to return to their *municipio* when called, or pay someone else to do their work. Otherwise, they can lose their local property rights, and family members left behind in Oaxaca can lose their access to electricity, water, and other government services.

Many Oaxacans believe that migrants get rich in the United States, while shirking their duties at home. Accordingly, *municipios* often expect expatriates to pay a premium if they do not return when summoned. Residents can buy their way out of their civic obligations for less than $100 per year; expatriates often must pay ten times that amount and more.

Migrants call these inflated payments extortion. They also complain that the number of new public offices has proliferated, enabling villagers to assign more jobs to migrants as a way to fill local coffers.

Supporters of the *usos y costumbres* system respond that mandatory service is essential to preserve their traditional way of life. As one local put it, "This is how we're a community." Another added that no amount of money is an adequate substitute for service, and that to be a citizen, "One has to give a bit of oneself."

REPRESENTATION AND REPRESENTATIVE DEMOCRACY

Because liberals value liberty more than freedom, representative government is the natural choice for liberal democrats. Representatives spare citizens the day-to-day burdens of governing, while remaining true to the principles of limited and accountable government.

Representative democracy replaces citizen-legislators with professional politicians who govern in the people's name. Ordinary people do not make the big decisions – their representatives do.

Representatives can either be *instructed delegates*, who vote according to the perceived will of their constituents, or *free agents*, who vote according to their own experience, conscience, and judgment. The American House of Representatives leans toward the instructed delegate model. Small congressional districts and biennial elections encourage House members to pay close attention to their constituents and the public mood.

The Senate hews toward the free agent model. Senators enjoy six years between elections, represent states instead of small districts, and have millions, rather than thousands, of constituents. These factors insulate senators from immediate accountability, allowing them to chart a more independent course.

Elected officials usually have professional administrators – civil servants – to assist them in running the government on a day-to-day basis. *Civil servants* are government employees who are largely exempt from direct democratic accountability, but must answer to the people's representatives and to the law.

Citizens in representative democracies are free and sovereign only on election day, after which they return to their private lives and surrender their freedom to their elected representatives. Many liberal democracies provide at least some additional opportunities for popular participation, including jury duty, the right to petition the government, the right to recall representatives, and voter initiatives, propositions, and referenda.

Some problems common to representative government include:

1. *Is Representative Government Democratic?* The Athenians thought that elections were a defining characteristic of aristocracy, not democracy, because as a practical matter only the rich (or their surrogates) can afford to run for office. Other free democrats dismiss representative government as, at best, democracy once removed.

2. *Special Interests.* Critics contend that rich and powerful individuals and groups have disproportionate influence in liberal democracies. Politicians pay special attention to those who make large contributions to their election campaigns and those who support public officials with money, information, and other resources while they are in office. Wealthy benefactors are rewarded with privileged access to public officials, and have a greater say in policy decisions than ordinary constituents might reasonably expect.

3. *Representative Government Encourages Citizen Irresponsibility.* Representative government encourages citizens to abdicate their civic responsibilities, by delegating important political decisions to others. Rousseau compared it to hiring mercenaries to fight wars, and called the practice lazy, weak, and unmanly.

4. *Low Participation Rates.* In liberal democracies, the word "politics" is often used in a pejorative sense, and political participation is considered a distasteful duty rather than a cherished right. Not surprisingly, participation rates often fall below 50 percent in liberal democracies, even though voting every few years is hardly burdensome.

   Liberal democrats rarely lose sleep over low voter turnout, and liberal democracies often have little real incentive to raise participation rates, because: (1) fewer demands placed on the system means that the government can conserve scarce resources and be more efficient; (2) voter decision-making is better, because active participants are usually better educated, better informed, and more highly motivated than nonparticipants; and (3) nonvoters are presumably content with the status quo.

   The alternative explanation is more worrisome – that people do not participate because: (a) there are barriers that discourage or prevent

FIGURE 4.2 Is democracy a community event or a private function? Original illustration by Ian Zell.

people from voting; and (b) people feel alienated from the system and do not think that their votes matter.

5. *Mutual Disengagement.* Low participation rates lead to a mutual disengagement between citizens and representatives. As citizens disconnect from politics, politicians become increasingly insulated from the electorate, and government grows more unresponsive and unaccountable (Figure 4.2).

THE SELECTION OF PUBLIC OFFICIALS

Because it is impractical in a large nation-state to ask citizens to decide every public issue, all modern democracies rely on representatives and civil servants to make at least some major policy decisions. Whatever these officials are called – executives, ministers, legislators, magistrates, administrators, selectmen, managers, judges, or jurors – they have delegated authority to articulate and execute the collective will of the people. How these representatives are selected inevitably has an impact on the nature of government.

Random Selection

Using random selection, or sortition, to select public officials yields a statistically representative cross-section of the eligible population. There is no advantage to being rich, highborn, well connected, good looking, charismatic, or popular. For that matter, there is no benefit to being inspired, intelligent, experienced, competent, honest, ethical, or otherwise fit for office. It all comes down to the luck of the draw.

To the Athenians, democracy meant selecting most government officials by lot. Every male citizen had an equal chance to hold public office, and any Athenian boy could grow up to become a leader of men. Only a few offices, notably the military Archon (*strategos*), were thought to require special expertise, so were elected.

Today, Australia, Canada, New Zealand, the United Kingdom, the United States, and other common law countries use sortition to create jury pools that provide a representative cross-section of the community. Although jury pools and venires are randomly selected, the final jury often is not. Lawyers can challenge potential jurors for bias, conflict of interest, or other good reasons (challenges for cause), and many jurisdictions also give lawyers the right to strike a limited number of potential jurors without having to state any reason at all (peremptory challenges). In the United Kingdom and in U.S. federal courts, jury selection has been streamlined so that challenges are rare and most juries are more or less randomly drawn. In contrast, most U.S. states have purposive selection procedures that allow lawyers to use their challenges to shape juries more to their liking.[7]

Elections

Most modern democracies elect their legislators and chief executives. There are different ways to do this, and we will look briefly at six types of electoral systems: proportional representation, first past the post, hybrid, preferential voting, indirect elections, and purposive representation. We will also consider term and tenure restrictions, and appointment.

---

[7] American defendants have a constitutional right to a representative jury pool, but there is no corollary right to a representative jury. One problem is that most lawyers do not want representative juries – they want sympathetic juries, and voir dire enables them to exclude potential jurors who might not be sufficiently attuned to their clients' interests. Lawyers often seek to exclude entire categories of persons from jury service, thwarting the ideal of broadly representative juries. The most egregious example of this sort of behavior occurred through the 1960's among Southern ·prosecutors, who routinely used peremptory challenges to exclude black veniremen in order to ensure all-white criminal juries.

Proportional Representation

Proportional representation (PR) allocates legislative seats according to the percentage of votes each political party receives. If a party earns more than a predetermined minimum percentage of the overall vote (usually 5–10 percent), it will earn the same percentage of seats in the legislature. If a party fails to earn the predetermined minimum, however, it will not get any seats.

For example, if a legislature has 100 seats and Party A gets 10 percent of the vote, then Party A will take ten seats. If Party B gets 5 percent of the vote, then it will take five seats. But if the minimum vote threshold is 5 percent and Party C receives 4.99 percent of the vote, then Party C will not get any seats.

PR makes it easier for smaller political parties to be represented in government. It encourages multiparty systems, where a broad spectrum of parties represents a diverse array of ideological, ethnic, religious, single-issue, and other discrete constituencies.

PR also strengthens the hand of political parties and party leaders. Voters usually vote for a party list rather than for individual candidates, and party leaders control the order in which candidates are listed on the ballot.[8] This means that party leaders, rather than voters, control who represents the party in the legislature.

Critics charge that PR can cause or exacerbate political instability, by encouraging political polarization and discouraging moderation, negotiation, and compromise. Parties can afford to appeal to a small but passionate voter base and still secure meaningful representation in government. This means that radical, fringe, and single-issue parties often have little incentive to negotiate, compromise, or court mainstream voters. To the contrary, niche parties often maximize their popularity and influence by making hyper-partisan appeals to core supporters, and attacking the moderate policies and compromises that mainstream parties must make in order to govern.

Because of the complex mix of parties that PR systems tend to produce, they often result in coalition governments, where mainstream centrist parties must accommodate smaller fringe parties in order to secure a legislative majority. In such circumstances, even the smallest and most intransigent party can wield disproportionate influence. It is not uncommon for a fringe party with just one or two legislative seats to hijack the political agenda by making extravagant demands and threatening to bring down the government if it does not get its way.

Italy, the poster child for this sort of chronic instability, has had more than sixty different governments since the end of World War II. Other PR countries,

---

[8] In most PR systems, party leaders place candidates on the ballot in rank order. The name at the top will receive the party's first legislative seat, the second candidate gets the second seat, and so on.

　　This contrasts with the U.S., where single-member districts mean that there is no party list. Party leaders cannot control who can file papers to run for office, and individual candidates often organize, raise money, and campaign on their own, without significant party support.

including Belgium and Israel, have had similar problems with marginal extremist parties sometimes driving government policy.

Some PR systems try to soften these destabilizing effects by raising minimum representation levels and creating incentives to compromise. Belgium and the Netherlands actively encourage broad coalition governments and consensual decision-making. This approach has generally worked better in the Netherlands than in Belgium, where longstanding tensions between the Dutch-speaking Flemish and French-speaking Walloon populations make cooperation and compromise difficult.

First Past the Post/Winner Takes All

In a first-past-the-post system, also called a winner-takes-all or plurality voting system, the candidate with the most votes wins, even if she or he receives less than 50 percent of the vote.[9] When combined with single-member districts, this usually leads to a two-party system, because it amplifies the power of moderate centrist parties with broad mainstream support, and penalizes fringe parties.

Third parties are at a structural disadvantage in first-past-the-post electoral systems. This is because most elections are contested near the center of political opinion, and the most successful parties are those that can claim the center-left and center-right of the political continuum. Parties positioned toward the extremes of the political spectrum are squeezed out in the process.

Third parties can play a spoiler role, by siphoning off support from one of the major parties. This can be considered a crime of passion, because third parties invariably hurt the mainstream party they are closest to in terms of ideology.

The United States and United Kingdom are two leading examples of first-past-the-post systems. The United States has had a stable two-party system for more than two centuries. The UK has what some refer to as a two-and-a-half-party system: the Labor and the Conservative parties trade power, while a third party – in recent years, the Liberal Democrats – and a handful of minor regional parties exert some marginal influence.[10] The UK periodically considers new electoral rules designed to strengthen the hand of third parties, but so far the two major parties have been able to block these efforts and preserve the status quo.

The main advantage of a winner-takes-all system is that it encourages elections to be contested in the middle of the electoral mainstream. Candidates must appeal to the political center to win, which tends to result in moderate

---

[9] Some first-past-the-post systems require a runoff election if no candidate earns more than 50 percent of the vote. This ensures that the winning candidate has a popular mandate, but it also makes elections more complex, expensive, and time-consuming.

[10] In the 2010 general election, Social Democrats earned 23 percent of the vote but took only 57 seats in parliament (8.3 percent out of a total of 650 seats). Labor received 29 percent of the vote but took 258 seats (39.6 percent).

governments with relatively broad popular support.[11] In a PR system, a party that polls at 3 percent can make or break a government; in a winner-takes-all system, a party that polls at 3 percent is irrelevant.

The most significant cost of the winner-takes-all system is that it does not represent minority interests as well as PR systems. Third parties that would enjoy significant legislative representation and influence in a PR system are regularly co-opted, ignored, or locked out of the political process. Moreover, because candidates must move to the center to win general elections, both major parties begin to look and sound alike, as they try to court the same moderate voters. This limits voter choice and alienates those who are outside of the political mainstream.

Hybrid Systems

Japan and a few other countries try to split the difference between PR and first-past-the-post rules by combining them in various ways. This is sometimes referred to as a mixed-member proportional voting. In Japan's bicameral diet, 300 of the 480 seats in the lower house (the House of Representatives) are directly elected in single-member districts using winner-takes-all rules; the remaining 180 seats are apportioned through a party-list system using proportional representation. In the upper chamber (the House of Councilors), 146 members are from winner-takes-all single-member districts, and 96 are selected through PR. Spain, Germany, Bolivia, Venezuela, and New Zealand also have hybrid systems.

Preferential Voting

The third type of electoral system is preferential voting, sometimes referred to as alternative, choice, or single transferable voting. In this system, people vote not only for their preferred candidate, but also for alternative candidates in descending order of preference – first choice, second choice, third choice, and so on. If no one receives more than 50 percent of the initial tally, the candidate with the fewest votes is eliminated, their voters' next preferences are plugged in, and the votes recounted. This process is repeated until a candidate receives more than 50 percent of the vote.

Preferential voting combines the multiparty approach of proportional representation with a nod to the electoral center, as less popular candidates are systematically eliminated in favor of those with broader appeal. One weakness of this system is that the winning candidate might be the second, third, or fourth choice of most voters – hardly a resounding mandate.

---

[11] In primary elections, candidates often appeal to the more extreme fringes of their partisan base, because highly ideological party activists tend to dominate primary elections, while moderate voters stay home and do not vote. For general elections, however, candidates in competitive races must move to the political center to appeal to moderate and undecided voters. The obvious political repositioning that goes on between primary and general elections inevitably undermines candidates' credibility and fuels voter cynicism.

Ireland, Australia, and Malta are leading proponents of preferential voting systems. In the United States, this system was used in city elections in Boulder, Cincinnati, Cleveland, New York, and Toledo, and it is still used in Cambridge, Massachusetts, for city council and school board elections. In 2011, British voters overwhelmingly rejected a national referendum that would have transformed their first-past-the-post system into a preferential voting scheme.

Indirect Elections

Rather than directly electing representatives, voters in indirect elections select intermediaries, who then elect the actual representatives. It is representation once removed.

The American political system has always relied heavily on indirect representation. Colonists used indirect elections during the Revolutionary era to select delegates to the two Continental Congresses, the Constitutional Convention of 1787, and all thirteen state ratification conventions.[12] The Constitution, in turn, established indirect elections for president, vice president, and senators.[13]

In presidential and vice-presidential elections, voters elect intermediaries, called electors, who travel to their respective state capitals on the appointed date in December to elect the president and vice president.[14] If there is a tie in the Electoral College, the House of Representatives selects the president and the Senate chooses the vice president.

State legislatures originally controlled the selection of U.S. senators.[15] This system remained in place for more than 100 years, until Oregon pioneered the direct election of senators in 1907. Nebraska quickly followed suit, and other like-minded states soon joined them. In 1913, the 17th Amendment stripped state legislatures of their power to choose senators and required direct elections. The appointments of cabinet members, most major executive officials,

---

[12] In 1787, Rhode Island voters rejected the draft constitution in a state referendum by a margin of ten to one. After all of the other states approved the Constitution in state conventions, Rhode Island called its own state convention in 1790 and was the last of the original thirteen colonies to approve the Constitution, on a vote of thirty-four to thirty-two.

[13] The Electoral College was originally designed to ensure that a small number of presumably wise elites from each state had the final say as to who would become president. In most states, presidential electors were originally selected by state legislatures. As late as the election of 1800, state legislatures in eleven states chose presidential electors, and only five states allowed for the popular election of electors.

[14] Most states use a "short ballot" that lists only the presidential and vice-presidential candidates' names, rather than the individual electors' names. Despite appearances, voters in these states do not vote directly for a candidate, but vote for a preselected slate of electors pledged to vote for the named candidate. Only a handful of states still list the electors' names in a "long ballot."

On the Monday after the second Wednesday in December, electors gather in their home state capitals to vote for president and vice-president. Despite its name, the Electoral College never meets as a single body. The sitting vice-president formally announces the official results to a joint session of Congress on January 6th.

[15] "The Senate of the United States shall be composed of two Senators from each State, chosen by the Legislature thereof." Article I, sec.3, cl.1.

and federal judges are by indirect selection. These officials are nominated by the president and confirmed by Senate vote.

Most modern democracies rely heavily on indirect elections. In parliamentary systems, the prime minister is almost always indirectly elected. Australia, the Baltic states, Canada, the Czech Republic, France, Germany, Hungary, Italy, Lebanon, Spain, and the United Kingdom all use indirect elections and/or "democratic appointments" to select government ministers and at least some legislators (usually members of the legislature's upper house).

Purposive Representation

Some democracies consciously shape election results through the use of quotas and other forms of assured representation for protected groups. Purposive representation takes proportional and indirect representation a step further, by guaranteeing representation for some groups irrespective of popular will.

Consociational democracies do this systematically, usually to maintain social cohesion in the face of ethnic, religious, or other sociopolitical conflict. In Lebanon, a country long divided along sectarian lines, the president is always a Maronite Christian, the prime minister is Sunni, the speaker of the parliament is Shi'a, and the Druze and other smaller religious and ethnic groups control lesser offices. The country's parliament is apportioned along similar lines.

In Hong Kong, the British established a system of "functional constituencies" for the local legislative council (Legco). Half of all Legco members were directly elected; various local organizations – businesses, unions, and professional organizations – selected the other half. China has preserved these functional constituencies, presumably because they allow the Chinese government to limit local autonomy by diluting democratic representation. Some 16,000 organizations, consisting of just 211,000 individuals (out of a total population of 7 million) currently select 30 members of the 60-seat Legco.

Many countries reserve legislative and government seats for groups that have been historically discriminated against or chronically underrepresented. Quotas for women are especially popular. Among the countries with representational quotas for women are Afghanistan, Bangladesh, Belgium, Bosnia, Burkina Faso, India, Iraq, France, Jordan, Mexico, Nepal, Pakistan, Rwanda, Slovenia, and Uganda. Scandinavian countries set aside between 15 percent and 50 percent of legislative seats for women. Eleven of nineteen Latin American countries have mandatory quotas for female legislators. Some countries, such as Brazil, require political parties to field a minimum percentage of female candidates for elective office, but do not require representational quotas – all nominees must earn their seats in open elections.

Term and Tenure Restrictions

Term and tenure restrictions determine how much time representatives have in office before the next election, and how long they can stay in office before being compelled to step down and move on. Most political offices have a set maximum term, although parliamentary systems often allow for interim (snap) elections called at the government's discretion. Shorter terms, from six months to two years, encourage representatives to be especially sensitive to constituent demands; longer terms, from four to six years or more, allow representatives greater insulation and autonomy from short-term public opinion.

Some jurisdictions also impose term limits on office holders. This is done, in part, to check the political advantages of incumbents and encourage political turnover. Term limits allegedly support the ideal of "citizen legislators," and avoid the emergence of a ruling class of professional politicians. Supporters claim that term limits make the electoral system more competitive and government more responsive. Term limits also allegedly help limit corruption and rein in rogue representatives.

Term limits can, however, cause or aggravate other problems. They result in less experienced and arguably less competent representatives, as seasoned political veterans are forced from office. They can increase the power of special interests, because inexperienced lawmakers rely more heavily on lobbyists and other self-interested "experts" for information and support. Finally, term limits restrict contestation rights and deprive constituents of the opportunity to elect representatives of their own choosing.

At the other extreme, a few countries, including the UK and Canada, have upper legislative chambers where the seats are either hereditary or carry a lifetime appointment, sometimes subject to a mandatory retirement age.[16]

Appointment

In most democracies, at least some important government positions, including judicial and administrative officials, are appointed rather than elected. In Britain, the prime minister appoints members of the House of Lords to life terms. Historically, the House of Lords has consisted of both hereditary peers and life peers, but this is changing as hereditary peers are being phased out. A few seats are reserved for notables with ex officio rights, such as ranking bishops in the Church of England. In Canada, the governor general appoints federal senators to life terms on the advice of the prime minister.

In most countries, judges are appointed rather than elected. Japan and many U.S. states (although not the federal government) are among the few jurisdictions where judges are either elected or subject to systematic public review.

The theory behind most appointment schemes is to select public officials on merit rather than popular appeal, and to insulate them from political pressures so that they can base their decisions on calm reflection, wisdom, fairness, professional expertise, and dispassionate judgment, rather than reacting to the

---

[16] Canadian Senators must retire at age 75.

public temper of the moment.[17] There are inevitable gaps here between theory and practice, and the appointment process itself is often highly politicized.

To insulate key government workers from political pressures, developed democracies rely heavily on a professional civil service. Although some civil servants serve at the pleasure of those who appoint them, most have job tenure protections – either for a set term of years or indefinitely on good behavior, perhaps subject to a mandatory retirement age. This is done to encourage professional and impartial administration based on the rule of law, rather than on will, whim, connections, corruption, political pressure, or expedience.

Finally, there are patronage appointments. In the United States, President Andrew Jackson institutionalized patronage appointments, which became known as the *spoils system*.[18] Unlike the professional civil service, the intent here is to make officials more dependent on their political sponsors. The right to appoint and remove large numbers of federal officials at will remains one of the most important presidential powers.

---

[17] Most U.S. states elect judges, and/or require some sort of periodic public approval while on the bench. Federal judges are not subject to any review beyond the initial Senate confirmation process, except upon impeachment.

    Worldwide, direct popular oversight of judges is rare. Japan is one of the few countries to require periodic referenda, called "people's reviews," for Supreme Court justices. These plebiscites occur every ten years, until the justice reaches the mandatory retirement age of seventy. No Japanese justice has ever been removed following a people's review.

[18] From the American saying, "To the victors go the spoils." The quote is attributed to New York Senator William Learned Marcy's 1832 speech extolling Jackson's landslide victory in 1828.

5

Inclusion

This is what I hate about democracy: everyone gets a voice.

– Greg Proops[1]

ELITE AND INCLUSIVE DEMOCRACIES

How open is the political process? Who gets to participate, and who is excluded? Broadly speaking, democracies can be either elite or inclusive. *Elite* systems limit political rights to a relatively small percentage of the adult population; *inclusive* systems grant near-universal adult suffrage and guarantee open contestation for offices. Historically, free democracies tend to be more exclusive than liberal democracies, although this is in part because inclusive democracies of any stripe are a relatively recent phenomenon.

Athens limited political rights to male citizens. Women could be citizens but had no political rights. Foreign residents (metics) had economic rights but no political rights, and slaves had neither economic nor political rights. Noncitizens, including metics, slaves, and their descendants, had no alternative path to citizenship. This meant that even during the golden age of Athenian democracy, only 12 percent of the population had political rights.[2]

Women were excluded from the political process almost everywhere until the end of the nineteenth century.[3] This limited political rights even in the most

---

[1] *The Smartest Man in the World Proopcast* (Podcast-iTunes) March 13, 2013.
[2] At its height, Athens had about 150,000 citizens (including women and children), plus 50,000 metics (foreign residents) and thetes (hired laborers), plus 50,000 slaves, for a total population of about 250,000. Of this figure, approximately 30,000 were adult male citizens with political rights.
[3] The exception was New Jersey, which allowed women to vote from 1776–1807. New Jersey women lost their right to vote in 1807, after a bitterly contested public vote on whether to

open democracies to less than 50 percent of the adult population. The most common justification for denying women political rights was that they allegedly lacked the capacity for rational thought, and remained locked in a perpetual childlike state of nature.[4]

New Zealand was the first nation to allow women to vote, in 1893. American women won the right to vote in 1919, at roughly the same time as in the United Kingdom and Northern European democracies. France did not extend the franchise to women until 1945. Switzerland barred women from voting in national elections until 1971, and a few cantons did not allow women to vote until the early 1990s.[5] Women are still excluded or actively discouraged from exercising political rights in some parts of the developing world, although this is rapidly changing almost everywhere, except in fundamentalist Islamist states such as Saudi Arabia and the Taliban-controlled parts of Afghanistan and Pakistan.[6]

Sidebar 7: Aung San Suu Kyi: A Woman's Work ...[7]:

Genuine tolerance requires an active effort to try to understand the point of view of others; it implies broad-mindedness and vision, as well as confidence in one's own ability to meet new challenges without resorting to intransigence or violence. In societies where men are truly confident of their own worth, women are not merely tolerated, they are valued. Their opinions are listened to with respect, and they are given their rightful place in shaping the society in which they live.

---

build a new county courthouse in Newark or Elizabethtown. Allegations of voter fraud, plus the questionable motives of an influential state legislator, John Condict – who was apparently angry about the large number of women who had voted for his opponent in an earlier election – led the state legislature to disenfranchise women. Surprisingly, there was little backlash to the new law from either women or men. Judith Apter Klinghoffer and Lois Elkis, "'The Petticoat Electors': Women's Suffrage in New Jersey, 1776–1807," 12 *Journal of the Early Republic* 159 (1992). Some women were allowed to vote in New York, Massachusetts, and New Hampshire prior to the Revolution, but these rights were revoked between 1777 and 1787.

[4] Former Speaker of the House Nancy Pelosi (D-Cal.) cites as a turning point in her life the day when she was a member of her school debate team, and the question tabled for discussion was, "Can Women Think?"

[5] Appenzell-Ausserrhoden agreed to allow women to vote in 1990. Neighboring Appenzell-Innerrhoden held out until the Swiss Supreme Court forced the issue in 1991.

[6] In Lebanon, women must prove that they have had at least an elementary education before they can vote. Men are not subject to the same requirement. Voting in Lebanon is compulsory for men, but not for women. The only states that still explicitly disenfranchise women are Saudi Arabia, Brunei, and Vatican City.

[7] Excerpts from Aung San Suu Kyi, Opening Keynote Address to the NGO Forum on Women, Beijing, China, August 31, 1991.

There is an outmoded Burmese proverb still recited by men who wish to deny that women too can play a part in bringing necessary change and progress to their society: "The dawn rises only when the rooster crows." ... The intelligent rooster surely realizes that it is because dawn comes that it crows and not the other way round.

There is an age-old prejudice the world over to the effect that women talk too much. But is this really a weakness? Could it not in fact be a strength? Recent scientific research on the human brain has revealed that women are better at verbal skills, while men tend towards physical action. Psychological research has shown, on the other hand, that disinformation engendered by men has a far more damaging effect on its victims than feminine gossip. Surely these discoveries indicate that women have a most valuable contribution to make in situations of conflict, by leading the way to solutions based on dialogue rather than on viciousness or violence?

The history of racial and ethnic exclusion tells a similar story. In the United States, although free black men were allowed to vote in some states after the Revolution, the vast majority were disenfranchised, especially in the South. After the Civil War, Reconstruction governments empowered southern freemen to exercise their new voting rights to elect black representatives to Congress and various state offices. When Reconstruction ended, however, southern states once again systematically deprived black men of their participatory rights, and things only got worse from there. The sole motivation for often-vicious racial oppression was prejudice, clothed in faith-based arguments about divine judgment and blatantly racist theories about intelligence and reason. Racial barriers to political inclusion in the South finally began to fall in the mid-twentieth century, and the Voting Rights Act of 1965 marked the effective end of state-sanctioned exclusions on the basis of race and ethnicity in the United States.

CITIZENSHIP AND FOREIGN RESIDENTS

Almost all democracies restrict political rights to citizens and deny voting rights to foreign residents and transitory visitors. Many countries also place strict limits on citizenship. In modern Germany, legal residents of Turkish descent, most of whom immigrated to Germany as invited guest workers beginning in the early 1960s, were legally barred from becoming German citizens, even if they were born in Germany to families who had lived there for generations. The government softened this blanket exclusion in 2000, although the rules for naturalized German citizenship remain labyrinthine, especially for people who lack German blood. Germany, along with Italy, China, Japan, and many other countries, base citizenship on jus sanguinis (law of blood) rather than jus soli (law of land, or citizenship based on birthplace).

Sidebar 8: I Hear You Knocking...[8]

Being born in Switzerland is not enough to make one Swiss. Switzerland follows the *jus sanguinis* theory of citizenship, and there is no right to citizenship based on place of birth. For those without the required quantum of Swiss blood, the only alternative path to citizenship is naturalization, and Switzerland has some of the toughest naturalization procedures in the world.

Applicants must live in Switzerland at least twelve years, speak the local language, and prove that they understand Swiss law and culture. Citizenship is considered a political and a social question, which means that local communities decide who can become a citizen. In most places, applicants must appeal directly to the community in which they reside and secure the consent of a majority of local citizens in a public referendum. Government officials may make recommendations, but citizenship is granted only by popular vote.

Anti-immigrant feelings run high in Switzerland, and ethnic Turks, Slavs, and Africans have found it especially difficult to gain citizenship. Not long ago, the conservative Swiss People's Party (SVP) ran an anti-immigration campaign with posters showing black and brown hands grasping at Swiss passports.

Elias Ego is an ethnic Turk who lives with his family in Schwyz, a small town of 14,000 in central Switzerland. Despite being born in Switzerland, living legally in Schwyz for twenty years, passing all of the citizenship tests, and being recommended by local authorities, the townspeople rejected Mr. Ego's citizenship application three times. Western European immigrants are routinely granted citizenship, he complains, while longtime residents from other parts of the world are routinely rejected.

"How can they do it?" he asks. "They just look at our pictures and our nationality, and for them that's enough to decide our future? It's not fair.... I feel Swiss. I was born here, all my friends are here. For me, this is like my country, my identity."

In 2003, the Swiss Supreme Court changed the rules, to require that local votes on citizenship be conducted by secret ballot rather than by a public vote. The change made a difference in Mr. Ego's case; after ten years of trying, the people of Schwyz finally granted him citizenship in 2008.

The United States follows the more inclusive jus soli theory of citizenship. American citizenship is the birthright of any child born on American soil, regardless of parental citizenship. Children born outside the United States are citizens by right if either parent is an American citizen. The United States also

---

[8] Excerpted and adapted from *BBC News*, May 31, 2008, retrieved from *http://news.bbc.co.uk/go/pr/fr/-/2/hi/europe/7427865.stm*.

has relatively open naturalization procedures for legal residents who remain in the United States for more than five years. There are, however, more than 11 million illegal immigrants currently living in the United States who cannot legally vote, run for office, serve as jurors, or apply for naturalized citizenship.

Few democracies extend to noncitizens the right to vote, run for office, or otherwise participate in politics. Nor is there any observable trend toward greater inclusion – if there is a trend, it is to eliminate such privileges where they exist.

British Commonwealth countries granted voting rights to citizens of other Commonwealth countries for much of the twentieth century, although only a few still allow the practice. Australia allowed residents from other Commonwealth countries to vote until 1984. Some Canadian provinces still allow resident British citizens to vote in local elections. In the United Kingdom, citizens of other Commonwealth countries, Irish citizens, and European Union (EU) citizens have limited voting rights.

France, Ireland, and Spain grant limited voting rights to legal residents from other EU countries. Scandinavian countries recognize mutual voting rights for resident citizens of other Nordic Passport Union countries. Israel allows some resident aliens to vote. Swiss law permits individual cantons and political subdivisions to allow foreign residents to vote in local elections, and a few jurisdictions have done so.

In America, many individual states allowed foreign residents to vote in the eighteenth and nineteenth centuries, but all of these laws were repealed between 1900 and 1930.[9] There have been occasional attempts to allow noncitizens to vote in local elections, but with few exceptions these efforts have failed. In 2004, San Francisco voters defeated an initiative that would have allowed noncitizens with school-aged children to vote in local school board elections, and they rejected a virtually identical measure again in 2010. In 2009, the Maine legislature voted down a bill that would have allowed noncitizens to vote in municipal elections, and the following year voters in Portland, Maine, killed a similar proposal.

Swimming against the tide, Chicago allows noncitizens to vote in some school board elections. A few Maryland towns allow noncitizens to vote on local issues.[10] In 2013, the California legislature passed a bill to allow all legal residents, including noncitizens, to serve as jurors, but Governor Jerry Brown vetoed it. The New York City Council is currently considering extending voting rights in municipal elections to noncitizen residents.

---

[9] Among the states that at one time allowed foreigners to vote in state elections: Alabama, Arkansas, Colorado, Indiana, Kansas, Mississippi, Nebraska, Oregon, South Dakota, Texas, and Wisconsin.

[10] Ron Hayduk, *Democracy for All: Restoring Immigrant Voting Rights in the United States* (Routledge 2006).

OTHER LIMITS ON POLITICAL RIGHTS

Citizens are also sometimes denied or stripped of their political rights. Although this presumptively seems like a bad idea, there are sometimes legitimate, or at least defensible, reasons for limiting participation rights among citizens. First, a country might restrict participation rights to keep the number of voters manageable, or reinforce social cohesion. Second, a country might limit political rights to those with sufficient intelligence to exercise their rights sensibly. Third, states might restrict political rights to those who are sufficiently invested in the community, either psychologically or materially, to exercise their rights responsibly. Fourth, participation rights might be contingent upon meeting certain easily quantifiable factors – age, education, wealth, or property ownership – that serve as indirect measures of intelligence, virtue, reason, responsibility, or legal capacity. Whereas any of these limitations might seem reasonable, it is worth noting that all of these exceptions have been used in the past to rationalize invidious discrimination.

The most common exclusion is based on an alleged lack of capacity for mature reason, judgment, and responsibility. This is why children do not have full political rights until they reach the somewhat arbitrary age of majority. It is also why some – but not all – countries deny political rights to the mentally handicapped and insane. Most U.S. states allow mentally ill adults to vote, in part because drawing a bright legal line regarding mental capacity has proved to be difficult.

Wealth, property, class, and education have all been used at various times as proxy measures to determine whether to grant or deny political rights. Aristotle proposed that only the wealthiest 6,000 male citizens be allowed to participate in Athenian politics. He assumed, as have many other serious political thinkers, that wealth is an excellent indicator of intelligence, if not virtue. In the nineteenth century, progressive liberals such as Jeremy Bentham sought to require juries to contain at least one gentleman, to offer déclassé jurors enlightened leadership and exemplary role models. As late as the twentieth century, many European democracies, including the United Kingdom, denied political rights to the poor and working classes. Some countries still have literacy tests or other educational threshold requirements to vote.

Finally, many democracies deny political rights to those convicted of serious crimes. This loss of freedom is usually temporary, although Florida, Virginia, and ten other U.S. states permanently bar felons from voting and jury service.[11]

One persistent problem in the United States and other countries is vote suppression – public or private efforts to discourage eligible voters from exercising

---

[11] The twelve states are: Alabama, Arizona, Delaware, Florida, Iowa, Kentucky, Mississippi, Nebraska, Nevada, Tennessee, Virginia, and Wyoming. Whether by design or accident, this policy has a disproportionate exclusionary effect on black men. See, "Felon Voting," retrieved from www.felonvoting.procon.org.

their political rights. In the old days, devices such as poll taxes and literacy tests were widely used to deter nonwhite and poor citizens from voting. Today, some states, including Arizona, Florida, Georgia, Kansas, North Carolina, Texas, and Pennsylvania, impose stringent requirements on voters to prove their citizenship before voting. Supporters claim that such laws prevent voter fraud. Critics counter that in-person voter fraud is virtually nonexistent, and that these laws are intended to discourage the poor, elderly, college students, and minority groups from voting.

Finally, democracies sometimes restrict participation rights to those who pay taxes or otherwise demonstrate that they have a sufficient financial stake in the community to vote responsibly. Representation on local Dutch water boards (*Waterschappen/Hoogheemraadschappen*) is apportioned according to the different financial responsibilities of local landowners, leaseholders, and other residents who depend on the local polders for land reclamation, flood control, fresh water, and sewage disposal. In the United States, many jurisdictions required voters to pay a poll tax before they could vote, until the 24th Amendment banned the practice in 1964. Voting rights in some special district elections, such as power and water districts, are still limited to taxpayers or ratepayers.

6

Equality

After inclusion, the next question is whether everyone participates on an equal basis, or whether some people are more equal than others. There are two distinct types of equality to consider: political-legal equality and socioeconomic equality.

Liberal democrats focus on political-legal equality, which is closely tied to individual liberties, including rights to think, speak, and organize, and equality before the law. Most liberals believe that people are born to equal rights, and assume that equality is the natural state of things. Because equal rights are, in effect, a preexisting condition, government does not have a significant role to play in creating or maintaining equality, especially with respect to socioeconomic rights.

Government has a responsibility to ensure that everyone has equal opportunities and equal justice, but otherwise should leave people alone to make their own way. If people choose well and prosper, then they have the right to the fruits of their labor. If they choose poorly and fall behind, then they must take responsibility for their actions and accept the consequences.

Equal opportunity does not ensure equal results. Although people might be born equal, they are destined to unequal outcomes, and this is OK. Economic inequalities, in particular, do not violate the liberal sense of justice, unless they are the result of some fundamental unfairness, such as fraud, duress, or coercion.

Free democrats also believe in political-legal equality, but they are more likely to go the extra mile to demand socioeconomic equality in the form of a social democracy. In contrast to liberal democrats, most free democrats believe that people are naturally unequal at birth. Inequality is the natural state of things, because we are all born to different circumstances and different fortunes. Equality is a purely human construct, tied to freedom and community. Citizens in a free society are equal if and only if people choose to treat each other as equals.

In a social democracy, government has the ultimate responsibility to establish and maintain a broadly egalitarian society. Government not only guarantees political-legal equality, but also seeks to eliminate gross distinctions of wealth, class, and status. Social democrats believe in distributive justice, including the redistribution of resources to limit gaps between the richest and poorest citizens. Social democrats not only want equal opportunities, they also want equal – or at least equitable – results that allow everyone to share fully in all aspects of community life.

POLITICAL AND LEGAL EQUALITY

Equal Representation: Egalitarian and Weighted Systems

In *egalitarian* democracies, individuals have an equal vote and an equal voice in the political process. In *weighted* systems, some votes and voices are worth more than others.

Although Athens was an exclusive democracy, it was extraordinarily egalitarian. Every male citizen had an equal voice and vote, and because the Athenians filled most public offices by lottery, every eligible citizen had an equal chance to serve as a public official in almost any capacity. Athens was the rare exception; weighted systems are the norm.

The Roman Republic was explicitly class conscious. Public assemblies were divided according to class and tribe, with wealthier classes and favored tribes having greater influence through weighted voting and other procedural advantages. Elite classes, for example, had the right to vote before members of lesser classes in public assemblies.[1]

In modern times, the United States has always had a highly unequal political system. Political inequality is built into the federal system, which gives the citizens of some states significant advantages over citizens of other states in federal elections. In Senate and presidential elections, voters in the least populous states carry far more weight than voters in heavily populated states.

In the Senate, states are equal rather than people, so the electoral principle of one person, one vote does not apply. Wyoming, with a half-million people, has the same representation as California, with 37 million people. This means that one Wyoming vote is worth seventy-four California votes. In Senate deliberations, senators representing less than 10 percent of the American population can block any proposed law or prevent the Senate from conducting normal business.

In presidential elections, each state's electoral votes are determined by adding the number of the state's Representatives to the number of Senate seats,

---

[1] Alexander Yakobson, *Elections and Electioneering in Rome: A Study in the Political System of the Late Republic* (F. Steiner 1999).

meaning that the least populous states are guaranteed at least three electoral votes. In presidential elections, one Wyoming vote is worth four times as much as a California vote.

Even the supposedly egalitarian House of Representatives had a long history of weighted voting among congressional districts. The main reason for the constitutionally required decennial census was so that House seats could be regularly reapportioned to match internal population shifts. In practice, however, states often failed to redraw district lines to keep up with intrastate migration. By the mid-twentieth century, votes in rural congressional districts were often worth ten times more than votes cast in urban districts.[2]

Malapportionment among state legislative districts was even worse. In California during the early 1960s, one rural state Senate district had a mere 14,000 voters, whereas Los Angeles's only state Senate district had more than 6 million voters – a ratio of 428:1. In Vermont, the smallest state assembly district had just 36 people; the largest had 35,000 – a ratio of 1,000:1.

These gross imbalances ended in 1964, thanks to two landmark Supreme Court decisions in *Wesberry v. Sanders* and *Reynolds v. Sims*.[3] *Wesberry* established the one person, one vote principle for federal congressional districts; *Reynolds* required *all* state legislative houses to be apportioned according to the one person, one vote standard.[4] The two justices most responsible for these rulings, Earl Warren and William Brennan, considered these two cases to be the most significant decisions of their careers – even more important than *Brown v. Board of Education.*

In the United Kingdom, members of parliament (MPs) traditionally represented an eclectic mix of constituencies, including counties, boroughs, and universities. Privileged voters, including university professors, often had more than one vote, because they were members of multiple constituencies. For example, a university professor might vote for one MP to represent their home district, and vote for another MP to represent their university. Leading liberals, including Jeremy Bentham and John Stuart Mill, endorsed this practice on the ground that it allowed the better sort to have a greater, and presumably more intelligent, say in election outcomes.

Britain's *rotten boroughs* are perhaps the most notorious examples of weighted voting. Boroughs are towns established by royal charters that grant residents the right to elect a specified number of members (usually two) to the House of Commons. Borough boundaries were almost never altered after the original charter was issued, so even if a borough lost population it retained its right to return the same number of MPs. By the nineteenth century, some

---

[2] This was not necessarily the result of carelessness or incompetence. Rural interests lobbied against reapportionment efforts in order to maximize their own political clout.

[3] *Wesberry v. Sanders*, 376 U.S. 1 (1964); *Reynolds v. Sims*, 377 U.S. 533 (1964).

[4] Chief Justice Earl Warren, writing for the Court, concluded that the federal Senate was a unique exception to the one person, one vote rule. It was a singular compromise necessary to save the republic, and its peculiar historical circumstances were not applicable to state legislatures.

boroughs had as few as 7 residents, and at one point 72 percent of all MPs (293 out of 405) represented constituencies with fewer than 500 voters. Reform legislation finally dismantled the rotten borough system in the mid-nineteenth century.

Today, the City of London ("the City") still allows plural voting. The City is a small district in the heart of London's commercial quarter. It consists mostly of office buildings, and has only 8,000 full-time residents. City residents have the right to vote in local elections, but so do local businesses and commercial interests. These businesses get to select individuals to represent their interests and vote on their behalf. There is no rule that these representatives must reside in the City, which means that nonresident representatives vote twice: once in the City, and a second time at their official place of residence. The City also grants voting rights to local businesses and other special interests to elect the members of the City of London Corporation – the City's main governing body. Finally, the City's twenty-five wards have substantially unequal populations, but each ward elects one alderman. All of this leads critics to call the City of London the last of the rotten boroughs.

Britain honors weighted voting of another kind in selecting the House of Lords. The House of Lords is one the least representative legislative bodies in the world. It was, and remains, specifically designed to represent the aristocratic few rather than the democratic many. Traditional democratic considerations, including voter equality, accountability, and regional representation, are legally irrelevant.

Canada's senate is similar to the House of Lords in terms of selection and appointment, but unlike Britain's upper house it requires a degree of regional representation. Representation is heavily weighted, however, to favor some provinces over others, with little regard for population or proportionality. Unlike the U.S. Senate, the Canadian senate does not recognize the principle of provincial equality; the number of senators apportioned to each province and territory varies widely, and is not tied to population. British Columbia has 4 million residents and 6 senators; Nova Scotia has a population of 1 million people and 10 senators.

The Australian senate, like its American counterpart, is apportioned on the principle of equality of states. Each state elects 12 senators, which means that Tasmania, with 500,000 citizens, has the same number of senators as New South Wales, with more than 7 million residents. Federal and state legislatures in Australia are all consciously apportioned to favor rural voters over urban residents, in part to prevent city voters from overwhelming rural interests.

Most other modern democracies have weighted electoral systems, either by choice or through historic inertia. After World War II, Japan proved unwilling to reapportion its legislative districts as required by law, which eventually led to severe malapportionment in favor of rural voters. This has had a profound influence on Japanese politics, including Japan's longstanding and often militant agricultural protectionism. After repeated Japanese supreme court decisions requiring the government to respect the one person, one vote rule, the legislature reluctantly began to resolve these structural inequalities. A series of half-hearted reforms in the 1980s and 1990s partially reapportioned national legislative districts, but considerable inequities remain. In 2009, the House of Representatives had a disparity of more than 2:1 between the most and least populated districts; the House of Councilors had a bias of more than 5:1.

Spain systematically favors small and rural provinces over heavily populated urban electoral districts. In the lower house, the Congress of Deputies, the maximum disparity is 5:1 between rural Soria and urban Madrid; in the Senate the figure is almost 9:1 favoring sparsely populated Castilla y León over the more numerous madrileños.

In many countries, including the United States, special-purpose districts and other quasi-governmental entities routinely weigh votes unequally. In business improvement districts and special tax districts, votes are weighted according to the value of property owned or the amount of taxes paid. Weighted representation is also common in the private sector, the best example being corporate shareholder meetings, where votes are apportioned according to the number of shares owned.

Weighted Voting in Government: The Votes That Count?

Weighted voting also occurs within governments. A vote in the U.S. House of Representatives is worth less than one-quarter of a senator's vote, because the House is more than four times larger than the Senate. This is one of the reasons why the House is sometimes referred to as "the Zoo," and the Senate as "the Club."

The judiciary is even more exclusive. The lowliest state or federal trial judge can strike down a law on constitutional grounds, nullifying the collective will of the government and people with the stroke of a pen.

In 1992, Colorado voters overwhelmingly passed Amendment 2, repealing all existing gay rights ordinances and prohibiting any new laws that would make homosexuals a legally protected class. The amendment passed with 54 percent of the vote, but the U.S. Supreme Court struck it down on a 6–3 vote in *Romer v. Evans*.[5]

In 1997, 59 percent of California voters approved Proposition 187, denying public education, health care, and other government assistance to an estimated 1.3 million illegal immigrants. Federal District Judge Mariana Pfaelzer ruled that Proposition 187 was unconstitutional, and when Governor Gray Davis refused to appeal, the law quietly died.[6]

In 2008, 52 percent of California voters approved Proposition 8, banning gay marriage. Federal District Judge Vaughn Walker ruled that Prop 8 was unconstitutional, and the 9th Circuit Court of Appeals affirmed. The Supreme

[5] *Romer v. Evans*, 517 U.S. 620 (1996).
[6] *League of United Latin American Citizens v. Wilson*, 997 F.Supp. 1244 (1997).

Court dismissed the appeal on procedural grounds, leaving the 9th Circuit's decision intact and gay marriage legal in California.[7]

In 2000 the Supreme Court voted 5–4 in *Bush v. Gore*[8] to stop Florida's vote recount in that year's disputed presidential election. The decision effectively declared George W. Bush president.[9] In the end, five Republican justices were the votes that counted.

In most countries that recognize judicial review, only special constitutional courts have the right to declare laws unconstitutional, and then only under limited circumstances. Restricting the right of judicial review to a special court is typical of civil law countries, including France, Germany, Russia, Egypt, Brazil Peru, and Mexico. Some common law countries, such as South Africa, follow this practice, but others follow the American custom of allowing any court to interpret and enforce the national constitution.

Some countries, including Finland, New Zealand, and Malaysia either do not allow judicial review of national legislation, or allow only limited review under exceptional circumstances. The United Kingdom and Netherlands have historically refused to recognize any right of judicial review, but both now seem prepared to accept it on a limited basis with respect to EU human rights law.[10]

At the other end of the spectrum, Iran's Grand Ayatollah and the twelve-member Council of Guardians, the country's unelected supreme body of Islamic clerics and jurists, wield an absolute veto over all government decisions and have the unchecked authority to disqualify any candidates for any public office for any reason. Whereas ordinary Iranians formally elect the representatives to the national legislature (Majlis), in the final analysis the only votes that truly count are those cast by the Council. Whether this is a weighted democracy or a faux democracy is debatable.

Finally, many putatively democratic international organizations weigh members' votes unequally. The United Nations gives a veto power to the five permanent members of its Security Council (Britain, China, France, Russia, and the United States). The International Monetary Fund weights votes on the basis of each country's financial contributions (known as its quota), based on the country's perceived economic power.

---

[7] *Perry v. Schwarzenegger*, 704 F.Supp. 2d 921 (2010); *Perry v. Brown*, 671 F. 3d 1052 (2012); *Hollingsworth v. Perry*, 570 U.S. ___ (2013).

[8] 531 U.S. 98 (2000).

[9] Howard Gillman, *The Votes That Counted: How the Court Decided the 2000 Presidential Election* (University of Chicago Press 2001).

[10] The United Kingdom accepted a limited form of judicial review for the first time in 1966, when it accepted the jurisdiction of the European Court of Human Rights, which has the right to review members' domestic laws. In 2005, the British government established a new national supreme court, with limited powers of judicial review. That court cannot overturn an act of Parliament, but can review executive and administrative actions to determine whether they violate the intent or scope of authorizing legislation.

The Netherlands voted narrowly in 2010 to move for the first time toward establishing a limited form of judicial review, with legislation passing in the lower house by just one vote, 37–36.

Benign Weighting

Some political systems employ so-called benign weighting to guarantee greater opportunities and better results for disadvantaged or underrepresented groups. Affirmative action programs seek to redress past discrimination on the basis of gender, race, ethnicity, class, religion, or other group identity.

Along with representation, hiring, promotion, education, and training preferences governments might also provide money, legal advice, and other resources to help disadvantaged groups compete on a more level playing field. In 2012, Brazil enacted an affirmative action law requiring public universities to reserve half of their admissions slots for poor students and students of African descent, with the government promising to extend its affirmative action programs to other areas in the next few years.[11]

Affirmative action programs are controversial, in part because it is not always clear whether they remedy past discrimination, or perpetuate discrimination by systematically favoring some groups over others. Some critics charge that affirmative action programs can create a stigma by reinforcing the notion that beneficiaries are incapable of making progress without institutionalized favoritism. Even supporters of affirmative action programs worry that quotas intended to help disadvantaged groups might become a ceiling, rather than a floor, in terms of representation or assistance.

Opponents also allege that affirmative action programs offer windfall benefits to individuals who are not actual victims of past discrimination, solely because they happen to belong to a protected class. Should President Obama's children be able to take advantage of government affirmative action programs because of the United States's past mistreatment of African Americans? The answer is not self-evident.

A related concern is that affirmative action programs might reinforce separatist identification and behavior, stir resentment among excluded groups, and aggravate, rather than relieve, underlying social conflicts. If this happens, affirmative action programs might slow progress toward establishing a more egalitarian, pluralistic, and just society.

Perhaps the worst-case scenario is that the oppressed become oppressors. In an attempt to protect unique and presumably vulnerable local ethnic groups, the Nigerian constitution grants special rights and preferences to *indigenes* – tribes considered native to each region. Protected status quickly became a license for local indigene tribes to consolidate their privileges and systematically discriminate against rival clans. In much of Nigeria, indigenes monopolize local civil service jobs and university positions, and control public access to government services. Competing tribes are shut out, even if they have lived in the area for centuries.

---

[11] Simon Romero, "Brazil Enacts Affirmative Action Law for Universities," *New York Times* (August 30, 2012).

Qualified Democracies

Qualified democracies grant special privileges to a dominant, rather than a disadvantaged, religion, ethnicity, race, or other faction. Powerful groups, backed by state power, use their institutionalized advantages to promote their own interests and limit the influence of competing groups, relegating rivals to second-class citizenship or worse. The most egregious modern example of this was South Africa's apartheid regime. Other current examples of qualified democracies include the Islamic republics of Afghanistan, Bangladesh, Iran, Iraq, Mauritania, and Pakistan, and the Jewish state of Israel.[12] Most constitutional monarchies, including Great Britain, offer institutionalized privileges to the resident royal family and aristocracy.

Many democratic states explicitly advertise their specific racial and/or ethnic origins, which can serve to marginalize other groups symbolically, even if the law does not actively enforce this favored status. This has been a particular problem in countries such as Japan and Korea, which routinely celebrate their relative racial and/or ethnic purity. Many states' names explicitly identify with a particular ethnicity, among them Afghanistan, the Czech Republic, Denmark, Germany (Deutschland), England, Finland, France, Ireland, Pakistan, Romania, Scotland, Serbia, Slovakia, Thailand, Turkey, and Uzbekistan. Although these names are often only vestiges of long-gone ethnic enclaves, they retain symbolic power and can serve as an unsubtle reminder to immigrants and nonconforming groups that this land is not their land.

An Equal Political Voice: Access and Influence

An equal vote does not necessarily mean an equal voice. Even if a political system respects the principle of one person, one vote, some people will have privileged access to the media, political candidates, and government officials that gives them disproportionate political influence.

There are several ways to address this problem directly, including imposing limits on campaign contributions and spending, or instituting public campaign financing. The United States has taken some tentative steps in this direction, placing limits on campaign contributions and offering a public financing option to presidential candidates. The Supreme Court, however, recently dealt these modest efforts a series of hard blows, striking down federal and state laws intended to equalize political contributions and spending, and nullifying a state

---

[12] A few qualified democracies, notably Israel, make good faith efforts to respect the rights of nonconforming groups. The perception remains, however, that when the chips are down, the interests of the dominant group will take precedence over competing interests.

Other qualified democracies offer symbolic respect to select minority groups. Iran, for example, reserves five seats in the national legislature (Majlis) for Christians, Jews, and Zoroastrians. Such token representation does not compensate for the pervasive social, economic, political, and legal discrimination these groups routinely face.

THE INTRICATE MECHANICS OF GOVERNMENT

PUBLIC ENTRANCE

LOBBYIST ENTRANCE

FIGURE 6.1 NON SEQUITUR © 2010 Wiley Ink, Inc.. Dist. By UNIVERSAL UCLICK.
Reprinted with permission. All rights reserved.

law that sought to use public funds to equalize massive expenditures by wealthy, self-funded candidates. These cases will be discussed in more detail later.

In the last twenty years, running for federal office in the United States has become so expensive that candidates must be independently wealthy, sponsored by wealthy patrons, or actively engaged in full-time fundraising efforts, even if the next election is years away (Figure 6.1).

Other countries have been more successful in managing campaign financing by limiting donations, expenditures, and campaign length. Australia, Germany, Japan, and the United Kingdom use a combination of public and private campaign funds, and impose strict limits on private contributions to political candidates. Japan and the United Kingdom try to limit active campaigning to the six weeks leading up to an election,[13] although candidates in both countries face

[13] In the United Kingdom, during the six-week run-up to an election, governments are not supposed to introduce significant or controversial new policy proposals. This pre-election grace period is called "Purdah," from the Farsi word for the curtains that conceal women from the world of men.

growing pressures to engage in more extensive fundraising efforts to finance increasingly expensive campaigns. To lessen these fundraising pressures, the United Kingdom offers candidates free campaign advertising during the official six-week election season.

Canada relies on a comprehensive public financing scheme for its political parties. First, the government grants political parties generous subsidies on the basis of previous voting results. This is called the *direct public subsidy*, or *government allowance*. Second, the government also reimburses political parties for about half of their actual election expenses, regardless of the election results.

In Hong Kong, candidates for the unicameral Legco apply to the government for postelection rebates for campaign expenses. The rebate rate is the same for all candidates, usually set at about $10 per vote earned.

One of the most useful indirect ways to limit the effects of unequal access to candidates and government officials is to require full transparency in campaign financing, including public disclosure of all political donations and expenditures. Reporting requirements do not directly resolve the underlying inequalities, but they do allow everyone to see who gives money to whom. American election laws and the federal tax code are generally effective at maintaining a reasonably transparent campaign finance system, although a significant loophole exists at the federal level for nonprofit social welfare organizations, which are not required to identify major donors.

Once elections are over and successful candidates enter government service, privileged access to these officials becomes even more problematic. Well-connected individuals and groups can disproportionately influence public policy, and in some cases can tap directly into the public treasury.

Again, perhaps the most effective remedy for this is enforced transparency. An especially effective example of this approach is California's Brown Act, which requires all government bodies to post meeting agendas at least seventy-two hours in advance, and requires officials to conduct all government business in open, public sessions. Some states require or encourage government officials to open their calendars, so that the public can see with whom officials meet and the subjects of those meetings. Transparency does not directly solve the problem of unequal access and influence, but it does compel government to do the people's business in full public view.

Legal Equality

Legal equality means that everyone has the same rights, meaningful access to the courts, and entitlement to impartial justice. It means that laws are applied fairly and consistently – that like cases are treated alike, without favor or prejudice on the basis of wealth, status, class, connections, ethnicity, race, gender, or other extraneous factors. Legal equality means that the poorest and least educated, least popular, and least consequential person stands before the law on substantially the same footing as the wealthiest, most intelligent, most popular, and most influential.

Most Americans think of this as their right to have "their day in court." There is no guarantee of a particular result, but it should be a fair fight, and everyone should have an equal opportunity to plead their case before an impartial magistrate or a jury of their peers.

Legal equality includes due process. *Due process* requires that investigatory, trial, and appellate procedures are accessible, clear, reasonable, and fair.[14] This might require government to take positive steps to ensure equal justice, such as guaranteeing effective legal representation in criminal cases.[15]

Legal inequalities can be formal or informal. *Formal* (de jure) inequalities are created or maintained by law. Examples include the rule in some Muslim countries that a woman's testimony is worth half a man's, and the rule barring atheists from testifying at all.[16]

Informal (de facto) inequalities are not created or consciously enforced by law, but in practice distort the course of justice. In the United States, the most persistent de facto inequality is wealth. It is the best single predictor of success in civil litigation, and in criminal cases a defendant's wealth significantly affects his or her chances of obtaining a favorable verdict or lighter sanctions. This is especially true in capital cases, where the death penalty is reserved almost exclusively for the poorest defendants.

SOCIAL AND ECONOMIC EQUALITY

Social democrats are not satisfied with political-legal equality and equal opportunity; they also want socioeconomic equality, with equal or equitable results. Free democrats are more likely to be enthused about socioeconomic equality than liberal democrats because it squares with their views about community building and social solidarity.[17]

Most liberals now accept the limited idea that the state should address *absolute* poverty. This means that government should ensure that no one suffers from a lack of essential resources – food, clothing, shelter, and perhaps minimal health care. State-supervised food programs, homeless shelters, and urgent care clinics are examples of government programs designed to mitigate

---

[14] Due process is not always strictly neutral. In criminal cases, for example, there is a designed imbalance regarding the burden of proof: the state bears the burden of proof at all stages of investigation and trial.

[15] *Gideon v. Wainwright*, 372 U.S. 335 (1963).

[16] This rule remains common practice in the Middle East and elsewhere. In the United States, although the U.S. Supreme Court has ruled that barring atheists from testifying is unconstitutional, four Southern states (Arkansas, North Carolina, Tennessee, and Texas) and two Northern states (Pennsylvania and Maryland) still have laws on the books that prohibit atheists from testifying in court or holding public office.

[17] Liberal democrats can also be social democrats. Some members of Britain's Liberal Democrat party consider themselves to be social democrats. In the United States, the late Republican Congressman Jack Kemp (R-Cal.) referred to himself as a "bleeding heart conservative" because of his social democratic leanings.

FIGURE 6.2 Who's Sorry Now? Absolute Poverty versus Relative Poverty. Original illustration by Ian Zell.

absolute poverty and ensure that no one starves, dies of exposure, or suffers unnecessarily from common and easily curable injuries or diseases.

Social democrats embrace the broader view that government should tackle *relative* poverty. They believe that gross differences in wealth and class are not only unjust, but also cause serious political and social problems. The state plays the role of equalizer, to limit class and status distinctions. It provides redistributive justice by limiting wealth differentials between the richest and poorest citizens, and offers benefits to lift the poor, weak, and needy. These are positive rights, or entitlements, intended to level society, strengthen the middle class, and encourage social cohesion (Figure 6.2).[18]

---

[18] Negative rights limit the government's power (and sometimes also limit the power of private parties) to infringe on liberties; they are "leave me alone" rights. Positive rights mean that the government is obliged to provide specified goods or services; they are "help me" rights.

Some rights can be negative *or* positive, and have different meanings depending on context. The right to travel, an implied right in the American Constitution, has always been interpreted as a

Some socioeconomic entitlements are universal and available to everyone on an equal basis, regardless of wealth or status. Every child, for example, might have the right to a free public education, regardless of family wealth.

Other entitlements guarantee equal benefits, but require those who can afford to pay more to do so, while the government subsidizes others on the basis of their perceived ability to pay. Everyone might have a right to a specified level of health care or child-care, but the rich must pay for it, while the government subsidizes low-income families. This sort of means testing has a secondary leveling effect on society.

The third category of government assistance involves *indirect redistribution* programs, such as tax credits or subsidies. These include farm subsidies, investment credits, redevelopment funds, business subsidies, and tax breaks for charitable donations. Such indirect redistribution programs are often justified on the grounds that they strengthen the middle class, protect jobs, help family farmers, and encourage charitable giving. Critics argue that these programs are often counterproductive, because in practice government subsidies and tax breaks usually disproportionally favor the rich and powerful, as they are often able to manipulate the rules to their advantage.

The fourth type of government aid is *direct wealth redistribution*. The government plays Robin Hood (an ironic role, given the original story), taking from the rich and giving to the poor. Examples include wealth and property, progressive income, luxury, and estate taxes. In some cases, the government might seize private property through imminent domain or other legal devices.[19] The government then redistributes these resources through aid and assistance programs, including welfare, social security, aid for dependent children, and other mechanisms designed to limit socioeconomic inequality and encourage the development of a strong middle class.[20]

---

negative right, meaning that states cannot erect arbitrary barriers to hinder interstate migration. A positive right to travel might oblige government or another third party to *facilitate* travel under some circumstances, perhaps requiring government to provide transportation subsidies, build roads, or provide other means to allow people to move about. Public roads and freeways might be considered a positive right, but the use of public roads is usually considered to be a privilege, not a right.

[19] Land seizure and redistribution programs are common in the developing world, especially in Latin America and Africa. In South Africa, land redistribution requires full and fair compensation to property owners, although white farmers complain about growing intimidation and unjust compensation for seized white-owned farmlands.

   In neighboring Zimbabwe, land seizures are often carried out with little or no compensation. Landowners are harassed until they abandon their property, and farmers are sometimes murdered so that their property can be confiscated. Seized property routinely goes to politically connected black elites, rather than to the poor or to actual victims of injustice under the old, white-dominated regime.

[20] Some of these redistributive programs are not intended to favor the poor or weak, but are designed to benefit those with natural, earned, or inherited advantages. Few object to merit-based scholarships, which favor intelligent and accomplished students. Legacy admissions at private and public universities are more controversial, because they disproportionately privilege wealthy and well-connected families.

In the United States, a leading example of direct government socioeconomic leveling was Franklin Roosevelt's G.I. Bill of Rights. The law provided veterans with unprecedented access to government resources, including federal mortgage subsidies and generous federal payments for college and professional education. The G.I. Bill, along with other similar government programs, helped create the middle-class society that drove the post–WWII economic boom.[21]

Social democrats use such policies to provide for the general welfare, with the idea that people in a solid middle-class society are more likely to have common core values and share a personal investment in the system. By limiting the gap between rich and poor, they seek to reinforce social solidarity and provide the greatest good for the greatest number.

There is a common misperception that social democracy is synonymous with socialism or even communism. In fact, social democracies in Sweden, Norway, Finland, Denmark, Iceland, Holland, and other countries combine socioeconomic leveling with a strong commitment to free markets and capitalism. Creating a predominately middle-class, egalitarian society is a democratic policy preference, not a Marxist manifesto.

Critics of social democracy offer two arguments why government has no business undertaking such large-scale social engineering projects, no matter how appealing they might seem. First, the job is beyond the remit of limited government, and will lead to a powerful, intrusive, and oppressive state. Second, government will inevitably botch the job, and in the long run make matters worse rather than better.

Liberals argue that giving government broad powers to level and reshape society comes at a steep price in terms of restricting liberty and private choice. Comprehensive government social programs not only dangerously empower the state, but also encourage a culture of dependency that undermines individual responsibility and initiative. At best, such programs will result in a benign but intrusive nanny state; at worst, they will lead to a top-down command state.

British Prime Minister Margaret Thatcher once claimed that there is no such thing as society. Society, she argued, begins and ends with individuals and families. Individuals are ultimately responsible for their own lives and problems; they must first care for themselves and their families, and only then should they try to help their neighbors.[22]

---

[21] In the 1980s, the federal government shifted its economic strategy to promote the interests of the wealthiest Americans as the new engine of economic growth. These reforms reversed earlier New Deal and Great Society policies that sought to drive the economy by strengthening the middle and lower classes.

[22] *Women's Own Magazine*, Oct. 31, 1987. See also, e.g., Claire Berlinski, *There is No Alternative: Why Margaret Thatcher Matters* (Basic Books 2008). The idea is reminiscent of flight attendants' instructions on commercial airplanes to secure one's own oxygen mask before helping others.

Thatcher's underlying point was that society is not to blame for what goes wrong in our lives, and we should not expect – or want – the state to protect us from all harm or cure every ill. Not all problems are government problems, and government cannot create new laws, regulations, or entitlements to remedy every citizen complaint. If we focus on what we think society owes us, rather than actively looking out for ourselves, we will end up with an oppressive government that taxes rich Peter to pay whiny Paul.

The second liberal argument against government-run social leveling is that no matter how well intentioned the government is, it will inevitably fail to do the job well. Government is simply not up to such a delicate and complex task, and its efforts to level and improve society will not only fail, but will have serious unintended consequences.

John Stuart Mill argued that government is inherently too big, slow, and dumb to fix complex social problems. Private initiatives are, as a rule, more effective at providing essential public services, including education, food banks, homeless shelters, and health care. Government should let individuals and private organizations take the lead when it comes to social welfare programs, and intervene only when necessary, as the ultimate safety net if the private sector fails to respond adequately to serve the public good.

Sometimes it is difficult to say which worries liberals more – competent government or incompetent government.

De Tocqueville warned of the risks of focusing on equality, rather than on freedom and liberty. Well-intentioned social engineers who push single-mindedly for socioeconomic equality are often willing to sacrifice everything else to achieve it. This is a serious problem, because it is always easier to drag the rich down than it is to pull the poor up, so this is what usually happens. Liberals fear that egalitarian policies will succeed only in making the rich poorer, rather than uplifting the poor or increasing overall social wealth.

De Tocqueville worried that most people would rather live equal as slaves than be free but unequal.[23] If people succumb to temptation and choose equality over liberty or freedom, they will lose both liberty and freedom, and gain only the equality of shared poverty. But if people focus first on their freedom and liberty, de Tocqueville promised that equality will inevitably follow.

In the debate over government services and socioeconomic equality, the United States has remained true to its core liberal values. Americans overwhelmingly prefer equal opportunity to equal results, and remain suspicious of ambitious, government-led social leveling projects. One troubling side effect of the U.S.'s dedication to liberal values is that although the United States has never had an entrenched class system, it has the most polarized wealth distribution curve in the developed world, on a par with some of the poorest Third World countries (Figure 6.3).

---

[23] Another apt simile is that people are like crabs in a barrel; if one crab tries to climb out, the others grab it and pull it back in, condemning all of them to the boiling pot.

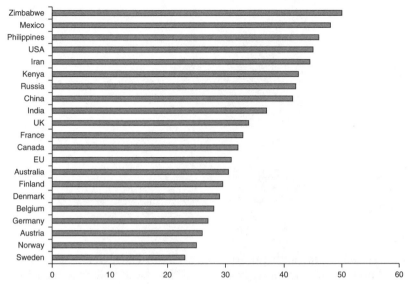

FIGURE 6.3 Gini Index: Income Distribution by Country.

Although the gap between rich and poor in the United States is immense and increasing, one possible silver lining is that the idea of the American success story – poor people working hard and growing rich through their own initiative – remains a powerful animating force in American society. It is a common perception among rich and poor alike that with hard work, it is easier to move up the socioeconomic ladder in the United States than anywhere else in the world. As Machiavelli noted, perception is often more important than reality when it comes to politics ... and economics.

7

Power

Power is, by definition, a threat to liberty. Accordingly, liberal democrats mistrust all power, and state power most of all. They seek to limit and channel government power through a system of checks and balances consisting of any or all of the following: (1) a constitution or basic law that defines and limits power; (2) fundamental rights that are beyond government's lawful reach; (3) separation of powers, whereby state power is divided among different departments; (4) a federal system that diffuses power among national and regional governments; and (5) a rule of law system that ensures fairness and requires everyone, especially the government, to follow the rules.

Free democrats expect more from government, and are willing to give it greater power to meet its broad responsibilities. Free democrats are comfortable with a robust state, because in a participatory society the government and people are one and the same thing, and government needs to be able to do whatever the community decides to do. A strong state, however, does not mean a state with unlimited or unchecked power.

Federalism is one aspect of government that both liberal and free democrats value, although for different reasons. Liberals see federalism as one of several useful checks on state power; free democrats see federalism as the indispensable means to make participatory democracy work in a world of nation-states. Federalism preserves freedom on a large scale by ensuring that power begins at the local level and works its way upward. It allows any number of small towns, communities, counties, and provinces to be linked together to create a nation of any size, preserving the core free democratic principles of direct popular participation and subsidiarity – the idea that decisions should be made at the most local levels practicable.

In this section, we will examine four basic questions about state power: (1) should power rise, like smoke, from the bottom up, or should it pour, like water, from the top down; (2) should government responsibilities be narrowly or broadly defined; (3) should government power be concentrated or diffused; and (4) should major political decisions be on the basis of majority rule, isocracy, or consensus?

WATER OR SMOKE

Most political theorists assume that sovereign authority is inherently indivisible and must reside in a single, undivided superior power – subject to no law, but a law unto itself. In this view, the state is the ultimate source of political power, and power flows like water, from the top down. This is Hobbes's social contract – a vertical agreement, whereby the ruler agrees to rule and the subjects agree to be ruled. This approach creates *constituted*, or organized, power, which is hierarchical and authoritarian.[1] When constituted power assumes a democratic character, by combining a powerful centralized state with popular institutions and processes, it can take the form of a statist or guided democracy.

Modern democratic theory, in contrast, accepts the principle of popular sovereignty and idea that power should rise, like smoke, from the bottom up. This was the essence of Locke's social contract, Montesquieu's theory of federalism, and Jefferson's conception of natural rights and democratic subsidiarity.[2] Individuals are the source of all legitimate power, and they may freely choose to join together with others to create a social contract among equal citizens to establish a government and political commonwealth. This is a *constituting*, or organizing, power.[3] Power originates with the people, and is either exercised directly by them, or is delegated to representatives who hold the people's power in trust and subject to their consent. Note that many democracies embrace Locke in theory, but follow Hobbes in practice.

NARROW OR BROAD RESPONSIBILITIES

Democratic government is a genie (liberals might say a monkey's paw) that uses the people's own power to grant their wishes. The key question is what people want from their government, because the answer will determine how much power government needs to do its job. Liberal democrats worry about expecting too much from government; free democrats caution against expecting too little.

---

[1] Hannah Arendt, *On Revolution*.

[2] Although many democratic theorists accept the idea of a social contract as the proper foundation of political society, some political theorists, including David Hume, argue that political communities are founded not on contract, but on some other basis. Hume thought that societies spontaneously generate from humanity's natural sociability.

[3] Arendt, *On Revolution*.

Liberal democrats believe in energetic but limited government. Government has as few as five responsibilities: to protect individual rights; prevent or remedy fraud, duress, coercion, and violence; enforce contracts; establish the rule of law; and conduct foreign relations. This is a minimal, or night watchman, state – a cop on the corner who keeps the peace and treats everyone fairly, but who otherwise stays unobtrusively out of the way.

Free democrats have greater confidence in government's ability to solve complex problems and be a positive, progressive social force. Government is not a necessary evil to be tolerated because the alternative is even worse; it is an indispensable partner to build a better society and improve everyone's quality of life.

In practice, the modern trend in both liberal and free democracies is toward bigger and more powerful government. Even in the United States, the great redoubt of classical liberalism, the federal government has gradually assumed broad new responsibilities that extend far beyond its traditional limits. The federal government has, by degrees, become involved in all manner of concerns, including education, transportation, health, economics, fiscal policy, public safety, and the environment. This bigger, more vigorous version of liberalism is *progressive liberalism.*

Progressive liberals seek to strike a flexible, pragmatic balance between the classic liberal preference for limited government and energetic and proactive government needed to manage a modern economy, maintain popular social programs, and pursue public goods such as transportation infrastructure, environmental protection, and space exploration. This has changed the liberal ideal of government by consent to government on demand. As people expect more from government, the state will assume correspondingly greater power. There is, of course, some risk in this.

CONCENTRATED, DIVIDED, AND DIFFUSED POWER

Should government power be concentrated, or divided and diffused? Concentrated power makes government more effective, but also potentially more oppressive. Divided and diffused power limits government meddling and overreach, but comes at a cost in terms of government responsiveness and efficiency.

Free democrats are less concerned about concentrated power than liberal democrats. They want a responsive and effective government, but they also demand a government that respects local autonomy and the principle of subsidiarity.

Liberal democrats divide and diffuse state power, so that government is strong enough to protect individual rights, but not so strong that it threatens them. They prefer a moderately inept government to a ruthlessly efficient one, and happily accept a degree of government incompetence to avoid the more serious threat of tyranny.

Concentrated Power and Unitary States

Plato, Hobbes, Jean Bodin, and other strong-state theorists promote the idea of indivisible sovereign authority with unlimited potential power. They tacitly accept Thrasymachus's view (despite Plato's denial) that justice is the will of the stronger. The result has been a 5,000-year parade of emperors, emirs, kings, popes, princes, potentates, pashas, dictators, juntas, theocrats, caliphs, imams, ayatollahs, Mandarins, Brahmins, nobles, and chiefs.

Unlike the United States, which began life as a democracy, most of the world suffered under an unbroken procession of authoritarian rulers until the great wave of democratization washed over the world in the twentieth century. As Europe, Latin America, Asia, and Africa began to democratize, most states simply grafted democratic institutions and procedures onto pre-existing authoritarian rootstock, with varying degrees of success. One consequence of this is that although more than 150 nations now self-identify as democratic, in most cases political power remains highly centralized and concentrated in relatively few hands.

A *unitary state* is a country where sovereign power is fully concentrated in the central authority. Local and regional governments might exist, but they have little or no autonomous power – they are legal creatures of the national government and subject to its will.

France is the prototype of strong unitary democracies – Bodin's idea of an indivisible and all-powerful state, leavened by democratic institutions and procedures. The result is a stable, centralized democracy, with a national government that has plenary authority to govern virtually every aspect of French life. It is the spirit of the ancien régime repurposed to serve liberty, equality, and fraternity.

Liberal fear of such concentrated state power was the basis for Prime Minister Margaret Thatcher's visceral distrust of Europe and the European Union. As Thatcher saw it, France and other continental European countries have an understanding of political power that is fundamentally alien to the Anglo-American traditions of liberalism and limited government. Thatcher worried that French presidents still sing softly to themselves, "*L'etat c'est moi*," when they think that no one is listening.

Despite its democratic architecture, Thatcher warned that Europe and the EU remain attached to its traditional model of an all-powerful command-and-control state. If the rise of European democracy has harnessed state power and rendered it benign, to classic liberals such as Mrs. Thatcher, even the most beneficent state with unlimited potential power poses a clear and eventual danger to liberty.[4]

---

4 When Prime Minister Thatcher made her remarks, Britain was, ironically, a unitary state with an all-powerful parliament. Britain remains a unitary state in theory, although it has devolved significant powers to regional governments in Scotland, Wales, and Northern Ireland. Parliament remains supreme, however, and may alter the terms of devolution at will. It has repeatedly done

Guided and Advisory Democracies

Guided democracies are relatively common in the developing world. They are usually one-party states – developmental dictatorships with democratic trim. Election ballots might have just one name listed for each office, the ruling party's approved candidate. Such a closed electoral system might still be plausibly democratic if elections, although not freely contested, are honest, transparent, and treated as plebiscites on the ruling party and its candidates. This means that if a nominee does not earn a clear majority, the party must respect the result and present a new candidate for public approval.[5] Examples of guided democracies include China, Cuba, Laos, Turkmenistan, Vietnam, and North Korea.

Some democracies, such as South Africa, do not have one official governing party, but are nonetheless effectively one-party states. Since the fall of the apartheid regime, the ANC has dominated the national government, and it remains to be seen if it will tolerate a truly competitive opposition party, or whether it will yield power if and when it loses an election.

One hint as to how South Africa might evolve can be found in Mexico. After the revolution of 1917, Mexico became a relatively stable guided democracy, with the Institutional Revolutionary Party (PRI) controlling all aspects of the national government until the presidential election of 2000, when the conservative National Action Party (PAN) and its candidate, Vicente Fox Quesada, won a free and fair contest, and finally broke the PRI's political monopoly. The PRI surprised some observers when it peacefully ceded power to the PAN. Six years later, another PAN candidate, Felipe Calderon, won the 2006 presidential election to extend the PAN's rule for a second term. Perhaps the most significant moment of PAN's twelve-year rule came with the election of 2012, when the PAN's candidate, Josefina Vazquez Mota, lost, and PAN quickly passed political power back to the PRI and its winning candidate, Enrique Pena Nieto. Having two consecutive peaceful and routine exchanges of power between competing political parties has helped to institutionalize democracy in Mexico.

Advisory democracy is another amalgam of authoritarian and democratic practices. In an *advisory democracy*, ruling elites solicit public input, but reserve the right to ignore it. This allows for limited democratic participation, while giving the ruler or governing elites the final word.

Although both guided and advisory democracies often claim to be true democracies, in reality they are often, although not always, a subspecies of illiberal democracy. China, for example, has lately become a developmental dictatorship with some democratic trappings. Party leaders pay attention to what they condescendingly refer to as "the masses," but do not answer to them. There is limited public consultation, but no public accountability.

---

so in the recent past, for example, suspending the Northern Irish Assembly four times during the Troubles. Devolution is, accordingly, not the same as federalism, either in theory or practice.

[5] Richard L. Sklar, "Democracy in Africa," 26 *African Studies Review* 11 (1983).

Chinese authorities now allow a degree of liberty, including the right to speak one's mind in private, or even online. But they remain quick to suppress any hint of unsanctioned public demonstrations. In short, the Chinese government is relatively tolerant when it comes to individual liberties, but remains deeply suspicious of political freedom. Political dissidents have been jailed for years merely for using the word "citizen" to describe Chinese subjects, and for claiming a right to gather with others in a public place to protest or demonstrate without official sanction. Even so, the regime enjoys, for now, a high degree of reported public confidence: nearly 80 percent of politically informed Chinese still trust the state to do the right thing.[6]

Russia is another example of a modern authoritarian-democratic hybrid. Despite its democratic aspirations, Russia remains, for the most part, an illiberal democracy dominated by authoritarian, top-down decision making. The old habits of its ancestral Soviet and Tsarist regimes permeate the vast state apparatus, which remains the main driving force of domestic political life.

The old Soviet Union's single-minded drive to modernize through a centralized command economy had at least one beneficial side effect: it created a highly educated "technical intelligentsia" that became, by default, the country's approximation of a stabilizing middle class. The technical intelligentsia was an influential political force during the closing days of the Soviet Union and the early years of the Russian Republic, when it supported Gorbachev's perestroika program in the 1980s and threw its weight behind the post-Soviet democratic reforms in the 1990s. Unfortunately, this group remains dependent on the state for its privileged existence. This has limited their ability to challenge the status quo, and has allowed Russia's political and economic oligarchs to maintain a firm hold on power in a corrupt authoritarian state.

Saudi Arabia offers an interesting example of an unapologetically authoritarian and proudly undemocratic regime making its first tentative concessions to democratic governance. In 2000, King Fahd created a Consultative Assembly (Majlis Al-Shura), and an advisory council of 150 members (including, at present, 6 women), all appointed by the king. The king consults the Shura at his sole discretion, and is perfectly free to ignore its advice.

It is easy to criticize authoritarian states such as China, Russia, and Saudi Arabia for their limitations and deficiencies. Before we get too smug, however, we should remember that all modern democracies make significant compromises regarding the top-down nature of state power, and governments routinely treat public opinion as advisory rather than binding. In most democracies, including the United States, elected representatives are top-down rulers

---

[6] Edelman Trustbarometer, retrieved from *www.edelman.com/*. These annual "informed public" surveys sample educated and successful people who say that they closely follow the news. Identical polls in other countries show considerably lower levels of trust in government: United States 41 percent, Germany 41 percent, Russia 40 percent, United Kingdom 35 percent.

with expiration dates. The voice of the people is the voice of God only on election day; in between elections, representatives have considerable autonomy to govern as they see fit, regardless of popular will.

In the United States and most other mature democracies, "public comment" sessions have become the norm before important laws or regulations take effect. During public comment periods, citizens are free to speak their minds about proposed laws, and lawmakers are free to ignore them.

Elected representatives cannot always dismiss public opinion without fear of consequences, however, especially if an election looms just around the corner. But incumbents have significant advantages over challengers in most elections, and lawmakers often try to make a virtue out of being leaders of public opinion, rather than its followers.

Most modern democracies allow advisory referenda, usually at the government's discretion. Many European countries hold advisory referenda prior to joining any major new EU treaty.[7] In Latin America, Brazil held a nonbinding referendum in 2005, to measure public support for a proposed government ban on the private sale and possession of firearms. Brazilians voted overwhelmingly in favor of private gun ownership, and the government dropped the idea. The United States is the exception, in that its laws do not provide for any form of national referendum, advisory or otherwise.

Legal institutions are the least democratic part of government, so it is not surprising that advisory democracy often plays a role here. In India, juries render advisory verdicts that trial judges may ignore. In most other common law countries, including the United States, juries often play an advisory role, but one with teeth. As a rule, judges cannot simply disregard jury verdicts and substitute their own judgments. Most jurisdictions, however, allow judges in civil cases to modify jury awards, or nullify a jury's verdict and order a new trial. In criminal cases, juries usually offer sentencing recommendations following conviction, which judges have at least some discretion to modify or ignore.[8]

Divided and Diffused Power

Dividing and diffusing government power requires an effective, comprehensive system of checks and balances. Divided (or separated) power apportions state authority *horizontally* among different government departments. Federalism

---

[7] The Netherlands, Norway, Sweden, and the United Kingdom are among the countries holding recent nonbinding referenda on proposed EU treaties.

[8] In the United States, judges have less power to disregard jury verdicts in criminal cases than in civil cases. As a rule, judges in criminal cases may impose a lighter but not more severe sentence than the jury recommends. This is especially true in death penalty cases: forty-seven states allow the trial judge to disregard a jury's recommendation of death and impose a lesser sentence, but only three states – Alabama, Florida, and Delaware – allow the trial judge to ignore a jury's recommendation of a life sentence and unilaterally impose death. Except in capital cases, U.S. juries in federal criminal cases do not have a formal say regarding punishment; sentencing decisions are left to the judge, subject to federal sentencing guidelines.

diffuses sovereign authority *vertically* between the central government and various semiautonomous regional governments. Both can serve as bulwarks against unrestrained centralized power, but also make government less efficient, decisive, and nimble.

In classical democratic theory, small is beautiful. Athens and the Roman Republic were unitary states writ small – compact city-states with relatively simple and straightforward political institutions. The same was true of medieval European city-republics, including Machiavelli's beloved Florentine Republic.

At the beginning of the sixteenth century, Machiavelli was among the first to realize that the emerging kingdoms of France and Spain represented something entirely new on the political landscape – nation-states. He also recognized the threat these behemoths posed to the patchwork of small city-states along the Italian peninsula that still foolishly considered themselves rich and powerful. Yet although Machiavelli understood the game-changing nature of nation-states, he made no effort to adapt traditional republican principles to fit the new political reality. Instead, he merely advocated restoring the old republican city-states to their former glory – a surprisingly naïve view for the founding father of political realism.

Not that it mattered. Europe ignored Machiavelli's call for the rebirth of city-state republicanism and moved decisively in the opposite direction – embracing the new model of highly centralized, authoritarian nation-states. Florence and other city-republics quickly found themselves overwhelmed and undone. The world had changed, and the continent's once-great city-states were either conquered, or isolated and rendered irrelevant.

Two hundred years later, Rousseau renewed Machiavelli's republican battle cry, rejecting the brave new world of nation-states and seeking a return to the lost utopia of small free republics. Rousseau's back-to-the-future ideas inspired modern revolutions in Europe, Latin America, Africa, and Asia, although the most successful of these – the Marxist-Leninist regimes in Russia, China, North Korea, Cuba, Vietnam, and elsewhere – were not notably democratic and failed utterly to transform highly centralized regimes into autonomous local republics ("soviets") as promised.

In the 1960s, E. F. Schumacher once again revived Rousseau's provocative ideas in America, with his influential book, *Small is Beautiful*. Schumacher's mantra remains popular today among progressive social movements that emphasize community activism and small-scale, local, sustainable practices as an alternative to the noisy complexities of modern nationalism and globalization.

In *The Federalist Papers*, Hamilton and Madison laid out the opposing view. The idea that small is beautiful might be attractive in theory, they argued, but is catastrophic in practice. The problem with small democracies, Hamilton argued in *The Federalist,* No.9, is that they are inherently unstable, trapped in a state of perpetual vibration between chaos and tyranny. They are especially vulnerable to factional infighting, and are easily dominated by local elites. The allure of small-scale republicanism is a siren's song, luring democracies to break apart on the shoals of faction, anarchy, and tyranny. Despite the tempting vision of establishing a small, closely knit republic where everyone is a good neighbor and there are no factions or feuds, the truth is that in every small hamlet and town, bitter rivalries are plentiful, and a few rich families and powerful local interests always seem to run things. As Madison put it: "[Small, participatory] democracies have ever been spectacles of turbulence and contention; have ever been found incompatible with personal security or the rights of property; and have in general been as short in their lives as they have been violent in their deaths."[9] When it comes to democratic government, Madison concluded, small and simple is nothing more than a recipe for disaster.[10] History has repeatedly judged such governments and found them wanting. They offer a roller-coaster ride that is more dangerous than exciting, a brief exhilaration of freedom that ends all too quickly in a terrible crash.

In short, small might be beautiful, but only from a safe distance. When it comes to protecting individual liberties and ensuring political stability, big is beautiful.

Note that "big" does not mean all-powerful. It means a geographically large and demographically diverse society, with a complex, multilayered government. Madison's preferred model of a limited, effective, and stable government requires an intricate political clockworks, with a touch of Rube Goldberg, to ensure that government is strong enough to keep the peace, control the undesirable effects of faction, and protect individual rights – but not so powerful that it threatens the very rights and liberties that it is charged to protect.

WHO DECIDES? MAJORITARIANISM, ISOCRACY, AND CONSENSUS

When should the majority get its way, and when should the needs of the many yield to the needs of the few? The answer requires democratic societies to balance the competing principles of majority rule and minority rights. Some democracies are predominately *majoritarian*, where the few must yield to the many. Others are *isocratic*,[11] limiting majority power in various ways to protect minority and individual rights. There is a third possibility, rule by consensus, although this option is more problematic.

In majoritarian societies, 50 percent plus one can do pretty much anything they want. This is an instinctively compelling idea, and it has long been a standard shorthand definition of democracy. The underlying logic is simple and appealing: if the goal is to provide the greatest good for the greatest number, the best way to achieve this is to allow the greatest number to decide the matter for themselves.

---

[9] James Madison, *The Federalist Papers*, No.10.
[10] Madison argued that the smallest state, Rhode Island, would be the least secure as an independent state. James Madison, *The Federalist Papers*, No. 51.
[11] Meaning self-rule, or no rule.

The American Founders were deeply suspicious of majoritarian democracy, and as usual Madison offered the best explanation. Placing too much power in the hands of the many, he warned, is as destabilizing and tyrannical as any authoritarian government. Left unchecked, the many will quickly conclude that having their own way is the natural order of things. They will grow insufferably arrogant, intolerant, and oppressive, and will either overwhelm the few or incite rebellion and civil war. Majorities are rarely in doubt, but often in error. They routinely mistake their passionate pursuit of self-interest for the selfless quest to do what is best for everyone. This sort of delusional thinking is especially dangerous in a democracy, because there is no more powerful or threatening political force than a majority that has made up its mind.

Although any faction can cause trouble, majorities have the potential to do the most damage and are the most difficult to control. A united majority can usually check troublesome minorities, even the rich and powerful. The majority, however, has no natural constraint, and there is no limit to the damage that a cohesive and willful majority can do. Majority rule ultimately leaves minorities no way to defend themselves except forceful resistance.

The American Founders wanted to protect individual rights and liberties, not empower the majority to impose its will on everyone else. Rather than instituting a majoritarian system, they established an isocracy. The Constitution places fundamental rights and liberties beyond the reach of the majority, and empowers political minorities to check majoritarian decision making in various ways.

Anglo-American juries offer an excellent illustration of isocracy in action. Most people think of juries as an archaic bit of free democracy in an otherwise liberal democratic system. But the common law jury is an isocratic, not a majoritarian, institution, and it is perfectly consistent with the core principles of liberal democracy. A quick comparison of Athenian and American juries reveals the difference.

The Athenian jury was a majoritarian institution. Juries were selected at random and ranged from 200 to several thousand men, depending on the importance of the case. Verdicts required a simple majority vote, taken without deliberation. If the majority found a defendant guilty, a second simple majority vote, also without deliberation, determined the punishment.[12]

Common law juries, in contrast, require either unanimity, or a supermajority of 11–1 or 10–2.[13] Unanimous verdicts, and to a lesser degree supermajority verdicts, protect minority rights in two essential ways. First, they require jurors

---

[12] In Japan, juries of six citizens (*saibanin*) sit in combined panels with three professional judges. Decisions regarding guilt and punishment are by majority vote. Yuriko Nagano, "In Japan," *Los Angeles Times*, June 27, 2009, A-19.

[13] In England, juries must try to reach a unanimous verdict, but the trial judge may, after an unspecified time, accept a supermajority verdict. Supermajority verdicts change the behavior of juries and the nature of jury deliberations, by making it easier to ignore minority views and encouraging verdict-driven rather than evidence-driven deliberations.

to consider and accommodate minority views, by giving represented minorities an effective veto over majority will. Second, in criminal trials, the strict voting requirements ensure that the government must carry its burden to prove the accused's guilt beyond a reasonable doubt.[14] This is done to protect the rights of the least loved and least powerful minority of all – criminal defendants.

Although isocratic institutions and practices are designed specifically to protect minority rights, they also favor the status quo by allowing intransigent minorities to block any proposed decisions or reforms. An unreasonable minority of one can hang a common law jury. A similar principle applies in the U.S. Senate, where filibuster rules allow senators who represent as little as 10 percent of the national population to stop Congress dead in its tracks.[15]

Beyond majority rule and isocracy there is a third way: to require broad social consensus to determine public policy.[16] Although not overtly democratic, Confucianism, the main guiding social force in China for more than 2,000 years, seeks to avoid coercion and reach a social consensus through education and moral persuasion. In the West, Rousseau argued that all major political decisions should be made by common agreement among all citizens, or what he called the general will. More recently, the American Occupy movements have enthusiastically adopted Rousseau's ideas about consensual decision making.

Perhaps the best argument in favor of consensus is that it short-circuits the impulse to allow majorities to have their way. In majoritarian systems, the many can casually ignore the interests of the few, and steamroll anyone who dares to get in their way. If policy decisions require consensus, the majority cannot impose its will on the rest of society, but must actively seek everyone's participation and consent.

Whereas consensual decision making might work in small communities, it is unworkable in large and diverse societies, as Rousseau himself recognized. In contemporary democratic elections, majorities of 55 percent are considered landslides. Requiring consensus would virtually guarantee that nothing significant is ever decided or done, unless consensus is either circumvented or coerced.

[14] The fact that one or more jurors refuse to confirm a defendant's guilt might in itself be sufficient to constitute reasonable doubt. As a formal matter, however, U.S. law considers it a hung jury, which gives prosecutors the option to retry the case without running afoul of the constitutional rule against double jeopardy.

[15] A small number of Southern senators were able to block all civil rights legislation and maintain segregation for more than a decade after the Supreme Court's landmark desegregation ruling in *Brown v. Board of Education*. President Lyndon Johnson finally persuaded Congress to pass the first major civil rights laws in more than a century, the Civil Rights Act of 1964 and the Voting Rights Act of 1965.

[16] Consensus in this context is different from the common law jury's requirement of unanimity. First, Rousseau's concept of general will applies to an entire society, rather than a small subset of twelve individuals. Second, the common law jury is by design a representative body, which Rousseau categorically rejected as a source of true social consensus.

A small handful of modern nation-states have claimed to rule by consensus. These countries have been, without exception, faux or illiberal democracies ruled by compelled consensus. The Soviet Union, China, and North Korea all claimed (the latter still claims) that major policy decisions reflected the enthusiastic and unanimous support of the masses. Leaders rallied thousands, sometimes millions, of supporters to demonstrate undivided public support for the government. Dissenting voices were, of course, ruthlessly suppressed. Even today in China and North Korea, legislative unanimity to ratify Communist Party decisions remains the norm, confirming suspicions that their legislatures are, at least for now, paper tigers with rubber stamp paws.

In Iraq, former president Saddam Hussein claimed to rule by unanimous consent. He routinely won reelection with 99 percent of the vote, in a diverse country with more than 11 million eligible voters. In the 2002 presidential election, his last, President Hussein tallied more votes than there were eligible voters, making him the only presidential candidate in history to win with more than 100 percent of the popular vote.

8

The Case against Democracy

In Italy, for thirty years under the Borgias, they had warfare, terror, murder, and bloodshed, but they produced Michelangelo, Leonardo da Vinci and the Renaissance. In Switzerland, they had brotherly love, they had five hundred years of democracy and peace, and what did that produce? The cuckoo clock.

– Harry Lime[1]

What is wrong with democracy? Possibly quite a lot, as it turns out. This section presents some of the arguments against democracy and in favor of elite rule.

It might seem self-evident that democracy is the least bad form of government, but history indicates otherwise. The vast majority of civilizations have been ruled by the one or the few; the many have governed only a handful of states over thousands of years, and almost all of them quickly failed. There must be some good reasons for this, beyond the cynic's version of the golden rule.

Democracy is not the only defensible choice for a government, and it might not be the best choice in all circumstances. Other systems might be superior to democracy, or at least better suited to accomplish certain goals.

That assorted authoritarians, aristocrats, and politically ambitious religious leaders have their own reasons to disparage democracy goes almost without saying. But there is also an impressive list of serious political thinkers who consider democracy impossible, undesirable, unjust, or even absurd – including Socrates, Plato, Aristotle, Augustine, Aquinas, Confucius, Hobbes, Lenin, Mao, and Khomeini.

---

[1] American smuggler Harry Lime talking to his naïve friend Holly Martins, in Carol Reed's classic film, *The Third Man* (1949). Actor Orson Welles, who wrote the "cuckoo speech," was wrong about one thing: it was the Germans, not the Swiss, who invented the cuckoo clock.

THE VIRTUES OF ELITE RULE

Every justification of authoritarian government begins with the claim that there live among us a select few with superior qualities that justify their right to rule. The list of these claimed virtues varies, but includes any or all of the following: wisdom, courage, breeding, education, enlightenment, cleverness, vision, virtue, divinity, destiny, discipline, iron will, and all-around excellence.

Plato thought that the special virtue of those born to rule is wisdom. He came to the modest and not at all self-interested conclusion that philosophers should be in charge, because philosophers alone have the wisdom to know the truth when they see it, and the courage to do the right thing for the right reason. Only Plato's philosopher-kings have the right stuff to make society virtuous and just – a harmonious society where everyone does their job and minds their own business.

Another popular justification for elite rule is the idea of a chosen one – a ruler who is either divine or divinely inspired. This is rule by *divine right*. Notable adherents include the Pharaohs, Alexander the Great, most Roman emperors, British monarchs from King Arthur through James II, Joan of Arc, any French king named Louis, Napoleon, plus a host of faith-based dictators ranging from medieval popes through modern-day ayatollahs – all of whom, some perhaps sincerely, claimed to be on a mission from God.

Machiavelli summarily dismissed all of these justifications as self-interested, manipulative nonsense. He thought it far more important for an authoritarian leader to be clever than wise, and scoffed at the idea of divine right. To rule effectively, a Prince does not need virtue but virtú: the quick intelligence necessary to understand power, a single-minded ruthlessness in its pursuit, and the skills necessary to seize, keep, and wield it effectively. Machiavelli was profoundly skeptical of any other higher qualities claimed by princes, demigods, or philosopher kings.

In *Democracy in America*, De Tocqueville contrasted the virtues of aristocracy with the limitations of democracy. His argument boils down to a choice between excellence and mediocrity. *Aristocracy*, as de Tocqueville noted, means rule by the best. If a society values excellence in its laws, institutions, education, leadership, art, architecture, and culture, then aristocracy is in almost every way better than democracy. In aristocracies, the elite are literally born and bred to lead. They are better educated, trained, and connected, and more experienced, cosmopolitan, cultured, constant, focused, and competent than democratic leaders.

Unlike democracies, aristocracies are prone to think strategically, and seek long-term results rather than short-term profits. This makes aristocratic laws, policies, and institutions especially good – they are thoughtfully designed, well executed, consistent, constant, and closely matched to desired ends.

As a bonus, de Tocqueville noted, aristocracies also produce cultural excellence. The tasteful few appreciate deep culture, and are willing to invest heavily in fine art and architecture, as a quick visit to any of the great European capitals will attest. Democracies, in contrast, are constrained by popular culture and middlebrow sensibilities, and are naturally driven to produce commercial art that appeals to the broad, low, and fickle tastes of the many. Aristocracies produce fine art for the ages; democracies produce disposable pop art for mass consumption.[2]

The point of aristocratic government is to allow the best and brightest to run things. This begs the obvious question: if there is a super-talented elite embedded in every society, who are these people and how do we find them?

Plato advocated testing everyone, not just to find the best leaders, but also to make sure that everyone finds his or her proper place in society.[3] He outlined a comprehensive system of state-run education and universal testing that would identify the wisest and most courageous citizens, who would then be cultivated to lead. The wise would rule, the brave would defend, and everyone else would obey.

Those who seek divinely sanctioned leaders look for supernatural omens announcing the next incarnation of the chosen one. It might come in the form of an oracle's prophecy, magic sword, mystical birthmark, preternatural ability to solve supernatural puzzles, or an unbroken chain of command dating back to an original divinity or prophet.

Hereditary aristocracies have their own way to ensure that society's cream rises to the top. Noble and aristocratic families are, not surprisingly, convinced that excellence is mostly a matter of genetics; virtue runs in families, and leadership skills are hereditary. Leaders are born, and they are born into the best families.

Aristocrats invariably deny that they rule in their own interests. They do not ask to lead or want to lead; it is their duty to lead. This is *noblesse oblige*. They are happy to point to various theories about natural selection and selective breeding to ensure passing along the requisite intelligence, temperament, will, leadership, and other superior qualities that define the ruling class. All of these attributes are admirable, although they are remarkably similar to the breed description for German shepherds. Moreover, hundreds of years of careful selective breeding among the European aristocracy resulted in a ruling class full of hemophilia, idiocy, insanity, and unnaturally large ears.

---

[2] Many of the most famous examples of splashy excellence and wealth in U.S. society, from its best private universities to its giant skyscrapers, are not testimonies to republican virtues, but signs of America's latent aristocratic tendencies. Great universities such as Harvard, Yale, and Stanford, and mighty buildings such as the Empire State Building and the Chrysler Building, are monuments to the ambition and ego of great men, and reflect elite reaction against egalitarian republicanism.

[3] Plato was uniquely open-minded in at least one respect: he advocated testing young girls on an equal basis with boys to see if they were made of the right stuff. For nearly two millennia, Plato was virtually alone among major political philosophers and theorists to offer women an equal opportunity to participate in public life.

That said, many democrats agree that the world would be better off if the best and brightest are allowed to run things. John Adams dismissed the idea of a hereditary ruling class, but swallowed whole the idea that every society has a natural aristocracy, and that the brightest lights of each generation should be identified, nurtured, and put in charge.[4] This nominally democratic ruling class would earn its place by merit, rather than claiming the right to rule on the basis of artificial considerations of birth, blood, or law.

THE LONG VIEW

De Tocqueville observed that aristocratic governments excel at strategic thought. They grasp the big picture and plan for it. Aristocracies think in terms of generations, and they are willing to undertake the difficult planning and investment necessary to produce long-term results.

Democracies live in the moment, and focus almost exclusively on immediate interests. Citizens are famously impatient, prone to believe that the only thing wrong with instant gratification is that it is not quick enough. This makes democratic governments nearsighted, reactive, and scattershot, forever scrambling to keep up with mercurial public demands, tracking polls, and daily headlines. What passes for long-term planning in democracies rarely stretches beyond the next election.

Property law provides an interesting illustration of the differences between aristocracies and democracies when it comes to long-term planning. For ages, the British aristocracy sought, with single-minded determination, to preserve the family property so that it would pass whole to uncounted future generations. To do this, they needed to ensure that each generation's heirs could not divest the ancestral estate. So they created a variety of legal devices, including life estates, trusts, remainders, fee tails, and other defeasible interests, so that property could not be sold off permanently, but would eventually and inevitably revert to the family.

In democracies – especially liberal democracies – everyone is expected to look after their own interests. This means treating real estate as just another commodity. Property is typically bought and sold without restriction – in legalese, fee simple absolute. This allows people to flip clear title to property quickly for immediate profit, without having to worry about complex deed restrictions, long-term consequences, or hypothetical future generations.

The ability to plan for the long-term is a clear advantage when it comes to government. For similar reasons, authoritarian management techniques remain common outside of government. Even in egalitarian societies, most private companies operate according to neo-feudal management principles, with leadership models that run the spectrum from Henry VIII to Attila the Hun.

---

[4] John Adams, "On Natural Aristocracy," letter to John Taylor of North Carolina, April 15, 1814; cf., John Adams, letter to Thomas Jefferson, November 15, 1813.

There are exceptions,[5] but most businesses in democratic countries are incongruously authoritarian in their management practices, in part because pseudo-aristocratic leadership models give corporations the stability, discipline, clarity, consistency, continuity, and focus at the top necessary to think, plan, and act strategically.[6]

RELIABLE PARTNERS

Authoritarian governments are, as a rule, more dependable and easier to deal with than democracies. In an authoritarian government, everyone knows who has power and can make things happen. The core leadership tends to be more stable, durable, certain, and predictable than democratic leadership, which is in a constant state of flux. Having a clear political hierarchy and stability at the top help to establish long-term trust and reliable partnerships.

Hussain Haqqani, a senior Pakistani diplomat, explained why dictators are better partners than democratic leaders when it comes to foreign relations. In a system where one person calls the shots, he noted, diplomats can be confident that the government will do what the leader says it will do.[7]

Democracies are a different story. With checks and balances, complex government structures, multiple competing authorities and interests, and constant turnover, no person or office is ever solely in charge of anything, and no one can commit to a proposal without first entering a perplexing maze of consultations, negotiations, and compromises. It is often difficult to figure out who has the authority to negotiate a deal, let alone secure a firm commitment from anyone who can reliably deliver the goods.

Allan Rabinowitz, a zoologist who works with developing countries to protect endangered species, agrees that authoritarian regimes are easier to deal with than democratic governments. Once a dictator can be persuaded to preserve local wildlife, good things happen in short order. Democracies are more mercurial, and although often well intentioned, they are difficult to deal with and much less likely to live up to their promises.[8]

The explorer's line, "Take me to your leader" can get you somewhere in an authoritarian state, but in a democracy it will only start a fight. Henry

---

[5] Major exceptions include some German, Dutch, and Japanese corporations that rely on institutionalized collaborative agreements between management and labor – a more cooperative model of corporate governance than the American practice of collective bargaining. Another alternative to the traditional top-down corporate model are co-operatives, which blur the traditional lines between management and labor by giving employees management responsibilities and making them joint shareholders.

[6] Ironically, given that corporations were created specifically to plan and invest for the long-term (as well as to take advantage of favorable tax rates and special protections from legal liability), shareholders and managers routinely sacrifice long-term prosperity for short-term profits.

[7] Ambassador Hussain Haqqani, speech to the Washington Center, Washington, DC, January, 2007.

[8] Allan Rabinowitz interview, *The Colbert Report*, June 10, 2008.

Kissinger's joke about the difficulties of dealing with the European Union – "Whom do I call if I want to talk to Europe?" – is a problem common to all democracies, because it is often impossible to figure out who has ultimate authority. It seems like everyone either thinks that they are in charge or that they should be, but no one has the last word on anything.[9]

Even if our intrepid explorer manages to find the right person to talk to, democratic governments are notoriously fickle. Public opinion is a perfectly fluid foundation for public policy. Democracies change their leaders and their minds at a moment's notice, as popular opinion shifts with the breeze. The only dependable truth about democracy is that the people responsible for making decisions today will not be in power tomorrow, and their successors will have new priorities and be inclined to disavow the previous administration's decisions as a matter of course. In seeking reliable partners, there are advantages to having the same government in power for forty years, rather than four.

ECONOMIC DEVELOPMENT

Some leading political theorists, including Hannah Arendt and Samuel Huntington, hypothesize that only relatively rich countries can afford to be democratic. Developing countries need sustained economic growth, and democracies are too unfocused, unstable, and undisciplined to support an emerging economy. By default, the only realistic choice for underdeveloped countries is a developmental dictatorship that can provide the leadership, organization, focus, discipline, determination, stability, and will to develop the national infrastructure and build the economy. Until this happens, democracy is not a realistic alternative.

China is a textbook example of the potential of developmental dictatorship. After the political and economic horrors of the Mao era, Communist Party leader Deng Xiaoping single-mindedly resolved to transform China into an economic powerhouse, by unleashing the country's latent entrepreneurial and productive potential. The results fell somewhere between being amazing and miraculous. In less than a generation, China went from rampant poverty and mass starvation to become the world's second-largest economy. Even today, the country's nominally Marxist-Leninist leaders remain economically ambitious. They recently embarked on an unprecedented project to link major urban areas with a complex system of bullet trains. The ambition, scale, and risks of the

---

[9] Newly elected American presidents are always disappointed to discover how little power they really have, although one would think that word would have gotten out by now. Everyone calls the American president the most powerful person on earth, but it is hardly the case. Presidents might have the world's best bully pulpit and access to the country's nuclear launch codes, but they cannot directly or unilaterally order anyone outside of the White House staff to do much of anything. Most of the president's power is persuasive, not declaratory. Moreover, the president is not the same, nor nearly as powerful, as the presidency. Most presidential orders must be conveyed through official channels, and the president has surprisingly little say in the day-to-day operations of most executive agencies.

project are breathtaking – it is something that no rational emerging democracy would dream of attempting.

This is one of the advantages of developmental dictatorships. China's leaders do not have to ask anyone's permission to act. They have unchecked access to unlimited treasury funds and a massive, largely passive workforce. They do not have to consider anyone's rights or interests in pursuing their policies. They do not need to worry about petitions, protests, or lawsuits. Absent a jasmine revolution or a serious scandal too big to cover up, they will never be held publicly accountable for their actions or abuses. They do not need to balance competing interests or compromise with opposition parties. They do not require a popular mandate. They are not obliged to seek the greatest good for the greatest number. They have considerable leeway to do whatever they want to do.[10]

There is a certain appeal to this sort of a can-do command economy, as long as the government in question does not want to knock down *your* home – or hometown – without legal recourse, just to build a high-speed railway, dam, factory, or nuclear power plant.

Sidebar 9: Monty Python on Developmental Dictatorship

Monty Python offered a send-up of developmental dictatorship in their movie *The Life of Brian*. The brief excerpt below is from a conversation among a hapless group of Palestinian revolutionaries fighting Roman occupation during the first century AD. The group's strategy sessions usually involve sitting around complaining about Roman rule, without actually doing anything about it. This time, however, their customary litany of grievances takes an unexpected turn:

- *[The Romans] have bled us white, the bastards. They've taken everything we had ... and what have they ever given us in return?*
- *The aqueduct?*
- *Oh, yeah – they did give us that. That's true, yeah.*
- *And the sanitation.*
- *Yeah, sanitation. Remember what the city used to be like?*
- *All right, I'll grant you the aqueduct and sanitation are the two things the Romans have done.*

---

[10] This is not to say that Chinese Communist Party leaders never worry about factional interests or public opinion. Although political pluralism does not exist in China and public protests are rare, the number of public demonstrations against the government is increasing, and unquestioning deference to political elites is in decline. Chinese leaders now face a growing possibility that their legitimacy might prove fragile, and that they might one day be judged in the court of public opinion. The odds of this happening seem remote at the moment, thanks to sustained economic growth, the continued loyalty of the Red Army, and the ability of dissatisfied Chinese to immigrate (which serves as a useful political relief valve). But the status quo could change quickly, depending on economic developments, the growing potential power of the new middle class, and the emerging *virtú* of the Chinese people.

- *And the roads.*
- *Well, yes, obviously the roads. The roads go without saying, don't they? But apart from the aqueduct, the sanitation, and the roads...*
- *Irrigation. Medicine. Education. Health.*
- *Yeah, yeah, all right, fair enough.*
- *And the wine.*
- *Yeah – that's something we'd really miss if the Romans left.*
- *Public baths.*
- *And it's safe to walk in the streets at night now.*
- *Yes, they certainly know how to keep order... let's face it – they're the only ones who could in a place like this.*
- *All right, all right... but apart [from all that] what have the Romans done for us?*
- *Brought peace...*
- *Shut up!*

THE FOIBLES AND FAILURES OF THE MANY

Human Nature

Some arguments against democracy are based on theories about human nature. Circle as many as apply to the following list of congenital human defects. People are, by nature, too: wild, selfish, hedonistic, passionate, dumb, undisciplined, shortsighted, gullible, greedy, untrustworthy, dishonest, irascible, intolerant, and ignorant to be capable of self-government. Here are some of the more persuasive arguments concerning the inherent failings of *homo democraticus*.

The Many Are Unwise

Plato believed that most people stand just one rung of the ladder above wild animals, and like animals are governed by their appetites rather than by reason. The best that the many can be expected to do is control themselves just enough to mind their own business and obey their betters.

Because the many are genetically incapable of wisdom, courage, or any other high virtue, the very idea of democracy struck Plato as not only unwise but absurd. The congenital ignorance and hedonism of the many will inevitably rule in a democracy, and in such an irrational and decadent society there will be no wisdom, courage, discipline, harmony, justice, or peace.

The Many Are Selfish

Thomas Hobbes rejected Plato's class snobbery out of hand, but agreed that human nature makes democracy unthinkable. He did not suffer from any of Plato's delusions about the claimed virtues of philosophers, aristocrats, or other self-proclaimed members of team *homo superior*. Hobbes was fiercely egalitarian when it came to human nature, although only in a negative sense: he believed that everyone is made of the same rotten stuff, and that, thanks to the leveling effect of guns (a relatively new and revolutionary technology in the mid-seventeenth century) everyone poses an equal mortal danger to everyone else. Hobbes's pessimistic view of human nature led him to conclude that the many are incapable of self-government. Unlike Plato, Hobbes had no moral objection to democracy; he just did not think it was a credible option, given our mutually destructive instincts.

The fatal flaw of human nature, in Hobbes's view, is that we are all radically and irredeemably selfish. Our shared imperative is to look out for number one, and we are perfectly willing, if not compelled, to do anything to anyone to further our own cause. This single-minded pursuit of self-interest makes us a danger to one another. In a state of nature (that is, in a world without government) people will inevitably plunge headlong into a savage war of all against all, where life is solitary, poor, nasty, brutish, and short. Life in a state of nature is a game with only one rule: win or die.

You cannot stop human nature – you can only hope to contain it.[11] Individual selfishness and savagery can only be held in check by a superior power – a Leviathan – that is powerful enough to save us from ourselves and protect us from our equally nasty neighbors, friends, and families. The Leviathan is not necessarily wise, enlightened, or virtuous, but it does not have to be – it just has to be strong enough to make us behave.

The Many Are Idiots

Comedian George Carlin often asked his audiences to contemplate how stupid the average American is, and then to remember that half the country is even dumber than that. Professional curmudgeon H. L. Menken claimed that no one ever went broke underestimating the intelligence of the American people, and he contemptuously dismissed the middle class as "the booboisie." My lawyer friends privately refer to jurors as "rocks in a box." Of course, Carlin, Menken, and my friends were talking specifically about Americans, but they could just as easily have been talking about people anywhere.

The common perception, even in democratic societies, is that ordinary people are idiots. The majority are, often by choice, uneducated, uninformed, and uninterested in public affairs. They do not read, reflect, or care much about politics or the world around them. They are focused solely on their own interests, and have little curiosity about anything beyond their own immediate concerns. Why would anyone in their right mind trust such people with the responsibilities of self-government?

The Many Are Disorganized

Machiavelli agreed that the many are by nature selfish and uncooperative, and that they need strong leaders to get them organized and moving in the right

---

[11] With apologies to sportscaster Dan Patrick.

direction. For Machiavelli, one of the main functions of a virtuous Prince is to create good laws and good institutions – things that the many are incapable of doing on their own.

James Madison used a similar argument to explain why a small elite group of men met in secret in 1787 to write the American Constitution. It must always be this way, he explained, even in democracies. Lawgivers are invariably elite, from Solon to (ahem) Madison, because there are some things that ordinary people just cannot do. All societies, even democracies, need elites to organize things and lead the way.

The Many Are Intolerant

There is a long line of kings, queens, aristocrats, religious leaders, and philosophers who would be quite happy to explain why ordinary people cannot be trusted with political power. Interestingly, many democrats share at least some of the same suspicions. Liberal democrats are among the first to admit to democracy's limitations and warn against allowing too much democracy. It is not always clear whether such relentless self-criticism is a strength or a weakness.

John Stuart Mill was openly conflicted about democracy. Like most upper-class philosophes, he had little confidence in the middle classes, let alone the lumpen-proletariat, to protect liberty or nurture a progressive society. Democracy empowers the base middle and lower classes, but it does not change their nature to be suspicious, intolerant, ignorant, closed-minded, parochial, boorish, selfish, apathetic, and xenophobic. Such unenlightened attitudes endanger liberty and progress, and need to be checked. Mill found an unlikely ally in anarchist Peter Kropotkin, who thought what although democratic states might tolerate interesting or eccentric people, they will not put up with radical people or ideas.

THE WEAKNESSES OF DEMOCRATIC GOVERNMENT

Democratic leaders and governments reflect the collective character of the many. If ordinary people are selfish, stupid, intolerant, oppressive, materialistic, quarrelsome, and incapable of strategic thought, then their leaders and governments will share the same qualities writ large.

Amateur Hour

As Anacharsis put it, democracy is the system where wise men speak, but fools decide.[12] Free democracy, in particular, is premised on the idea that ordinary people are equally capable of assuming high public office and making important policy decisions. Democracy is the apotheosis of the amateur, in an age where everything else that matters is entrusted to experts and professionals.

---

[12] Plutarch, *Greek Lives*.

In response, free and participatory democrats are instinctively suspicious of those who claim special wisdom, expertise, or competence. Most people dislike and mistrust people who claim to be smarter, better educated, or just plain better than they are, and this can give democratic societies something of an anti-intellectual bias. Free democrats are not only fiercely proud of their amateur status; they enjoy bringing so-called experts down a peg or two.

Although this sort of populist egalitarianism might sound appealing, critics charge that the result is an incompetent government dominated by tinkerers and dilettantes. Democracy is political amateurism run amok. It is literally unprofessional, and it produces leaders and decisions that are as pedestrian and inept as the average voter. It is a truism of democratic politics that C students run the country,[13] and for those who value political experience, expertise, pragmatism, wisdom, and competence this is not a comforting thought.

Most people know little about politics and care even less. Expecting the average voter to make sound policy decisions is like asking your dog to do brain surgery; no matter how lovable and well intentioned it might be, it is not going to end well.

Sidebar 10: Tinker, Tailor, Sculptor, Soldier

In the movie, *The 300*, the allied armies of Greece prepare to face Persian King Xerxes's overwhelming invasion force. They are dismayed when Sparta delivers a mere 300 men to help guard the critical pass at Thermopylae. Most Greek armies were composed of citizen-soldiers, drawn from all walks of life. Sparta did things its own way. The excerpt below occurs when Daxos, Commander of the Arcadian army, is stunned to see the token Spartan contingent, led by King Leonidas.

Daxos: You bring only this handful of soldiers against Xerxes? I see I was wrong to expect Sparta's commitment to at least match our own.

King Leonidas: Doesn't it? (Turning to address the Arcadians): You, there – what is your profession?

1st Arcadian Hoplite: I am a potter, sir.

Leonidas: And you, Arcadian – what is your profession?

2nd Hoplite: Sculptor, sir.

Leonidas: And you?

3rd Hoplite: Blacksmith.

Leonidas (Turning to face his own men): SPARTANS! WHAT IS YOUR PROFESSION?

The 300 close ranks, stomp, brandish their spears, and roar in unison: HAROO! HAROO! HAROO!

Leonidas: You see, old friend? I brought more soldiers than you did.

---

[13] Commonly attributed to President Harry Truman, although apocryphal.

Democratic Leaders

De Tocqueville explained why aristocratic leaders are in almost all respects better than democratic leaders. They are born and bred to lead. They come from the best families, receive the best education, have worldly experience and global connections, and represent a multigenerational commitment to public service. They do not need to seek public office for money or power, as they already have both, and so they are uniquely positioned to live up to the aristocratic ideal of doing the right thing for the right reason.

The democratic ideal that anyone can grow up to be president should be cause for worry, not celebration. In most democracies, age and citizenship are the only formal qualifications for office, and all it takes to win is to be slightly more popular than the other candidates. There is little to nothing in the way of objective vetting or quality control, and the results are predictably poor. Popularity is not necessarily the best litmus test for fitness to hold public office.

De Tocqueville noted two other reasons why democratic leaders are, on the whole, an unimpressively mediocre lot. First, people do not want to elect their betters to public office. This is not out of fear, but out of general distaste and lack of affection for such candidates. Voters prefer leaders they can relate to on a personal level – candidates with whom they would like to have a beer. This also might not be the best test of a good leader.

Second, the best leaders rarely seek office in democracies. Elections are difficult and demeaning (all those hands to shake and babies to kiss), and once in office there are too many demands and too many limits on power. Ambitious and talented people find things more to their liking in business, where they can do things their own way.

Aristophanes viciously mocked Athenian leaders in his plays *The Clouds* and *The Wasps*. He portrayed Cleon, one of Athens' greatest politicians, as a transparently shallow, self-serving, corrupt jerk. But the many worshipped Cleon, or so Aristophanes claimed, because they were too thick to see through his obvious masquerade – a thief and a charlatan disguised as a man of the people and heroic defender of truth, justice, and the Athenian way.

According to Aristophanes, Cleon excelled as a democratic leader because he had a certain roguish charm, knew how to prey on popular anxieties, and because he shamelessly flattered the masses and pandered to their base desires. Democracies are especially susceptible to such callow leaders – superficially charming, self-promoting, manipulative con artists. Successful democratic leaders quickly learn to tell people what they want to hear, not what they need to hear.

What motivates democratic leaders? For starters, political office offers a direct path to power and riches, providing successful politicians with an unequaled opportunity to wring private profit from public office, thanks to the incestuous ménage à trois that exists among executive officials, legislators, and private businesses.

Politicians and bureaucrats are uniquely positioned to solicit favors from the private sector and tap the public treasury to promote their own interests. Campaign contributors become political investors, with donations purchasing special access to candidates and government officials. This allows big donors to influence public policy and enrich themselves at public expense. Politicians and civil servants routinely enact laws and regulations to their own advantage, and have access to privileged information that can profit themselves, their sponsors, and favored special interests.

Finally, public officials enrich themselves by using the revolving door that spins between government and the private sector. Powerful special interests offer connected officials lucrative jobs when they leave office, and after a while encourage them to reenter government in strategic positions. Rotating jobs between government and the private industries that they are supposed to regulate allows politicians and their staff to enjoy lucrative parallel careers in government and business. These are some of the reasons why so many politicians begin their careers scraping by on modest government salaries, but retire as rich as Croesus.

Democratic Laws

If a camel is a horse designed by a committee, democratic laws are a hodge-podge of half-baked ideas, haphazardly slapped together by multiple committees into an absurd and inscrutable whole. Expedience, not principle, drives the legislative process. Laws reflect ad hoc, reactive attempts to deal piecemeal with immediate problems, with little regard for long-term consequences. Incessant partisan bickering results in laws being cobbled together at the last minute from mismatched parts, like Frankenstein's monster. Special interests drive the process, and when powerful lobbyists disagree, legislation is easily gridlocked through pointless bickering, and then clinched, if at all, at the eleventh hour through shady back-room deals.

The majority might ultimately shape the spirit of the laws, but they do not bring coherence to the process. The people's will is impulsive, constant only in its impatience. Majorities have little foresight but perfect hindsight. They are incapable of accepting blame, but quick to assign it. They will instantly absolve themselves of responsibility when things go wrong, but are singularly unforgiving of others. They rarely know what they want, but know that they wanted it yesterday. They have the collective attention span of a hyperactive three year old – what they desperately desire today will be forgotten tomorrow and replaced by some new obscure object of desire.

All of this makes democratic lawmaking careless, unfocused, ineffective, counterproductive, and often contradictory. Laws are uncertain and unstable, as legislators try to keep up with shifting public demands and simultaneously look after their own interests.

American lawyer and poet John Godfrey Saxe warned against watching laws or sausages being made. If forced to choose one, however, better to go with the sausages. Unlike legislatures, meatpacking companies are well organized, efficient, and accomplish precisely what they set out to do.

Tyranny of the Majority

Aristotle thought that the most dangerous form of democracy is a mob. He was almost certainly wrong. No matter how bad a mob might be, tyranny of the majority is worse. It is the most dangerous form of democracy, because there is no political force that can match the power of a determined majority.

Mobs are dangerous and destructive, but like other minority factions they are usually limited in scope and size, and can be readily checked by a resolute majority. Mobs are an acute problem with a relatively short half-life; as passions cool, they usually lose steam and are tamed in due course.

Minority factions are subject to the natural check of the majority; there is no equivalent natural check on majorities. Majorities have no peer in terms of their ability to marshal concentrated political power to destroy anything or anyone who might think about getting in their way, and they can cause considerable damage in the process.

Being part of a strong and cohesive majority is a powerful narcotic. Groups that are perfectly reasonable when in the minority quickly, and often unconsciously, become oppressive when they are in the majority. Religious, ethnic, and racial groups, political parties, and other factions, all of whom might be perfectly benign within the friendly confines of a pluralistic democracy, are susceptible to tyrannical behavior once they gain the whip hand.

Madison worried about tyranny of the majority more than any other political pathology. His classic essay in *The Federalist Papers* No. 51 offers an articulate warning about the dangers posed by unchecked majorities. Direct democracy empowers the majority to have its way, and society will suffer grievously as a result.

Emergencies

Machiavelli maintained that democracy's Achilles heel is its inability to deal effectively with crises that demand quick thinking and decisive action. If an airplane is in trouble, flight attendants do not have time to walk through the cabin asking passengers to debate the matter and then vote on what to do. Everyone has to trust that the pilot knows what she is doing. In a political emergency, the time and effort needed for democratic debate is an unaffordable luxury. A crisis situation requires one set of experienced hands on the wheel – a skilled political pilot, or in Machiavelli's terms, a prince.

No Democratic Decision Making in Business

Aside from government, there are few good examples of democratic decision making in our adult lives. The private sector rarely embraces democratic values and principles, so why does anyone think that it is the best way to run a government? Government is like a business, in that both require efficient, rational, sophisticated, and expert tactical and strategic decision making to solve complex problems in a challenging environment. Although businesses are well adapted to make such decisions rationally, democratic governments seem designed to stymie, rather than encourage, sound and efficient decision making.

The Illusion of Democracy: Mosca and Marx

In addition to arguments about why democracy is flawed, or why other forms of government are better, another line of argument is worth considering: that democracy is an illusion. The argument that democracy is a sham begins with the proposition that all societies have an elite class that actually runs things, including democracies. Aristocracies are up-front about who is in charge; democracies are egalitarian in theory but elitist in fact.

There are two major variations on this theme. Italian political scientist Gaetano Mosca argued that all societies have a ruling class that is ambitious, invested, connected, and endowed with the requisite organizational and leadership skills that empower them to dominate the political process. The nonpolitical classes, in contrast, are disorganized, atomized, have a low level of political sophistication and awareness, and are generally uninterested in public life.

For Mosca, the crucial difference between democracies and aristocracies is that in democracies the political elite is not monolithic, but composed of competing factions with divergent interests. Although democracies are never truly democratic, they have a diverse ruling class and benefit from regular turnover among government officials, as different interests compete for power.

The second perspective is Karl Marx's critique of bourgeois democracy. According to Marx, the state exists for one simple reason: to serve the interests of the dominant class. The ruling class inevitably creates the kind of state that best suits its needs, and the specific form that the state takes makes no difference in terms of its ultimate function. If it is in the interest of the dominant class that the state take the guise of democracy, then that is the form that it will take (Figure 8.1).

In capitalist societies, Marx theorized that democracy is a useful myth that allows the bourgeoisie to consolidate its power and minimizes the need for overt violence to maintain control. Claiming to operate an open, free, and fair political system mollifies the lower classes, lulling them into believing that they have a voice in government and can advance their interests peacefully through the ballot box. This resonates with Machiavelli's observation that it is easier to

FIGURE 8.1 Did they have a choice? Original illustration by Ian Zell.

control people by enticing them to comply voluntarily through trickery than it is to compel them to obey through force or fear.

In bourgeois democracies, Marx argued, concepts such as equality, liberty, and justice are symbolically powerful, but in practice invariably favor the rich. To the poor, the right to own property means the right not to own property, or to be trapped hopelessly in debt trying to buy property that they cannot afford. The right to equal justice does not stop the poor from being punished more severely than the rich. And the liberty to do as one pleases favors the rich, not only because their wealth gives them far more (and more pleasant) options; it also means that they do not have to feel responsible for the lack of opportunities available to the poor.

Democracy, Marx argued, is a façade – a game of political Three Card Monte that the ruling class cannot lose. Real power will remain forever out of reach, like a carrot dangled in front of a determined but thickheaded mule. Even if the many somehow threaten to seize power through the ballot box, the ruling class will simply change the rules or impose a more overtly oppressive regime to stay in power.

In *State and Revolution*, Lenin argued that in capitalist democracies the working classes are:

so crushed by want and poverty that they "cannot be bothered with democracy," and "cannot be bothered with politics;" in the ordinary, peaceful course of events the majority of the population is debarred from participation in public and political life.

Democracy for an insignificant minority, democracy for the rich – that is the democracy of capitalist society ... [where] the oppressed are allowed once every few years to decide which particular representatives of the oppressing class shall represent and repress them in parliament![14]

Can democracy ever advance the cause of the oppressed? Marx was skeptical, but acknowledged that it was possible. Although he thought that violent revolution was probably the only way to destroy capitalism and create a truly class-less democracy, he conceded the possibility of peaceful evolutionary change in two countries he considered exceptional – the United Kingdom and the United States. Marx implied that these two liberal societies might make a relatively peaceful transition to socialism through conventional political means, without suffering through a revolutionary bloodbath.

The idea of Anglo-American exceptionalism intrigued Marx, but bitterly divided his followers. After Marx died, two distinct lines of thought emerged about the potential of liberal democracies to deliver real social and economic justice. Lenin and Rosa Luxemburg argued that reform through the ballot box was impossible, and that violent revolution was the only alternative.

Other Marxists, including Karl Kautsky and Eduard Bernstein, were convinced that liberal democracies could be reformed peacefully by organizing the working classes, creating labor parties, using their strength of numbers to take control of government through elections, and passing new laws to promote working-class interests. They called for the gradual transformation of capitalism into what Bernstein called a "just, juster, and still more just" society.

Hannah Arendt had her own perspective on Marx. She argued that, despite his reputation as a radical thinker and revolutionary, Marx was just another conventional liberal – a mainstream Enlightenment philosopher who took the idea of socioeconomic equality more seriously than most. Like other liberals, Marx focused primarily on liberty, and viewed government as a necessary evil. His dream of ending exploitation, promoting equality, and shrinking government all amounted to little more than liberal wish fulfillment. Like other liberals, Marx conflated liberty and freedom. His stated goal was freedom for the working class, but in seeking to abolish the state, Marx would have destroyed freedom in the name of liberty. In the final analysis, Marx sought to liberate the working classes, not to make them free.

SUMMARY

So what is wrong with democracy? It is contentious, corrupt, decadent, disruptive, ignorant, incompetent, inconsistent, ineffectual, intolerant, materialistic, mediocre, messy, oppressive, partisan, reactionary, selfish, slow, small-minded, stupid, tyrannical, unjust, unstable, untrustworthy, unwise, violent, and xenophobic. It might also be a ruse to trick the masses into passive acceptance of elite rule. Otherwise, no complaints.

[14] Lenin, *State and Revolution*, chapter 5.

9

The Case for Democracy

The case in favor of democratic government is presented here in two parts: theoretical and moral arguments, and some claimed practical benefits. We begin where most political theory begins, with some assumptions about human nature.

POLITICAL THEORY AND MORAL ARGUMENTS IN FAVOR OF DEMOCRACY

Human Nature

Plato and Hobbes aside, most leading models of human nature are perfectly compatible with self-government. Here are five leading examples:

1. Machiavelli thought that there are two kinds of people: the few and the many. It is the nature of the few to dominate others; the many just want to be left alone. People are, metaphorically, either sheepdogs or sheep. Machiavelli advocated republican government as the best way to accommodate the natural drives of both groups. Republics accommodate the few by allowing them to lead, but limit their power through a system of checks and balances, where ambition checks ambition and power checks power, as the few jealously watch each other.

The many pose a different set of problems. Their single-minded attachment to their own interests makes them naturally selfish and uncooperative. Machiavelli saw two ways for a republic to check the tendency of the many to be uncontrollable – use religion to scare them into behaving, or instill popular virtú through political participation.

Machiavelli assumed that ordinary people will eventually grow too sophisticated to be cowed into good behavior by threats of hell and damnation, so although religion might be an effective means of social control in the short run, at some point it will no longer serve. This leaves political participation as the only long-term alternative to oppression.

For Machiavelli, freedom in a republican government has the added benefit of building public virtú. Through political participation, the many learn how self-interest and the public good are intertwined. They learn, in other words, to stop being sheep and become responsible citizens.

2. John Locke agreed that selfishness is intrinsic to human nature, but thought that its more destructive aspects are limited by our inherent capacity for reason and self-restraint. Our aptitude for rational self-control makes us naturally sociable, or as Locke put it, "easily domesticated." Accordingly, the many need only limited government to keep the peace and enforce the rule of law.[1]

3. Rousseau contemplated the state of nature while gazing out the window of his patroness's comfortable home in the bucolic French town of Chambéry.[2] Not unreasonably, Rousseau concluded that life in a state of nature is not a Hobbesian hellscape, but a pleasant, pastoral existence where people live happy, simple lives without the trappings and hubbub of so-called modern civilization. But the simple pleasures of an organic lifestyle were not enough for Rousseau. People living in a state of nature might be happy, but they are noble savages – pleasant and sociable enough, but ignorant naïfs. Participatory democracy, Rousseau argued, allows people to transcend the state of nature, where they are literally happy idiots, and ascend to the state of freedom, where they assume the highest form of humanity as fully engaged citizens.

4. During the nineteenth century, James Mill and Jeremy Bentham developed the theory of utilitarianism, arguably the most influential modern theory of human nature. Utilitarianism posits that people are rational creatures, with the congenital ability to make sophisticated cost-benefit calculations to guide their thoughts, decisions, and actions. This allows people to maximize their overall individual happiness, on the basis of reasoned self-interest.[3]

Utilitarian theory both presupposes and advocates rational decision making by individuals and societies. Individual actions cumulatively shape society through the invisible hand of the marketplace, with individual choices unconsciously promoting the common good. Sound public policy can further rationalize this process, to ensure the greatest good for the greatest number. Whereas utilitarianism is not inherently democratic in spirit, the utilitarian theory of human nature is perfectly consistent with self-government.

---

[1] "Wherever law ends, tyranny begins." Locke, *The Second Treatise of Government.*

[2] Madame de Warens.

[3] Utilitarian theory holds that human nature is constant and immutable. This view of human nature has been challenged by the notion that human nature is malleable, and with the right tools can be shaped at will. Some see this challenge to utilitarianism as a cause for optimism, in that human nature can potentially be changed for the better. But it is also cause for worry, because totalitarian political movements led by Stalin, Hitler, Mao, Kim Il-Sung, and others have repeatedly sought to change human nature for less noble purposes.

5. Finally, Hannah Arendt rejected the idea of human nature, and focused instead on what she called the human condition. Beyond genetics, two factors make us who we are: (1) individual reason and free will (internal factors that allow us to shape our own nature); and (2) the environment in which we live (external factors that shape our nature). These elements jointly determine who we are and might become. The underlying variables are infinitely mutable, which means that people are like snowflakes – everyone is made of the same stuff, yet each is the unique product of singular choices and circumstances.

The main problem, according to Arendt, is that societies and governments invariably seek to suppress individualism and encourage conformity, because they value order and predictability over eclecticism and true diversity. Because states and societies limit liberty and (often unconsciously) try to make everyone fit socially acceptable norms, most people never discover their own unique qualities, let alone have the opportunity to realize or develop them in order to live up to their individual potential.

Democracy is the only political system that allows everyone to interact with everyone else in a freewheeling exchange of ideas and collective action. It is only through this sort of interactive participation (Arendt called it "expressing, discussing, and deciding") that people have the opportunity to discover what they have in common with others and what makes them different. Freedom and liberty give people the chance to recover their singular individualism, and the opportunity to use their unique gifts to improve themselves and society. Through politics, ordinary people are born again as self-aware, reflective, autonomous, and free citizens. This empowers them to transcend the unthinking conformity of mass society, and act consciously to change the world.

We Do the Work, We Deserve Power

Athenian democracy was founded on the principle that those who work to defend the community earn the right to participate in politics. This idea originated with a literal sea change in Athenian military strategy during the fifth century BC.

At the time, Athens was an unstable aristocracy, characterized by chronic conflict between the established ruling class and upstart pro-democracy forces. One of the main justifications for aristocratic rule was that the upper classes did most of the work to protect Athens from her external enemies. Infantry troops – hoplites – had fought all of the decisive battles in all Greek wars to date, and soldiers were expected to provide their own armor and weapons. This was an expensive proposition, and it effectively restricted military service to wealthy families. The aristocracy argued that because they were Athens's main defenders, they deserved their monopoly on political power.

The last Persian War flipped this equation. In 481 BC, the great Persian king, Xerxes, launched a massive armada to conquer and subjugate Greece once and for all. Rather than waiting to fight on Greek soil, as they had always done in

"The Athenians are here, Sire, with an offer to back us with ships, money, arms, and men – and, of course, their usual lectures about democracy."

FIGURE 9.1 © Ed Fisher/The New Yorker Collection (1983).

the past, the Athenians determined this time to confront the invaders at sea. With a fleet of 200 ships, they met and routed the Persians off Salamis, sending the invaders home for good and leaving Athens as the dominant naval power in the Aegean.

So how did history's first great sea battle speed the birth of Athenian democracy? The navy depended on rowers, not infantry. The state provided the boats and oars, meaning that any able-bodied man could serve. And they did. Ordinary Athenians secured the victory at Salamis, and they returned home as heroes. Pro-democracy forces exploited their new leverage to argue that the demos had earned the right to rule as the city's new defenders. The aristocracy reluctantly yielded, and the golden age of Athenian democracy began (Figure 9.1).

Two millennia later, Abraham Lincoln echoed a similar theme during his famous debates with Stephen A. Douglas in 1858. Lincoln argued that those who do society's dirty work deserve political rights:

It is the eternal struggle between two principles, right and wrong, throughout the world. It is the same spirit that says "you toil and work and earn bread, and I'll eat it." No matter in what shape it comes, whether from the mouth of a king who seeks to bestride the people of his own nation, and live by the fruit of their labor, or from one race of men as an apology for enslaving another race, it is the same tyrannical principle.

Lincoln's point was not limited to slavery, but articulated the right of everyone who toils, works, and earns bread to enjoy the material and political fruits of their labor. Lincoln was hard at work on his plan to secure full political rights for freed slaves when he was assassinated in 1865.

A hundred years later, during the 1960s, the same sentiment prevailed once more. During the Vietnam War, the United States drafted thousands of eighteen-to-twenty-year-old men and sent them to fight in Southeast Asia, but denied them the right to vote until they turned twenty-one. This struck most Americans as unjust, and the result was the 26th Amendment, ratified in 1971, lowering the national voting age to 18.

PRACTICAL BENEFITS

The Greatest Good for the Greatest Number

The most compelling justification for democracy is also the simplest: it is the only political system that naturally seeks the greatest good for the greatest number. To many, this alone makes democracy superior to all other forms of government.

Aligning Self-Interest and the Common Good: Progress, Prosperity, and a Stake in the System

In authoritarian societies, people inevitably work for a master – the state, a dictator, a political party, or a dominant class. Such an arrangement is neither just nor especially productive. There was a joke in the old Soviet Union that the state pretended to pay the workers, and the workers pretended to work.

In democracies, especially in liberal democracies, citizens are expected to look after their own interests, which most people are all too happy to do. But individuals also benefit from the system of mutual promises of aid and support that democracy provides. When people do well individually, the community benefits; when the community does well, individuals benefit; and when people run into trouble, the community is pledged to step in and help. This means that beyond self-interest, everyone also has a personal stake in the system. When people are responsible for their own affairs, but also feel invested in society, they learn that self-interest and the common good are really two sides of the same coin. This is enlightened self-interest.

Successful democracies combine the restless energy that comes from the orderly pursuit of enlightened self-interest with the social consciousness and ethos of public service that come from being an integral part of a larger community. It is this balance between individualism and civic-mindedness that robber baron Andrew Carnegie embraced late in life, when he dedicated his fortune to good causes and declared that, "The man who dies rich dies disgraced."

Aligning self-interest and the common good encourages pride of ownership, not only in one's own possessions but in society as a whole. During his American travels, de Tocqueville noted that he found it impossible to criticize anything about the United States without sparking an argument, because Americans felt so invested in their country that they thought themselves responsible even for the weather, and were quick to take offense if an outsider complained.

Democratic societies that succeed in aligning self-interest and the common good are more vigorous, innovative, productive, and resilient than authoritarian states. People who labor in their own interest work harder than they otherwise would, which enriches both the individual and society. Moreover, if ordinary people feel invested in the system, they are quicker to respond to a crisis, and more willing to forgive the system's flaws when things go badly.

Democracies have some clear competitive advantages over aristocratic governments when it comes to new ideas and technological breakthroughs. Democracies have a restless energy that promotes innovation and progress; aristocratic states are naturally conservative, if not sclerotic. Over time aristocracies become, like Mr. Turveydrop in *Bleak House*, dissipated masters of deportment, pining for the lost glories of the old regime.

De Tocqueville contrasted aristocratic and democratic societies by comparing British and American naval forces as they were in the early nineteenth century. At the time, Britain had the clear advantage in terms of sea power; her magnificent warships were the envy of the world. British ships were designed by the best naval architects, built by the world's best craftsmen, made of the best materials, and equipped with the best sails, tackle, and weapons that money could buy. They were beautiful ships and technological marvels, built to last a century.

The American navy, on the other hand, was completely ramshackle. Her warships were poorly built, badly outfitted, and often barely seaworthy. In a head-to-head comparison, it looked like another clear win for aristocratic excellence over democratic mediocrity.

De Tocqueville argued, however, that the shabby quality of American ships was actually a sign of democratic superiority. The Americans knew that Yankee ingenuity and rapid technological progress would make the current generation of warships obsolete in just a few years, so it made no sense to build them to last longer than that.

De Tocqueville predicted that in the short term the British fleet would reign supreme, but that American warships would eventually eclipse Britain's and relegate the royal fleet to obsolescence – beautiful monuments to aristocratic excellence of an age gone by. The seemingly slapdash nature of the American navy revealed the true, although largely unplanned, genius of democratic enterprise – restless innovation and progress, fueled by individual initiative, a sense of common purpose, and a confident optimism about the future.

Inclusion and Moderation

All societies contain alienated and potentially violent individuals and groups. The question is what to do with them – whether to isolate, repress, or include them. Will inviting angry malcontents to participate in the political process lead to civil unrest, terror, or civil war? Or will including such groups moderate political discourse and soften destructive social impulses?

Although accommodating disaffected groups might increase social conflict in the short term, in the long run respecting the rights of the most radical dissidents to express their dissatisfaction peacefully and advocate alternative visions for society encourages greater tolerance, constructive engagement, mutual accommodation, and the moderation of extreme views. Even this modestly optimistic view, however, is complicated by a host of variables.

Some social conflicts might prove unbridgeable, and in these cases the inclusion/moderation hypothesis will fail. In the United States during the eighteenth and nineteenth centuries, pro-slavery forces were a small but powerful and disruptive minority. Early American history was dominated by a seemingly endless series of concessions to appease Southern slaveholders and accommodate their demands and sensibilities. Far from having a moderating effect, these allowances made slave owners and their allies more intransigent and unreasonable – an unsustainable situation that eventually led to civil war.

In the nineteenth and twentieth centuries, Marxist-Leninist movements consciously manipulated liberal toleration and inclusion in order to subvert existing regimes. In his book *State and Revolution*, Lenin forthrightly outlined his willingness to participate in the democratic process solely to sabotage Alexander Kerensky's social democracy and overthrow the freely elected Russian government.

The inclusion and moderation hypothesis also failed conspicuously when it came to the German National Socialist movement. Moderate German political parties naïvely thought that they could contain Hitler's brownshirts, and British Prime Minister Neville Chamberlain similarly miscalculated when he sold out Czechoslovakia in a doomed attempt to appease the Nazis and avoid a second great war. In Pakistan today, the Taliban use periodic peace and inclusion negotiations with the national government to recover, regroup, and rearm – breaking each cease-fire when it suits them and returning to the fight stronger than before.

Despite the problems and failures of the inclusion-moderation hypothesis, persistent efforts to bring dissenters, disruptive elements, rebels, and terrorists to the negotiating table often succeeds in restoring peace and reconciliation in democratic states. The United Kingdom's patient negotiations with the IRA over British rule in Northern Ireland ultimately led to the Good Friday Agreement of 1988, ending the IRA insurgency and bringing Irish republicans back into conventional politics. Spain's persistent efforts to negotiate with Basque separatists eventually paid dividends, allowing peaceful Basque nationalist factions to operate openly and gradually degrading terrorist elements within ETA (Basque Homeland and Liberty) and its political arm, Herri Batasuna (Popular Unity). Most impressively, after South Africa's apartheid regime fell in 1994, President Nelson Mandela's unequivocal policy of nonviolent racial inclusion and reconciliation helped the country make a peaceful transition to multiracial democracy – a result that, at the time, appeared to be highly improbable.

Sidebar 11: Nelson Mandela's First Presidential Inaugural Speech, Pretoria, South Africa, May 10, 1994:

The time for the healing of the wounds has come. The moment to bridge the chasms that divide us has come. The time to build is upon us.

We enter into a covenant that we shall build the society in which all South Africans, both black and white, will be able to walk tall, without any fear in their hearts, assured of their inalienable right to human dignity – a rainbow nation at peace with itself and the world.

We understand … that there is no easy road to freedom. We know it well that none of us acting alone can achieve success. We must therefore act together as a united people, for national reconciliation, for nation building, for the birth of a new world.

Let freedom reign.

The current acid test for the inclusion-moderation hypothesis is the Middle East, where the emerging democratic movements of the Arab Spring face unique challenges posed by Islamist factions, many of which violently oppose liberal democratic values and strive to impose their fundamentalist views on everyone else. Even in staunchly democratic Turkey, there is concern that moderate Islamists such as Recep Tayyip Erdogan see democracy merely as a convenient instrument to pursue distinctly nondemocratic sectarian ends. In 1995, Mr. Erdogan admitted that, "democracy is like a streetcar – You ride it until you arrive at your destination, and then you get off."[4]

So what is the best way to deal with such attitudes and draw the line between accommodation and appeasement? Authoritarian leaders predictably go with what they know – repression. Dictators tend to view all dissent as threatening, and treat even peaceful resistance as something to be eliminated by any means necessary. It should be noted that this approach often works, at least for a time (Figure 9.2).

If a government is relatively weak – whether authoritarian or democratic – the second preferred alternative is quarantine. This is the approach Pakistan has taken, by seeking to isolate and confine the Taliban in the so-called tribal areas, a policy that has so far achieved limited success, at best.

In the Middle East, there is still hope that the inclusion-moderation hypothesis will hold. Turkey, Lebanon, and Qatar have all served as early test cases, and each has been at least somewhat successful in bringing dissidents into conventional politics. The early signs following the 2011 Maghreb revolutions in Egypt,

---

[4] Nicole Dweck, "Democracy, Turkey's Double Edged Sword," *Ground Report*, June 10, 2007 (citing a *Turkish Daily News* interview from 1995), retrieved from *http://www.groundreport. com/World/Democracy-Turkeys-Double-Edged-Sword/2834027*; Matthew Kaminski, "Turkey's 'Good Dictator,'" *The Wall Street Journal*, June 10, 2011, retrieved from *http://online.wsj.com/ article/SB10001424052702304259304576375743249011516.html*.

FIGURE 9.2 DANGER! PACIFISTS (graffito, Segovia, Spain 2013).

Tunisia, Libya, Algeria, and Morocco are tentatively encouraging, with secular, liberal, and moderate Islamist groups all competing – for now – more or less peacefully for power within a relatively pluralistic political framework. Ongoing violence in Egypt and Libya, in particular, is worrying, although in Egypt the military, not the Islamic Brotherhood, is the main cause of continuing unrest.

Aggressively intolerant Islamist factions pose a serious challenge to emerging democratic movements in the region. Some Islamist groups seem willing to compete within an open democratic framework; others are intractably anti-democratic. The trick is to figure out which groups can be reconciled with democratic values, and which are essentially irredeemable. In its assessment of the situation, the Egyptian military seems to have made a serious miscalculation in deciding to crack down on the relatively moderate Egyptian chapter of the Muslim Brotherhood, potentially radicalizing the group and suffocating Egyptian democracy as it drew its first breath.

Sidebar 12: Will the Real Islamists Please Stand Up?

Which of these viewpoints represents the authentic Islamist position concerning democracy and cultural pluralism? The answer might determine whether the inclusion-moderation hypothesis will work in the Islamic world.

A. Muhammed Al-Zawahiri, former spokesman for the Egyptian Salafist Jihad movement:

We are of the view that democracy contravenes the true religion of Islam, as this places sovereignty outside of God's hands, and so we reject democracy and all its mechanisms and tools.[5]

B. Osama Bin Laden, former Al-Qaeda leader, on why he opposed democratic reforms in Iraq:

Islam is the religion of God, and [democratic legislatures] are the religion of ignorance. Those who have obeyed the commanders and scholars in making permissible what is forbidden – like entering the legislative councils – or making forbidden what is permissible (like jihad for His sake) has taken gods other than God and there is no strength or power save in God.[6]

C. President Muhammed Morsi, former Egyptian president and head of the Egyptian Islamic Brotherhood, on Egyptian democracy, before he was deposed in a military coup on July 3, 2013:

Egypt is now a real civil state. It is not theocratic; it is not military. It is democratic, free, constitutional, lawful and modern. We are behaving according to the Egyptian people's choice and will, nothing else.
[Americans should support] the right of the people of the region to enjoy the same freedoms that Americans have. [We have] a shared objective, each to live free in their own land, according to their customs and values, in a fair and democratic fashion ... including members of the Christian minority or those with more secular views.... I vow to uphold equal citizenship rights of all Egyptians, regardless of religion, sex, or class. Go Trojans.[7]

It is still unclear whether the mass protests that ignited the Arab Spring signal a coming democratic summer, or an unsettling prelude to an Islamist winter. Optimists see the Arab Spring as the new, best hope for democracy in the Middle East. The Arab street today appears to be less fundamentalist, more tolerant, and more pluralistic than it was in the aftermath of 9/11. People across the region are looking to replace traditional authoritarian rulers with new regimes that will respect individual rights and respond to popular demands.

---

[5] Waleed Abdul Rahman, "*Asharq Al-Awsat* Interview: The Other Zawahiri," Jan. 27, 2013. Retrieved from http://www.aawsat.net/2013/01/article55291413.

[6] *Messages*, 2005, p.208–209, "Quagmires of the Tigris and Euphrates," October 19, 2003, videotape delivered to *al-Jazeera*.

[7] David D. Kirkpatrick and Steven Erlanger, "Egypt's New Leader Spells Out Terms for U.S.-Arab Ties," *New York Times*, Sept. 22, 2012. President Morsi earned a Ph.D in Materials Science from the University of Southern California in 1982.

If the optimists are correct, then including moderate Islamist groups in the political process is probably necessary to secure and consolidate a broad, inclusive democratic settlement. Pessimists worry, however, that even so-called moderate Islamist parties are irreconcilable foes of democratization, and warn that these groups must be isolated or suppressed if democracy is to have any chance to take root in the region. The commitment of moderate Islamist groups to democracy will certainly be tested by setbacks such as the 2013 Egyptian coup.

When in doubt, inclusion is preferable to exclusion, because the long-term benefits of tolerance exceed the short-term benefits of repression or quarantine. In other troubled parts of the world, the inclusion-moderation hypothesis has been vindicated more often than not. Government forbearance and inviting dissenting – even belligerent – groups into the political process softens the political discourse, and encourages disaffected groups to come in from the cold and back to the bargaining table.

Vigorous dissent is a normal and routine part of the democratic process. It reflects public confidence that passionate but peaceful protest not only serves as a useful cathartic outlet for political passions, it can also lead to beneficial reforms. Mature democracies are at their best in such unsettled circumstances. They tolerate and even welcome peaceful dissent, which lowers the potential threat of uncontrolled violence posed by disaffected groups.

When there are effective social outlets to vent public frustrations and aspirations, factions that seek to foment violence and promote terror usually find little public support. Political violence is an aberration in mature democratic societies, not the rule. The main threat in these instances usually comes from government overreaction to a perceived threat, not from the violence itself, which is usually isolated and poses no real threat to social stability.

Organized and sustained programs of domestic political terrorism are, in contrast, more often a reflection of widespread feelings of hopelessness and social ennui that attracts fanatics, naïve romantics, and those who have given up hope for a better life by other means. It is a sign of a system in crisis, but it is usually a symptom, not the cause.

Democratic Peace Theory

Democratic peace theory holds that democratic nations rarely go to war, or resort to other belligerent, aggressive, or coercive acts against other democracies. Instead, democracies negotiate mutually agreeable settlements to resolve their problems peacefully and amicably.

Immanuel Kant hypothesized that democracies are naturally peaceful and unlikely to go to war without good cause, because the majority will not vote for war except in self-defense or for some other compelling reason. If all nations were democratic republics, Kant concluded, war would virtually disappear.[8] Alexis De

---

[8] Immanuel Kant, *Perpetual Peace: A Philosophical Sketch* (1795).

Tocqueville agreed to a point, noting that democracies seem less likely to declare war without good cause than other forms of government. Shared liberal values, including attachment to reason, reasonableness, and responsibility, help to explain the democratic preference for negotiation over war.

There is no shortage of critics, however, who question the validity of democratic peace theory. In *The Federalist Papers*, Jay, Madison, and Hamilton were openly skeptical of the idea, and cautioned that democracies are no less likely to go to war than other nations.[9] Most democracies, especially the most successful and powerful, have not been notably pacifistic.

Other detractors note that there is no established causal link between democracy and peace, and there is little positive evidence of the theory's validity. There are other, equally plausible, alternative explanations as to why modern, mature democracies have rarely gone to war against each other. Immanuel Wallerstein argues that "democratic peace" is an economic rather than a political phenomenon. It is the dominance of the global capitalist system, and shared economic interests among the core capitalist nations and the international capitalist class, that have kept the peace among the world's most wealthy democracies.

Democracies Attract Interesting, Eclectic, and Creative People

Democracies have the uncanny ability to attract hardworking and talented people, including immigrants from nondemocratic states. Gifted and unconventional people who chafe under the restrictions imposed by authoritarian regimes are drawn to the liberties, freedoms, and opportunities that democracies offer.

Democracies are perhaps less likely to produce excellence than aristocracies, because they seek the greatest good for the greatest number, rather than promoting the rarified interests of the few. Democracies are also less likely to produce excellence because individuals have the right to say no. Liberty means that people determine for themselves what to do with their lives, and how hard they will work at it. People in democracies have the right to choose; they cannot be compelled to do what the state wants them to do, nor forced to become what the state wants them to be. Individuals have fewer constraints and more choices, which make for a happier and more productive society, but it does not necessarily promote excellence.

---

[9] John Jay, *The Federalist Papers* No. 4; James Madison, No. 41; Alexander Hamilton, Nos. 6, 8. They had good reason to be skeptical, because American states were in constant, and not always peaceable, competition with each other. Jay did note one difference between democracies and monarchies. He wrote that all nations might go to war if they think that they have something to gain by it, but absolute monarchies will go to war even if the country has nothing to gain by it. Monarchs will declare war for purely personal aggrandizement – military glory, revenge for personal affronts, or to advance the narrow interests of the royal family.

Although democracies might not systematically produce, support, or appreciate excellence in the way that the most enlightened aristocracies can, they nevertheless unconsciously nurture excellence by liberating creative, talented, ambitious and productive people to do what they will. This is especially attractive to those who do not enjoy official approval and patronage in their home countries.

The contributions of foreign-born scientists, industrialists, academics, artists, inventors, entrepreneurs, and political leaders who sought refuge in the United States from authoritarian states are incalculable. All eight Nobel Prize winners of Chinese descent were native or naturalized Americans by the time they won their awards, or moved to the United States soon afterward. A top-ten list of European immigrants to the United States from authoritarian countries over last century might include Albert Einstein, Felix Frankfurter, Henry Kissinger, Madeline Albright, Hannah Arendt, Leopold Stokowski, Edward Teller, Enrico Fermi, Nikola Tesla, and Vladimir Nabokov.

Democratic Corruption < Authoritarian Corruption

All political systems are corrupt. Power is the shared heart of politics and corruption, and money is its lifeblood. There are, however, some good reasons to prefer democratic to authoritarian corruption.

Authoritarian regimes practice systemic, class-based corruption. They specialize in the sort of pervasive, organized fraud that can fill the ruling class's coffers for generations. Of course the ruling elites rarely consider what they do to be corrupt. They see their power and wealth as the natural order of things, and rationalize their conversion of public resources to private wealth as a modest and appropriate return for their selfless public service. In reality, they constitute a political *Cosa Nostra* – an entrenched, class-based family business that routinely uses the state treasury as their own private casino.

Corruption in democratic systems is no less common, but far less organized. It is usually based on individual greed rather than entrenched class interests, which makes it easier to discover, control, and remedy.

For various reasons, corrupt politicians cause less damage in democracies than in authoritarian governments. First, democracies limit the power of government, which in turn limits the consequences of corruption. Second, checks and balances mean that the different branches and levels of government monitor each other for bad behavior. Third, private interest groups keep tabs on government, and are quick to sound the alarm if they sense anything amiss. Fourth, in healthy democracies there is a regular turnover of elites, which limits the damage that any person or group can do while in office. Fifth, fundamental democratic liberties, including a free press and free speech, encourage government transparency and allow incriminating information to be readily gathered and disseminated. Finally, the rule of law limits corruption by building a sense of professional ethics among government officials, limiting their personal discretion, and establishing authoritative rules and procedures to investigate, expose, and punish wrongdoing.

Crisis and Patriotism

Machiavelli thought that democracies are especially vulnerable in a crisis. De Tocqueville disagreed, arguing that democracies are at their best during the times that try men's souls.

When al Qaeda terrorists hijacked United Airlines Flight 93 over Pennsylvania on September 11, 2001, passengers and flight attendants assembled at the rear of the plane to discuss their options. They debated their alternatives and then voted to rush the cockpit. Everyone understood that they were probably doomed no matter what they did, but they also knew that their only chance was to agree on a common course of action. They died not just heroes but free democrats – individuals who, when faced with an existential crisis, voluntarily joined together to act as one. They knowingly sacrificed themselves to save hundreds of other innocent lives.

Democracies spend most of their time in quarrel and division. In a crisis, however, they have a unique ability to transcend day-to-day partisanship and pull themselves together to present a united front against any perceived threat.

Fools and democracies seem to have their own guardian angels, but the palladium of democracy is neither mystical nor metaphysical. Democracies are uniquely strong and resilient in a crisis for a simple and pragmatic reason: they foster what de Tocqueville called rational, or reflective, patriotism.

Rational patriotism is attachment to one's country on the basis of enlightened self-interest, rooted in the understanding that self-interest and the common good are complementary. Rational patriotism gives people both selfish and selfless reasons to support and defend their country, because in defending their own interests they also defend their country's interests. For the same reasons, rational patriotism encourages people to be forgiving of their country's flaws and failures. This gives democracies unprecedented power, resolve, and flexibility during troubled times.

The alternative form of nationalism, *instinctive patriotism*, is a characteristic of authoritarian states. It is the attachment to one's country based solely on one's sense of affection for one's place of birth or residence. Instinctive patriotism can be a powerful political force, but it is a child's patriotism, based upon superficial, irrational, and emotional attachments. It is unthinking and unreflective – patriotism of the gut, not of the mind. Instinctive patriotism can be strong, but it is brittle. As people who struggle under authoritarian rule gain awareness that the system does not serve their interests, instinctive patriotism will weaken and – if given a sharp blow – shatter.

Machiavelli would call this popular awakening virtú. When a critical mass of people in an authoritarian state gain consciousness and begin to understand their true situation, instinctive patriotism will no longer suffice, and the state will be left with a stark choice – to oppress or yield. At this point the clock is ticking, because a people with virtú will not tolerate a regime that does not serve their interests.

Democracies have other advantages in a crisis. Their characteristic optimism, vibrancy, innovation, and productivity can prove decisive in moments of extreme peril. This was the case with the seemingly miraculous U.S. productive and fighting capacity during World War II.

There is also a characteristic spirit of independence and resistance to external threats unique to democratic states when they are attacked, invaded, or conquered. This spirit proved especially strong in Denmark, Holland, and Norway during the Second World War. These small countries struggled against the Nazi war machine, and if they could not avert conquest, they never quit resisting foreign occupation. Healthy democracies are difficult to conquer and virtually impossible to subdue. A people accustomed to liberty and freedom can be destroyed, but they cannot easily be enslaved.

One of the great mysteries of democratic government is why a system that produces such unexceptional leaders during peacetime seems to find great statesmen who rise to the occasion during a crisis. In democracies, the hour produces the man, or woman. Once again, there is a rational explanation for this apparent sleight of hand – "Now you don't see them; now you do!" During a crisis, the normal constraints placed on political leaders are suspended, as government assumes greater responsibilities to meet the perceived threat. The many are temporarily willing to accept better leaders, and better leaders are temporarily willing to step up, knowing that they will have greater power and fewer constraints.[10]

What Seems Like a Weakness Is a Strength

We've been kicking ass for 200 years. We're 10 and 1!

– Bill Murray, *Stripes*

One stealth advantage that democracies enjoy is that their enemies consistently underestimate them. Authoritarian states, from Persia and Sparta in the ancient world to Nazi Germany, Imperial Japan, the Soviet Union, China, and al Qaeda in modern times, confidently dismiss their democratic adversaries as weak and decadent, to their regret. Their lack of regard is understandable, although at some point one would think that they might catch on.

Prior to the Japanese attack on Pearl Harbor, Adolf Hitler considered the United States a degenerate, mongrel society that posed no threat to the Third Reich. During the Cold War, Mao Zedong famously called the United States a paper tiger, unable to withstand the wind or rain. Sayyid Qub, the dour Islamist whose bitter essays inspired the Muslim Brotherhood and al Qaeda, disparaged the United States as weak and debauched – corrupted by democracy, individualism, loose women, and jazz. Picking up where Qub left off, Osama bin Laden

---

[10] De Tocqueville, *Democracy in America*.

confidently predicted that the United States lacked the will to respond to 9/11. He dismissed the United States as a sick society, and claimed that most Americans are mentally ill. Any war, he assured his followers, would quickly destroy both the U.S. government and the last remnants of American civil society.

Dictators and would-be despots persist in deluding themselves that the vast majority of people who live in democracies secretly desire authoritarian leaders. Swiss philosopher Peter Bichsel insists that, "[the] Swiss long themselves for less democracy and more dictatorship."

Democracies invariably seem weak and decadent to critics, and there is often at least some truth to the charge. Democratic governments are naturally quarrelsome, ineffectual, unstable, and dysfunctional, which makes them look weak and dissipated. Democratic societies are prone to be selfish, spoiled, hedonistic, and anarchic. So it is hardly surprising that more tightly organized and disciplined authoritarian states fail to take them seriously.

Yet democracies have the signature ability to pull themselves together and rally when threatened, to their foes' seemingly perpetual surprise. Winston Churchill articulated what Hitler, Mussolini, and Tojo could not grasp – that democracy is the worst possible system of government, except for all the rest. The routine messiness of democratic government is all sound and fury, signifying nothing much.

Healthy democracies combine day-to-day turmoil with great underlying institutional and social stability. Rival factions engage in a noisy but ritualized struggle for power, which causes superficial instability, but also promotes a healthy circulation of power and prevents any one faction from dominating government or society. Constant tension among diverse interests ensures that multiple perspectives are brought to bear on problems, and this allows different skills to come forward as circumstances demand. Like pelagic sharks, democracies exist in a state of perpetual restlessness. Even in languorous times, democracies are rarely still for long, and nothing kills cozy nonpartisan cooperation faster than an approaching election.

All of this chaos and infighting seems like a weakness, but is in fact one of democracy's greatest strengths. Debate, discord, and dissent are not design flaws or signs of decay or imminent collapse; they represent the democratic virtues of social dynamism, adaptability, and resilience.

Authoritarian regimes have their advantages, but their perspective is limited by the leader's singular worldview. Dictators often fit the circumstances in which they come to power, but quickly outlive their usefulness as the world changes around them.

Democracies routinely make bad decisions and commit terrible mistakes, but they are able to change their minds, alter course, muddle through, recover, and learn from the experience. Whereas dictators indulge unchecked in whatever neurotic obsessions they invariably have, democratic leaders have hundreds of critics inside government, and millions in the general population, who are willing at a moment's notice to challenge their leaders, abuse them, disabuse them, and replace them. As a consequence, democracies learn and adapt. This was the spirit of Churchill's backhanded compliment about the United States, when he allegedly said (the quote is apocryphal) that he could always count on Americans to do the right thing, after they had tried everything else first.

No political system is more demanding of or less loyal to its leaders than democracy. Churchill's reward for his extraordinary leadership during World War II was to be booted from office immediately after the war by an ungrateful nation, just as he should have been.

Voters want to know what their leaders have done for them lately, and they are always looking to trade in the old model for something new. This disloyalty does not weaken democratic systems; it is a process of creative destruction that renews and reinvigorates them.

In modern democracies, politics is a game. It is a serious game, to be sure, but not only do today's losers live to fight another day, they might well win the rematch. This ceremonial struggle for power and influence enables democracies to harness political conflict in ways that would be highly destructive in authoritarian societies.

Factional infighting in authoritarian governments, in contrast, is a deadly serious business. The winners rule in luxury; the losers are routinely harassed, imprisoned, tortured, exiled, or liquidated. Even respectful dissent is treated harshly, because the gentlest disturbance can threaten state stability and imperil the ruling class's privileged position. Obsessive fear of dissent and instability leads authoritarian regimes to suppress political competition with the same enthusiasm that democracies embrace it.

People Might Not Be Idiots After All

For millennia, countless satirists and assorted pundits have earned a living mocking the alleged stupidity of homo democraticus. Ironically, democratic societies are quick to embrace the idea that ordinary people are fundamentally stupid and incapable of governing themselves. Part of this is democracy's good-natured willingness to laugh at itself, but it also reflects the universal tendency to think of one's self as clever but suspect that one's neighbors are morons.

The arguments have not changed much since Aristophanes savaged the Athenian middle class in his play, *The Clouds*. The aristocratic playwright presents a poetic description of the new model of democratic man: A WELSHER, famed as a TELLER OF LIES,
> a CHEATER, a BASTARD, a PHONY, a BUM,
> SHYSTER, MOUTHPIECE, TINHORN, SCUM,
> STOOLIE, CON-MAN, WINDBAG, PUNK,
> OILY, GREASY, HYPOCRITE, SKUNK,
> DUNGHILL, SQUEALER, SLIPPERY SAM,
> FAKER, DIDDLER, SWINDLER, SHAM,
> or just plain Lickspittle.[11]

---

[11] Aristophanes, *The Clouds*, p. 39, in *Aristophanes, Three Comedies* (Ann Arbor Paperbacks 1987).

To democracy's critics, it is irrelevant how intelligent or well-educated people actually are. In Aristophanes' day, ordinary Athenians were educated, cultured, and sophisticated, but that did not stop the aristocracy from declaring them to be hopelessly dumb, selfish, provincial, corrupt, greedy, and gauche.[12] Today, citizens in developed democracies are better educated, better read, more traveled, more sophisticated, and more cosmopolitan than ever, yet no matter how intelligent, reasonable, or worldly they are, it will never be enough for those committed to elite rule.

There is, however, another side to the story. Regardless of how smart or stupid ordinary people are, democratic decision making is arguably better than authoritarian decision making in three ways: democracy provides citizens with a practical experiential education that allows them to improve over time; it takes full advantage of the wisdom of crowds; and it encourages deliberative decision making.

Experiential Education

The educational effects of democracy are usually near the top of the list of the claimed benefits of democratic government. People learn by doing, and democracy offers the best sort of experiential education in self-government. As individuals learn and improve, so does society.

The apprenticeship of democracy is difficult. Error, excess, and instability are common, and the failure rate among young democracies is high. But people eventually learn that they are ultimately responsible for their own fate. As this happens, they stop being passive, infantilized subjects and become active, responsible, and enlightened citizens. In the long run, democratic societies flourish as ordinary people learn to discuss, decide, act, err, learn, moderate, adjust, and improve. The resulting combination of individual and social progress is unique to democratic systems, and serves as a powerful justification for democratic government.

The Wisdom of Crowds and Aristotle's Golden Mean

Do democracies make better decisions than authoritarian governments? Although authoritarian governments might be more decisive, democracies are more likely to make better decisions in the long run. One reason for this is that although individuals are often foolish, the community is wise.

---

[12] During the democratic era, the Athenian middle classes gained unprecedented access to education, thanks to a group of teacher-philosophers known as the Sophists. The Athenian aristocracy reviled the Sophists, because they made education, which had formerly been the exclusive preserve of the aristocracy, readily available to everyone. Thanks to aristocratic sniping by Aristophanes and others, the term "sophist" unjustly became an epithet.

In 1906, Francis Galton studied a popular guessing game at an English county fair. The contest invited fairgoers to estimate the butchered weight of a live ox. Galton tallied 800 individual guesses, and discovered that although no one correctly guessed the ox's weight, the mean average answer of 1,197 pounds was just 1 pound shy of the correct answer – much closer than any of the individual guesses or any of the professional estimates offered by local livestock experts.

Galton's study illustrates Aristotle's theory of the golden mean. Aristotle argued that the best answer to any political question is likely to be found near the midpoint of opinion. In the case of the unfortunate English ox, no individual knew the correct answer, but the community did. The extreme guesses on either end of the spectrum canceled each other out, leaving an average estimate that was remarkably close to the correct answer. This is the wisdom of crowds. Aristotle, although not a democrat, inadvertently provided a compelling argument for democratic decision making. Great authoritarian leaders – Solomon, Henry VIII, Louis XIV, Stalin, Mussolini, Mao, Castro, or Kim Il-sung – might make decisions much more quickly and with unshakable confidence. None of them, however, is likely to be as smart as a random group of English fairgoers.

Crowdsourcing is based on a similar idea, that soliciting opinions from a large community of interested people is a better source of information and ideas than relying on a few so-called experts. This is sometimes referred to as *participatory design* or *democratic design*. Social scientists have recently developed another predictive technique called *culturomics*, which treats the international news media as a democratic community, and uses the collective wisdom of international news archives to predict political events.

Sidebar 13: Crowdsourcing Baseball Strategy

One day in 1951, the St. Louis Browns' eccentric owner, Bill Veeck, asked the crowd to manage his baseball team, which was mired in last place and had lost four of its previous five games. A few days before the game, the local newspaper published a ballot to allow fans to select the starting lineup. At the game, everyone in attendance received a large placard with "YES" on one side and "NO" on the other. Attendants held up signs asking the crowd questions such as "Infield Back?" or "Steal?" and fans used their signs to vote, while the team's regular manager sat idly in a rocking chair perched on the dugout roof. The Browns won, 5–3.[13]

[13] Pat Borzi, "A Close Call? Better Use Crowdsourcing," *New York Times*, May 17, 2013, B.11.

Each of these approaches relies on community-based decisions and the power of the golden mean.[14] But crowdsourcing and culturomics focus on averaging individual, independent guesses taken without discussion or deliberation. They support the efficacy of group decision making, but shed little light on the merits of deliberative decision making.

The question remains: is it better to ask people to give individual answers independently, on the grounds that group psychology might drive public deliberations toward the flawed consensus of groupthink? Or was Pericles right that ideas that go undiscussed are likely to fail?

Deliberative Wisdom

In democracies, public debate is an essential part of the decision-making process. It ensures that all alternatives are raised and vetted before reaching a final decision. This is the marketplace of ideas, harnessed to serve the public good.

This approach is especially useful in pluralistic societies, where so many different perspectives are readily available for consideration. In democracies, no one has a monopoly on truth; it must fend for itself among competing points of view, with open debate the crucible to test clashing ideas and rival solutions.

One problem with encouraging such full-throated debate is the possibility of severe political polarization where, rather than having vigorous civil discussions to find practical solutions to common problems, both sides are content simply to yell at each other, or worse. In this case, political discourse can harden into hyper-partisanship, government gridlock, majoritarian bullying, social unrest, and, in the most extreme cases, civil war.

Another possible weakness of public deliberation is groupthink. *Groupthink* occurs when a decision-making body fails to consider all options, and too quickly settles on a premature and faulty consensus. But groupthink is primarily an authoritarian, not a democratic, disease. It is the result of top-down pressure to shut up and toe the party line. This is rarely a problem in healthy democracies, where diversity of opinion is valued and there is little expectation of reflexive deference to authority.

In a democracy, groupthink is most likely to be a problem during a crisis, when people are scared or angry, and willing to squelch debate and punish dissent. In such cases, short-circuiting the normal deliberative process is not so much the fault of democracy as evidence that normal democratic procedures have been compromised, owing to expedience, prejudice, or hysteria. Otherwise, healthy democracies often make mistakes, but only rarely because of lack of debate.

---

[14] Kalev Leetaru, "Culturomics 2.0: Forecasting Large-Scale Human Behaviour Using Global News Media Tone in Time and Space," 16 *First Monday* (Sept. 5, 2011).

Other Checks on Popular Passion, Mistakes, and Stupidity

Although democracies make as many mistakes as any other form of government, democracies have some advantages when it comes to avoiding hasty or ill-advised decisions. Democratic societies value the free flow of information and government transparency, both of which aid decision making and make it easier to discover and correct mistakes.

Most modern democracies have relatively sophisticated checks and balances systems, with structural safeguards requiring multiple decision makers to take a second, third, and fourth reasoned look at a proposal before it can become law. Many democracies require supermajorities for the most important decisions, reinforcing the need for discussion, persuasion, and accommodating minority views. Finally, the rule of law limits government overreach, protects minority rights, and establishes an independent judiciary to resolve disputes in a reasoned, dispassionate, and principled manner. All of this comes, however, at a cost in terms of decisiveness and efficiency.

POST-MATERIALIST BENEFITS

Democracy is the only political system in which ordinary people not only determine the course of their own lives, but also have a meaningful say about the direction of society as a whole. There is no predetermined telos for individuals or communities; in a democracy, each person, community, and generation decides where they want to go and how to get there. Democracy in this sense is a vehicle of self-discovery, self-improvement, self-empowerment, and self-actualization. Some people make fun of such things; others place a high value on post-materialist, quality of life issues.

10

Building a Stable Democracy

> In a republican nation whose citizens are to be led by reason and persuasion and not by force, the art of reasoning becomes of first importance.[1]

> – Thomas Jefferson

Every construction project needs the right materials, and converting an author-itarian regime into a stable democracy is no exception. What is needed to build a democracy? As with any undertaking, there is some flexibility in the details. Not everything mentioned in this chapter is necessary, although the more of the right stuff the better. Whether designing a free or liberal democracy, the fundamentals are the same. Building a stable democracy requires a sophis-ticated understanding of politics, history, economics, sociology, psychology, architecture, social engineering, and alchemy. After discussing the main paths by which authoritarian regimes democratize, the rest of the chapter is orga-nized according to three levels of analysis: individual, societal, and institutional requirements.

PATHS OF DEMOCRATIZATION

How do authoritarian polities become democratic? Political scientist Samuel Huntington identified three major pathways: evolutionary, cyclical, and dialectical.

The evolutionary path refers to the gradual, organic development of demo-cratic habits and institutions over time. It is sometimes called *linear develop-ment*, although in practice it is rarely a straight line, and democracy might be a long time coming. This slow-and-steady approach, however, is most likely

---

[1] Thomas Jefferson, Letter to David Harding, April 20, 1824. Quoted in Jon Meacham, *Thomas Jefferson: The Art of Power*, at 845.

to yield long-term stability. Switzerland, the United States, and the United Kingdom are leading examples of evolutionary democracies.

The *cyclical path* describes the situation when a state bounces back and forth between democratic and authoritarian rule like a ping-pong ball. Progress is uncertain, and gains are often short-lived. Pakistan and Nigeria have vacillated between democracy and military rule since each country gained independence, in 1947 and 1960, respectively. Much of Latin America followed a similar pattern, alternating between unstable democratic governments and equally volatile authoritarian regimes for more than a century following the continent's wars of independence, until democracy finally took root in much of the region toward the end of the twentieth century.

The third route is *dialectical*, or *revolutionary democratization*, which involves a quick, violent transition from authoritarian rule to democracy. The failure rate among dialectical democracies, not surprisingly, is high.

The French Revolution was the first modern example of revolutionary democracy, and a notable fiasco. It was the revolution that devoured its own children, and ultimately resulted in Napoleon I. The second and third French revolutions of 1830 and 1848 were less bloody but no more successful, leading to King Louis Philippe I, and Emperor Louis Napoleon Bonaparte (Napoleon III), respectively. Ironically, the French revolutionary model became the aspirational ideal for almost all later revolutionary movements. Marxist-Leninist revolutionaries, in particular, doggedly followed the trail blazed by the sansculottes, with equal success (Figure 10.1).

There is a fourth democratic pathway that Huntington alluded to, but did not discuss at length: externally imposed democracy. This approach has significant legal, moral, and practical problems, as well as a decidedly mixed track record. It does not work very well very often, but it has succeeded on occasion. America's overtly paternalistic efforts to democratize the Philippines in the twentieth century eventually bore fruit, and later efforts to impose democracy on postwar Germany and Japan succeeded beyond all expectations.

The most notable contemporary examples of externally driven democratization efforts are the recent U.S.-led attempts to democratize Iraq and Afghanistan. The wisdom of these policies is highly debatable, and even on their own terms it is too early to tell what their long-term effects might be, although the initial results are not encouraging.

Aside from the considerable legal and ethical problems of imposing democracy on another country, in a purely instrumental sense this pathway's potential for success is a closer question than conventional wisdom might suggest. Established democracies routinely encourage democratization in other countries through any number of direct and indirect means, including foreign aid, special trade agreements, training, advice, expert assistance, exchange programs, education, election observers, and security assistance. This sort of external support, as opposed to direct imposition, can be an effective democratization strategy. Even this soft-power approach, however, is susceptible to

FIGURE 10.1 Liberty leading the people ... to meet the new boss. Original illustration by Ian Zell.

charges of neocolonialism and illegal interference in the domestic politics of other sovereign states.

There are other practical problems to consider. Foreign aid programs are often haphazardly conceived and badly executed, and uncoordinated external assistance can have unintended consequences that undermine internally driven democratization efforts. Aid agencies that pour money into a developing country often do little more than enrich local elites, fuel corruption, distort the local economy, and inevitably favor some domestic factions over others. This can stir local resentments, exacerbate internal rivalries, and trigger blowback against even the best-intentioned programs.

Despite the risks, developed democracies have had some success in promoting democratization in other countries. In the 1970s, the European Commonwealth and its successor organization, the European Union, helped stabilize troubled emerging democracies in Spain, Portugal, and Greece. External assistance played a key role during the 1980s in assisting democratization movements in East Germany, the Baltic States, and the Balkans after the collapse of the Soviet Union. There have been similar successes in Asia, Africa, and South America, where external support has repeatedly proved to be an influential, if not a decisive, factor driving democratization efforts in South Korea, East Timor, Hong Kong, Tanzania, Kenya, South Africa, Chile, Colombia, Uruguay, and Haiti, among other countries.

INDIVIDUAL LEVEL

To build a stable democracy, citizens must embrace the three Rs of self-government: reason, reasonableness, and responsibility. What does it take to instill these core republican virtues? The answer is deceptively simple: education.

The First R: Reason

Self-government requires a people who choose *reason* to govern their actions, rather than appetite, instinct, dogmatic faith, or docile obedience. Reason is reflective thought, based on evidence and logic. It requires dispassionate analysis, with due consideration of alternative possibilities, to reach an informed opinion or calculate a rational course of action.

Appetite, instinct, faith, and obedience all have their place in democratic societies, but reason must inform, check, and balance these irrational qualities. Reason is a necessary prerequisite of democracy, because without it liberty becomes license, freedom becomes mob rule, faith becomes orthodoxy, obedience becomes servitude, and democracy becomes unsustainable.

One key question that any democracy must answer is: who has the requisite capacity for reason and who does not? At different times and places, entire categories of people have been denied political rights because they were thought to lack the capacity for reason. Among the usual suspects: women, disfavored racial and ethnic groups, and the poor.[2]

---

[2] The disqualification of women from political and legal rights was legally termed a "defect of sex."

Modern theories about reason and rights are more inclusive. In most established democracies, all adults are presumed to possess sufficient reason to participate in political life. The only people universally thought categorically to lack capacity for mature, reflective reason are children. In some countries the severely mentally handicapped and the insane are denied political rights, but in many democracies, including the United States, they retain their political rights, including the right to vote.

Reason is a necessary, but not sufficient, condition for a stable democracy. Lenin, Stalin, Hitler, Kim Il-sung, HAL 9000, and the Borg all had (or will have) a prodigious capacity for reason, but all were (or will be) monsters. Reason must be leavened by reasonableness.

The Second R: Reasonableness

At a minimum, reason is the ability to calculate self-interest through rational cost-benefit analysis, and the capacity to act accordingly. This minimalist definition is where most economists and libertarians stop. But defining reason solely as the ability to think and act out of narrow self-interest encourages a radical, narcissistic selfishness that, if left unchecked, will lead to an atomized society where people are self-absorbed, uncaring, isolated, and alienated – a society with Asperger's Syndrome.

Democracy demands more than the single-minded pursuit of objectivist self-interest. It requires *reasonableness* – the ability to consider, evaluate, understand, tolerate, and accommodate different perspectives. This includes taking into account other people's interests, and the common good, when calculating one's own interests. This is enlightened self-interest.

Being reasonable means being sensible, empathetic, and pragmatic. It means treating other people with respect, and evaluating what they say and do with an open mind. It means relying on persuasion, negotiation, compromise, and reconciliation to resolve disagreements, rather than coercion, compulsion, or violence. It means, in short, acting in accord with the golden rule.

Being reasonable means being willing to consider new ideas, new arguments, new evidence, and new solutions. Reasonable people realize that there is always a residuum of doubt in the answers that reason provides. This makes them slow to judge, and reluctant to reach unassailable conclusions. Reasonable people understand that the answers to life's problems are complex, nuanced, situational, and tentative. Being reasonable means seeing reality as a spectrum of alternative possibilities, rather than as the stark black and white of absolutes.

Reasonable people are by nature optimistic realists about human behavior. They have a presumptive confidence in other people's intentions, which leads to the sort of amiable sociability that makes civil society possible. Reasonable people assume that other people are also reasonable, until the facts prove otherwise. Such an approach is necessary in a democracy, where political life involves constant interaction with dissimilar people in an open and pluralistic environment.

The injunction to be reasonable has its limits. Unreasonable and unreasonably dangerous activities need not be tolerated, and reasonable people must always be prepared to act decisively against existential threats.[3] Although it is perfectly reasonable to oppose dangerous nonsense, it is worth remembering that what is considered nonsense today might be common sense tomorrow. It was not long ago that racial integration, female suffrage, and homosexuality were widely believed to be degenerate behaviors that directly threatened civil society, if not civilization itself.

The Third R: Responsibility

Reason and reasonableness in turn lead to responsibility. In politics, being *responsible* means being a good citizen. But what does that mean?

In authoritarian societies, being a good citizen means following orders. This was Plato's definition of virtue: do your own job, mind your own business, and obey your superiors without question. In Nazi Germany, being a good citizen meant unthinking obedience to power, regardless of reason, law, morality, ethics, judgment, conscience, or consequences.[4]

In 1962, psychology professor Stanley Milgram conducted a series of experiments on obedience. The trials took place in a Yale university laboratory, where volunteers met in pairs with a scientist ("the experimenter") to test whether learning could be facilitated through punishment. The experiment centered on a shock generator with more than a dozen switches on the front panel, labeled sequentially from 15 through 450 volts, with the most severe shocks cryptically marked "xxx."

At the beginning of each session, two volunteers drew lots to see who would be the teacher and who would be the learner. The experimenter took the learner into a small adjoining room and, with the teacher looking on, strapped the learner into a chair and attached electrodes connected to the shock generator.

The wall separating the two rooms was only partially soundproof. The teacher was instructed to use a one-way intercom system to read a list of multiple-choice questions to the learner. The learner was directed to answer the questions using a small panel of four buttons, marked one to four, which lit up

---

[3] Ideas can be unreasonable, but ideas alone cannot significantly infringe on others' rights, and should not be subject to content-based state control. Unreasonable actions, and actions that infringe on others' rights, can justly be regulated through reasonable time, place, and manner restrictions. Unreasonable people and ideas might be subject to informal social controls, such as shunning unreasonable people, ignoring unreasonable speech, or challenging unreasonable people and ideas with opposing arguments based on evidence and reason.

[4] Arendt, *Eichmann in Jerusalem: A Report on the Banality of Evil* (1963).

a numeric answer board in the main room. The learner, securely restrained in his chair, could move his hand just enough to reach the buttons.

Back in the main room, the experimenter handed the teacher a list of multiple-choice questions, explained the shock generator, and gave the teacher a mild sample shock. The experimenter then instructed the teacher: (1) to ask the learner the assigned questions; (2) to administer a shock for each wrong answer; and (3) to increase the voltage each time the learner made a mistake.

The first mild shocks caused the learner to vocalize brief pain, which the teacher could hear through the wall. With each wrong answer, the learner's verbal response increased, until at 250 volts he screamed in agony and begged to be released. At 330 volts, the learner gave a final, blood-curdling scream, then fell silent and failed to respond, even when the teacher administered more severe shocks. If the teacher tried to stop, the experimenter calmly reassured the teacher that the shocks were not dangerous and ordered the teacher to continue.

The teaching-learning experiment was a ruse. The shock board was a dummy, and the learner was an accomplice who did not receive any shocks. The lottery was rigged, so that the sole naïve subject always became the teacher. The learner's answers were programmed to include many wrong answers, and his screams were standardized on a tape recorder to match each shock's supposed intensity.

Milgram's intent was to see how ordinary people would react to orders to inflict pain on an innocent, helpless human being. The results were troubling.

Prior to the experiment, Milgram polled a panel of independent psychologists, who predicted that less than 0.1 percent would obey the experimenter's commands and shock the learner to the end of the board. In fact, 50 percent of the teachers complied fully with the experimenter's orders and shocked the learner to the end of the board. This led Milgram to conclude that most people will do what authorities tell them to do, regardless of conscience or consequences.

Milgram later conducted a series of follow-up experiments and discovered another significant, although less well-known, lesson about the limits of authority. In the original experiment, many teachers expressed qualms about administering the stronger shocks, and asked who would be responsible if the learner was injured. Following a prepared script, the experimenter took full responsibility, at which point most of the teachers continued to follow orders.

In a subsequent study, although the experimenter insisted that the shocks were harmless, he refused to take full responsibility for possible injuries to the learner. This led most of the teachers to break off and refuse to administer more shocks. It is the sense of personal responsibility that stirs Jiminy Cricket from his slumbers, and gives people the courage to disobey immoral orders. Teachers might have simply feared being sued, but the realization that *they* were ultimately responsible for their own actions animated their individual will to defy authority.[5]

Good citizenship in a democracy means that individuals must assume responsibility for their own actions. This includes questioning, and sometimes defying, authority. Individuals must respect the rule of law, but they must also: (1) make their own reasoned legal, moral, and ethical judgments; (2) refuse to engage in illegal, immoral, or unethical conduct, even if ordered to do so; (3) take personal responsibility for the consequences of their actions; and (4) balance their own self-interest with concern for others and for the common good. All together, this is what it means to be responsible in a democratic society. Such a people can be relied on to respect the social contract and exercise their rights in a reasoned, reasonable, and responsible manner.

Education

The human capacity for reason is genetic, but the decision to use it is voluntary. Reason is an intellectual muscle – it needs to be developed and exercised, or it will atrophy.

Democracies rely on citizens who take an active interest in the world around them. This requires an informed populace with the capacity to think critically and for themselves. The specific content of this education is less important than its breadth. Democratic education should be comprehensive; it should tap the range of human thought and experience, promote the consideration of alternative perspectives, and encourage citizens to make their own connections among diverse disciplines. There are good reasons why this is called a liberal education, although it could with equal justification be called a free education.

Emerging democracies need to establish a comprehensive, universal system of education, to ensure that everyone receives a primary and secondary education and that higher education is readily available. Developed democracies can support this process by helping institutionalize education in new democracies, and by inviting students from developing countries to seek higher education abroad if they lack sufficient opportunities at home.

Even the simplest literacy programs encourage the development of essential critical reasoning skills, because the ability to read and write opens doors to new possibilities. This is why the Taliban are so violently opposed to education

[5] Dr. Jerry Burger ran an updated version of the Milgram experiment in 2007, and found that 70 percent of today's teachers were still willing to shock the learner to the end of the board. Dr. Burger had to make one significant concession to modern sensibilities: his shock board went only to 150 volts, owing to concerns about subjecting test subjects to too much stress. In the United Kingdom, Dr. Abigail San replicated the Milgram experiment in full, with a shock board going all the way to 450 volts, and found levels of obedience similar to what Milgram observed. "People 'Still Willing to Torture,'" *BBC News*, Dec. 19, 2008. Retrieved from http://news.bbc.co.uk/go/pr/fr/-/2/hi/health/7791278.stm.

for young girls. They are afraid – quite rightly – that even a basic elementary education will open girls' eyes and break the cycle of ignorance and dependence that keeps women isolated and controllable.

In Nigeria, the ultraviolent Islamist group, *Boko Haram* ("Western Education is a Sacrilege") seeks to destroy the national educational system through mass murder and other acts of terror, precisely because they know that education promotes reason, liberty, and freedom – all of which the group views with fear and loathing.

Perhaps the least desirable form of education is the rote memorization of a single holy and unquestionably true text, whether it is the Bible, the Torah, the Koran, or Das Kapital. When we think of indoctrinational education, we usually think of fundamentalist madrassas, ultraorthodox yeshivas, and Marxist-Leninist reeducation camps. But it is worth remembering that there are fundamentalist schools in the United States where the Bible is the primary textbook in every class, including science and humanities courses.

Even a mind-numbing, one-book, indoctrinational education is better than no education at all. Limited literacy is always preferable to illiteracy, because people who are forced to read one book develop the ability to read other books of their own choosing.[6] The good news is that readily accessible elementary and secondary education is now available almost everywhere. Moreover, the Internet and other global communications systems place the greater part of human knowledge within reach of people in all but the most isolated corners of the world.[7] As a result, near-universal adult literacy is a realistic goal for the first time in history.

A democratic education is not necessarily confined to classrooms and campuses. International travel is easier and more accessible than ever, and immigration levels are at historic highs. As a result, almost every country is significantly more diverse and cosmopolitan today than a generation ago. The global economy has existed for centuries, but the idea of globalized culture is new. The world today is more interconnected than ever; on the whole, this has led to greater awareness, tolerance, understanding, and appreciation for different peoples from diverse cultures. The unprecedented mixing of nationalities,

---

[6] In the movie, *Zardoz*, Sean Connery plays a member of the illiterate servant class in a post-apocalyptic world, ruled by an elite with the blessing of God, who appears in the sky to give orders and keep the peace. Zardoz (Connery) stumbles across the ruins of a long-lost library, where he rediscovers books and gradually teaches himself to read. His worldview suddenly changes when he reads *The Wizard of Oz*.

[7] The exceptions are also among the most problematic regions in terms of democratization. Countries such as North Korea, and to a lesser extent Afghanistan, Burma, and Somalia, remain closed, isolated, and xenophobic, in part by circumstance but mostly by choice. These countries presently have little interest in engaging with the rest of the world. Their people have few opportunities for international travel or engagement, except as immigrants on a one-way ticket out of the country. It is especially difficult to reconcile the Taliban, al-Shabab, or the North Korean elite to democratic values when they remain willfully ignorant of, and hostile to, the world outside of their borders.

ethnicities, and races provides a useful practical education in cultural plural-ism. This process has one ironic side effect: it tends to result in a form of global homogenization, where formerly distinct cultures begin to blend together into a standard mélange.[8]

Civil Society

The three Rs of self-government make civil society possible, and civil society makes democracy possible. *Civil society* consists of all individuals and private groups that allow for the development of a cohesive, stable, and peaceable community apart from the state. A civil society is an essential precondition of democracy, because it is largely self-regulating and eliminates the need for an all-powerful state. With only limited government necessary to keep the peace, democracy – especially liberal democracy – can flourish.

Civil society contains three main components: (1) voluntary associations; (2) routine social interactions on the basis of the principles of pluralism, tol-erance, respect, trust, and good faith; and (3) nongovernmental, community-based mechanisms for peaceful conflict resolution. We will look briefly at each of these components in turn.

Voluntary Associations

Civil society begins with the elemental personal relationships that Edmund Burke called society's "little platoons." These include families, clubs, sports leagues, religious congregations, and neighborhood organizations where peo-ple develop their strongest and most intimate social bonds. Burke's conception of society as an army of little platoons dovetails perfectly with democratic federalism: small, local, organic, semiautonomous units that can be linked together from the bottom up to build a democratic system of any size.

Burke's little platoons form the foundation of the much larger interlocking network of private organizations that constitute civil society. De Tocqueville called these groups voluntary associations, Madison called them factions, and most people now call them *civic* or *special interest groups*. They are the count-less clusters of like-minded individuals who freely join together to pursue com-mon interests.

For de Tocqueville, voluntary associations defined American democracy and set it apart from all other systems. Although subjects in authoritarian states must await instructions from their superiors before acting, de Tocqueville noted that Americans hardly seemed to need government at all. They were compulsive

---

[8] In the United States, a similar process has rapidly narrowed regional differences. Cities and towns across the country have developed an increasingly familiar mix of people, stores, shops, and architectural styles, so that everything everywhere begins to look the same.

self-organizers, who spontaneously banded together to pursue common goals without government assistance, permission, supervision, or control.

American society today consists of myriad little platoons – and big battalions – of self-interested activists who organize themselves to solve problems and get things done.[9] Sometimes these groups consciously seek to shape society to their liking, but most of the time they affect society unconsciously and incrementally, through the cumulative effect of innumerable groups, each focused on its own particular agenda.

Voluntary associations serve as a useful social check on some of the biggest problems facing democratic states: individual selfishness, the exclusion of marginalized groups, inequality, and oppressive state power. They have a salutary dual nature, in that they instill a sense of individual efficacy among members, and simultaneously help forge a sense of common purpose. This helps democratic societies strike a healthy balance between individualism and community.

Voluntary associations also play an important role in fostering political inclusion and equality. They make it possible, at least in theory, for the weakest, poorest and least-loved individuals to band together to form a credible social force.

Finally, voluntary associations serve to limit state power. Because they are an institutionalized form of people power that is largely independent of state control, they can be an effective counterforce against an intrusive state, to ensure that government serves local interests, rather than the other way around.

Depending on the circumstances, voluntary associations can supplement, resist, or supplant state power. They even allow communities to bypass government entirely, in favor of direct private action. This is especially useful during a crisis, because local groups can mobilize quickly to meet a natural or man-made threat, rather than having everyone stand around waiting for the cavalry to arrive. Democracy is essentially a do-it-yourself project anyway, and voluntary associations reinforce the instinct to join together to do what needs to be done, with or without government help.[10]

Pluralism

We're all very different people. We're not Watusi. We're not Spartans. We're Americans. ... Our forefathers were kicked out of every decent country in the world. We are the

---

[9] Not all organizations are voluntary associations. Corporations, for example, are not organic, independent, private organizations. They are artificial creatures of the law, created, empowered, and supported by the state.

[10] The dual tragedy of 2005's Hurricane Katrina was that people in and around New Orleans initially waited for the federal cavalry to ride to their rescue, when the federal government had already decided, for ideological reasons, not to lead rescue, recovery, or cleanup efforts. By the time the scope of the problem became clear and the federal government reluctantly reversed course, a natural disaster had become a man-made catastrophe.

wretched refuse. We are the underdog. We are mutts. ... But there is no animal that is more faithful, that is more loyal, or more loveable, than the mutt.

– Bill Murray, *Stripes.*

Like any political community, it is essential for emerging democracies to establish an abiding sense of common identity and purpose. Does pluralism help or hinder this process?

Embattled politicians are quick to blame pluralism for their domestic political problems. They seek to shore up their popularity by circling the wagons around their core supporters and scapegoating rival groups. In more extreme instances, stronger factions will try forcibly to quarantine, remove, or liquidate competitors in order to create a more homogeneous society. This approach has led to violent ethnic cleansing campaigns in places such as Yugoslavia, Iraq, Lebanon, Rwanda, Somalia, and Sudan.

Sometimes rival groups agree to self-segregate. Yugoslavia's decomposition into ever-smaller monoethnic mini-states gave this phenomenon its name – *Balkanization.* In Bosnia today, Muslim, Croat, and Serbian children attend the same schools, but each group has a separate curriculum and students remain segregated during the school day. They share the same campus, but learn virtually nothing about each other. They are neighbors, schoolmates, and strangers – each group living in its own hermetically sealed cultural bubble.

Rwanda endured the most radical form of ethnic cleansing – genocide. For three months in 1997, Hutu tribal militias and extremist factions within the national armed forces systematically butchered 800,000 Tutsis and moderate Hutus. When the Tutsis retaliated and eventually gained the upper hand, more than 2 million Hutu refugees had to flee into neighboring Zaire (now the Democratic Republic of Congo).

Other problems commonly associated with pluralism are not so easily confined to the third world. Mature democracies routinely fret about the negative effects of "too much" diversity, and seek to limit or roll back racial, ethnic, and cultural mixing. One common concern is that immigrants threaten hard-won national identity and unity. The German and Swiss governments worry openly about the large number of Turks and other foreigners who began to arrive as guest workers in the 1960s and never left. The British fear that large numbers of Muslim immigrants from Central and South Asia are turning London into Londonistan.

In 2011, German Prime Minister Angela Merkel and British Prime Minister David Cameron jointly declared multiculturalism to be a failed experiment that had undermined civil society in both countries. Scandinavia and the Netherlands found that abandoning their traditional model of insular ethnic homogeneity in favor of increased immigration and cultural pluralism has greatly complicated their cozy consensual political culture.

Even in the United States, where immigration and pluralism are ingrained in the culture, many worry that recent waves of Latin American immigrants threaten the national identity, because so many of the newcomers congregate in large, segregated enclaves that resist the unifying crucible of the American melting pot.

In light of these and other related problems, countries sometimes look wistfully at the handful of relatively homogeneous countries that remain – notably Japan and South Korea – and see them as aspirational models of social cohesion. Yet however tempting it might be to promote social solidarity through cultural homogeneity, it is invariably a mistake.

Given the extraordinary mixing of cultures that has taken place around the world over the past century, it is probably too late to turn back the clock on global pluralism, absent genocide and/or radical cultural and economic isolation along the lines of a country such as North Korea. This has not, however, prevented new and continuing attempts at ethnic segregation. In Europe, even as the EU strives to make existing national barriers obsolete, it suffers from the contradictory tendency toward balkanization, characterized by the emergence of relatively homogeneous microstates dominated by a local ethnic group. Basques, Catalans, Scots, Walloons, and Flemings, among others, continue to press for autonomous ethnic homelands. Elsewhere, demands for exclusive ethnic enclaves are being aggressively, and sometimes violently, pursued by ethnic separatists in Chechnya, Palestine, Quebec, Sudan, Syria, and elsewhere.

There are some good reasons to resist these exclusionary impulses. On a practical level, closed and homogeneous cultures suffer from significant disadvantages compared to more open and pluralistic societies. For the most part, the newly emerging monoethnic polities are small, weak, unstable, and politically irrelevant – archaic city-states in a world of nation-states, with all of the structural and social problems that Madison warned about 200 years ago. They are especially vulnerable to unhealthy conformity and groupthink, and suffer from a limited worldview, with pronounced tendencies toward nativism, parochialism, cultural chauvinism, and xenophobia. They are prone to neurotic manias about outsiders, often framed in terms of wild obsessions about racial and ethnic purity.[11]

Homogeneous societies are by nature exclusionary and repressive when it comes to people and ideas that do not fit the accepted mold. Because they encourage unity through uniformity, they are inclined to take a dim view of eclecticism and dissent, and are reluctant to embrace new ideas or disruptive technologies. This makes them instinctively conservative and slow to adapt to changing circumstances, limiting their potential for innovation and progress.

---

[11] From the late nineteenth century through the 1960s, the American South attempted to make a pluralistic society into a patchwork of racially homogeneous communities, through de jure segregation. These efforts were fueled by a pathological fear of racial miscegenation and mongrelization. South Africa's apartheid regime was even more extreme, with the additional element of the white minority's fear of what would happen to them if the black majority were ever in a position to seize power.

Homogeneous societies suffer from other competitive disadvantages in the world marketplace. Japan and South Korea are in many respects economic powerhouses, but their lack of diversity limits their ability to engage fully in the global community. Ironically, their self-imposed and often self-satisfied insularity has made both countries more dependent on external support and protection, especially from the United States – the ultimate mongrel state.[12]

Healthy democracies do not fear diversity; they embrace it. Democracy, especially liberal democracy, is premised on eclectic individualism and pluralism, and is designed to reap the benefits of both. Despite the risks of factional conflict, diverse societies offer the best bet for long-term social and political stability.

One notable success story has been Benin, a small African country just west of Nigeria. Since its unexpectedly peaceful transition from Marxist-Leninist state to multiparty liberal democracy in 1990, Benin has become a model for African democratization. Although it has had its share of problems, including occasional election-day violence and postponed elections in 2011, Benin has seen a decisive electoral shift away from the ethno-politics that dominated the first national elections in 1991, and toward a consolidated pluralistic democracy where tribal and ethnic voting has largely disappeared. In the 2006 presidential elections, voters ignored local tribal loyalties and voted on the basis of candidates' individual politics, policies, and personalities. As a result, presidential candidates can no longer win by securing overwhelming support from their own ethnic group, but must appeal to a broad national cross-section of the electorate.

Pluralistic democracies see diversity as the natural order of things, and seek to accommodate all sorts of different individuals, ideas, and cultures. The constant mixing, jostling, competition, and compromise among different groups produces a vigorous society, open to experimentation and alternative possibilities. Pluralistic societies draw from a deep pool of people from different backgrounds, experiences, and expertise. Greater diversity also makes it more difficult for one faction to dominate all others. All of this makes pluralistic societies more open, dynamic, energetic, flexible, creative, and adaptable than homogeneous societies.

In the Old Testament, the story of Babel paints pluralism not just as a bad idea, but an affront to God. The indiscriminate mixing of races and cultures is arrogant human folly that invites divine retribution. Modern global society is Babel revisited, with the original moral turned on its head – it is the sunny side of Babel.

---

[12] Even so-called homogeneous societies are rarely as homogeneous as outsiders think. Japan and South Korea, although exceptionally homogeneous in many respects (with a large percentage of the population sharing the same race, ethnicity, language, and culture), are nonetheless quite diverse in other respects. This should not be a surprise; even the close genetic and environmental homogeneity of the nuclear family results in significant diversity among its members.

The global confluence of different peoples causes all sorts of problems, mostly of the nonbiblical variety. The initial mixing process can be difficult, as diverse groups compete for power, resources, and respect. Violent ethnic conflicts erupt sporadically everywhere from Northern Ireland to South Africa, from Quebec to Tierra del Fuego, from the Holy Land to the Ganges delta, and from Siberia to Tasmania. The long-term payoff, however, is enlightened tolerance, mutual accommodation, and peaceful coexistence – in other words, a dynamic civil society – although this ideal is not always quickly or easily realized.[13]

Finally, there are countries where different communities share the same home but choose to live in separate rooms. In Iraq, most Shi'a live in the south, the Kurds live in the north, and most Sunnis live in the middle. In Northern Ireland, Catholics and Protestants live in segregated neighborhoods, sometimes separated by concrete barriers. In Lebanon, Sunnis, Christians, Shi'a, and Druze live in ethnically exclusive enclaves. In Canada, Quebec and the First Nations fight to stay culturally insulated from the rest of the country. In the United States, some cities remain ethnically segregated, and many Indian tribes maintain a separate existence on semi-sovereign reservations.

Plural societies are not necessarily the same as pluralistic societies. True pluralism requires routine interactions among the various groups on the basis of mutual tolerance and respect – the topics of the next two sections.

Tolerance

Tolerance means being considerate of others, including those we do not especially like. It is a live and let live philosophy, endorsing the view that variety is the spice of life, and people's beliefs, preferences, and choices are nobody else's business, as long as they are reasonable and do not unduly infringe on others' equal rights. Tolerance does not imply approval of alternative values, choices, or lifestyles; it requires only a willingness to put up with them.

The most important lesson of toleration is to learn how to disagree without being violently disagreeable. To maintain a civil society, people must accept that diversity of opinion and profound disagreements are inherent to the human condition, without reflexively treating these differences as an existential threat to self, family, God, or country.

---

[13] This separation can be by law (de jure) or by private choice (de facto). The former would include the South Africa's apartheid regime and Jim Crow laws of the American South; the latter type of segregation would include Northern Ireland, where Protestant and Catholic populations are segregated, for the most part, by choice rather than by law.

In many American cities, different ethnic, religious, and racial groups live together in somewhat homogeneous enclaves, as the large numbers of Irish, Chinese, Latino, and gay neighborhoods attest. Because these neighborhoods are the result of individual choice, and are not encouraged, endorsed, or enforced by law, they tend to be more diverse and fluid today than they were in the old days of *de jure* segregation.

It is easier to advocate tolerance than to be tolerant, let alone create a tolerant society. The world favors intolerance in so many ways. The strong routinely oppress the weak, the aggressive abuse the meek, the loud overwhelm the quiet, the clever manipulate the trusting, and the shouts of self-righteous extremists drown out the gentler voices of moderation and compromise.

Most people want nothing more than to be left alone to pursue their own path in life. Yet intolerant people will insist on imposing their views on others, and they will use the power of the state to do it if they can. Sectarian societies are especially problematic in this regard, because nonconforming views are often harshly suppressed for no reason beyond prejudice.

Intolerance is a chronic problem, but once change begins progress can be surprisingly quick. After centuries of slavery and racial prejudice in the United States, a fundamental shift in mainstream attitudes about race has occurred over the past fifty years, leading to a significantly more tolerant and inclusive society. Social prejudices against homosexuality are fading even faster, moving from overt hostility to acceptance in a single generation in the United States.

Globalization promotes this sort of accelerated toleration, by exposing people to different cultures and promoting greater understanding among diverse populations. Not long ago, the people who lived in the next town down the road seemed strange and exotic. Globalization has raised our cultural awareness, so that people who once seemed weird, inscrutable, and presumptively dangerous now seem interesting and (mostly) non-threatening. As the world becomes more interconnected, we gain a greater appreciation for what we have in common, and our differences seem more natural and benign. The circle of the other shrinks; the spirit of toleration grows.

Respect, Trust, and Good Faith

In a mature civil society, people are more than grudgingly tolerant; they habitually treat each other with presumptive respect, trust, and good faith. Otherwise dissimilar individuals feel connected to one another by a mutual, substantive sense of community – the feeling of being part of a joint enterprise based on shared core values and common purpose, regardless of underlying differences in background, belief, interest, ethnicity, or ideology.

Civil society is calm, confident, and relaxed. Strangers are presumed friendly until proven otherwise. In a civil society, the first instinct on seeing a stranger is to walk up and say hello. In states lacking a civil society, the first instinct is to avoid eye contact, cross to the opposite side of the street, and prepare for immediate fight or flight. It is the difference between Locke's world, where reason, reasonableness, and responsibility govern – and Hobbes's world, where respect, trust, and good faith are fatal character flaws.

Community-Based Conflict Resolution

Social conflicts arise for two reasons: unreasonable people being themselves, and honest disputes among otherwise reasonable people. Along with state-sponsored conflict-resolution systems (which will be discussed separately), democratic societies usually develop non-governmental, local, community-based social mechanisms, to help control antisocial behavior and resolve disputes fairly and peacefully without direct state involvement. These might include community-based mediation, arbitration, neighborhood watch, gang-intervention, drug counseling, and youth mentoring programs. Informal social pressure can also moderate antisocial behavior.

Anarchists and communists depend exclusively on such community-based social mechanisms to control conflict and regulate undesirable behavior in stateless societies. In democracies, they serve as a useful supplement to – and an important check on – state power.

Social Checks on State Power

One of the most serious problems facing emerging democracies is the need to overcome the oppressive legacy of authoritarianism and all-powerful states. Three useful social checks can limit the crushing power of despotic government: popular virtú, a strong middle class, and a free market economy.

Virtú

According to Machiavelli, the most effective social check on state power is popular virtú – a people's love of liberty and freedom. If the many lack virtú, they will submit to a prince; but if they have virtú, they will not tolerate a prince and will demand self-rule. Either way, Machiavelli concluded, people ultimately get the government that they deserve.

Following World War II, India's independence movement launched a mass campaign of passive resistance to British rule, and it proved stronger than the concentrated power of empire. Although India was perhaps fortunate to have Great Britain as its colonial ruler, rather than a more ruthless master, this only affected the final body count, not the outcome.

In the Philippines, the People Power movement that toppled dictator Ferdinand Marcos in 1986 set the modern gold standard for spontaneous popular uprisings against oppressive regimes. Corazon Aquino's Yellow Revolution began a slow cascade of mostly peaceful mass insurrections against entrenched and presumably stable authoritarian states around the world. It presaged the fall of the Berlin Wall and the Soviet Bloc in 1989, the color revolutions in Central Europe during the 1990s, and the Arab Spring of 2011 in Tunisia, Egypt, Libya, Bahrain, and Syria – although how democratic any of these states will be remains to be seen.[14]

---

[14] These movements are not always successful. China's initial spontaneous popular uprising did not survive the Tiananmen Square massacre of 1989, and the Arab Spring has produced mixed results.

A Middle-Class Society

Another important social check on state power is a strong middle class. A vigorous bourgeoisie is by nature individualistic, assertive, and ambitious, and chafes under the constraints imposed by despotic governments. The key question is whether the shopkeeper class (Napoleon's condescending term) is large, cohesive, and determined enough to stand up to a repressive state.

In developing countries, the emergence of a robust middle class is critical to democratization. Economically polarized societies, burdened by a hyper-rich ruling elite and a vast impoverished underclass, are especially susceptible to authoritarian rule. The poor are rarely in a position to resist state power, and the wealthy have little incentive to do so.

For better or worse, democracy is a bourgeois political construct. The middle class is the backbone of all successful democratic states, and middle-class values define democratic societies. To predict which authoritarian states are most likely to democratize, one might first consider developing countries with a healthy middle class. Among the leading current contenders are two dark horses – Iran, with its strong *bazaari* (merchant) class, and Tunisia, a relatively rare example of an Arab country with a highly educated and potentially powerful bourgeoisie.

China offers an interesting case study of a country with an emerging middle class that seems less inclined with each passing year to submit passively to Communist party rule. Chinese leaders have so far successfully promoted economic liberty while repressing political freedom, but it is not clear how long the country's autocratic leaders can keep their balancing act going before internal pressure to democratize reaches critical mass. Party leaders have successfully forestalled grassroots democratization efforts by combining rapid economic growth with traditional authoritarian repression and open-door emigration policies that allow, and sometimes encourage, dissidents to leave. The rapidly growing middle class, however, represents the best hope for real political reform, and is probably the only social force in the country with the potential power to stand up to the state and the People's Liberation Army.

A Free Market Economy

The third major social check on state power is a free market economy. A free market economy means uninhibited trade through the open, competitive, transparent, fair, and honest exchange of goods and services. Free markets are, by definition, beyond the control of the state or anyone else. It is the antithesis of a command economy, dominated by the state, ruling political party, or powerful private interests.[15]

[15] Marx understood that a free market economy makes socialist revolution impossible, because in a free market no one controls the means of production. Marx theorized, however, that the capitalist class would, for entirely selfish reasons, encourage greater state regulation of the economy in the name of stability, predictability, and profits. In doing so, however, the capitalist class seals its own fate, because once the state becomes heavily involved in regulating the economy, the working class can take control of the means of production simply by seizing control of the state.

Free markets are not synonymous with capitalism or capitalist markets. In unregulated, laissez-faire capitalist markets, the only rule is caveat emptor. Crime pays, cheaters prosper, and the rich and powerful have great and perhaps insurmountable advantages.

Capitalism abhors the uncertainty of free markets. Businesses desire profits and predictability, and to secure those ends they will compulsively seek to control their environment, eliminate their competition, and dominate the marketplace. In a laissez-faire economy, free markets never stay free for long; the economy moves relentlessly toward its natural end: oligopoly and monopoly.[16]

There is something of a chicken-and-egg dilemma regarding free markets and state power. Although free markets serve as a useful check on state power, free markets require active but measured government policing and regulation to maintain open trade, market transparency, and fair competition. A free market economy requires an effective rule of law state, where the government enforces contracts, serves as an impartial judge in economic disputes, and takes the necessary and proper steps to keep free markets free.

Some states take additional steps to, for example, mitigate the costs of economic failure through progressive bankruptcy laws, or provide effective consumer protection and disclosure laws. Many democracies proactively try to maintain a level playing field, by offering assistance to disadvantaged groups (such as subsidies, expert advice, and other public resources) and limiting the economic advantages of the rich and powerful (such as antitrust laws). Such regulatory and remedial steps are not necessarily required, but they are consistent with the spirit and letter of free markets.

Just as democratic states need to maintain a healthy circulation of political elites, free markets need to encourage the free circulation of wealth, so that resources and economic power do not concentrate in too few hands for too long. Antitrust laws, progressive income and wealth taxes, estate taxes, and progressive property laws (such as the infamous rule against perpetuities) all help prevent the privileged few from amassing too much wealth and tying it up indefinitely.

Once again, some states go further to redistribute private wealth, strengthen the middle class, and limit the economic gaps between rich and poor. Democracy does not require economic egalitarianism, but narrowing extremes in wealth

---

[16] The American economy at the close of the nineteenth century was a classic example of a largely unregulated capitalist market, driving quickly toward oligopoly and monopoly under the control of corporate trusts. By the turn of the century, the American Sugar Refining Company controlled 98 percent of American sugar refining. *United States v. E.C. Knight Co.*, 156 U.S. 1 (1895). Similar trusts controlled the production of other basic products, including oil, iron, steel, aluminum, copper, and nitrates. By 1900, the situation was so dire that presidential candidate William McKinley and his running mate, Theodore Roosevelt, campaigned on a platform of trust-busting and economic reform. After McKinley was assassinated in 1901, one of President Roosevelt's first acts was to ask Congress for new legislation limiting corporate power to destroy free markets and seize control of key economic sectors.

disparities encourages social and political stability. The Scandinavian economic model has been particularly successful in this regard, skillfully combining free markets, capitalism, and egalitarian economic and social policies.

Reckless economic intervention, however, carries the risk that the state will seek to control rather than protect free markets. Instead of serving as an honest referee, or even as an intrusive but benign nanny state, the government risks becoming a bully state, directing a command economy that ultimately benefits only the state and those who control it.

Elites

Elites shape all societies well beyond their raw weight of numbers. The upper class tends to have a coherent collective character, and the specific nature of this identity matters. If a developing country's elites are sympathetic to democratic values, they will play a leading role in the democratization process. If they are determined to protect their own privileges against the interests of the many, they will be a barrier to democratization and will have to be dealt with through negotiation or other means.

The oldest and most successful democracies – Switzerland, the United States, Holland, the United Kingdom, Canada, Australia, New Zealand, Costa Rica, and India, were all fortunate to have had founding elites who supported democratic ideals. Like picking one's parents, this is mostly a question of luck, but cultural norms and historical circumstances also matter.

Elites inevitably play a decisive role in establishing democracies, not only because of their privileged position in society, but also because they invariably create the laws and institutions on which successful democracies are founded. Aspiring democracies that find their Solon, Publius, Cincinnatus, Washington, Figueres, or Mandela – enlightened elites who create democratic laws, procedures, and institutions and then step aside gracefully – are fortunate.[17] Proto-democratic movements dominated by faux populist leaders such as Robespierre, Lenin, Mao, Castro, Hussein, or Mugabe are notably less successful.

The United States was a product of its age, and the eighteenth century was an auspicious time to be an emerging republic. The American intellectual and political elite constituted an honor roll of Enlightenment thought, and for all their disagreements and flaws, most shared a common commitment to liberal democratic principles.

It has long been fashionable to dismiss the U.S. Constitution as an anti-democratic reaction against the more freewheeling democracy promised by the Declaration of Independence and the Articles of Confederation. French philosopher Nicolas de Condorcet memorably condemned it as the triumph of great men over the people.

---

[17] The founding leaders of: Athens, Rome, the United States, Costa Rica, and South Africa.

It is true that the Constitution was written by a small group of privileged men, who met in secret to bury the Articles of Confederation and replace it with a stronger and more stable federal government. But that does not necessarily make the Constitution a counterrevolutionary manifesto or a betrayal of democratic principles.

Madison, self-servingly but accurately, observed that elite leadership in creating democratic laws and institutions is not only inevitable but desirable, so long as: (a) leaders are sincerely committed to democratic principles; and (b) the people freely assent to any proposal through proper democratic procedures.

The Framers met in Philadelphia during the summer of 1787 to debate, write, sign, and present a new draft constitution for public approval. Once their work was done, they packed up and went home. They did not impose their will on the country, they reserved no positions of authority for themselves in the new government, and they never even considered the possibility of seizing power or establishing a provisional junta, directorate, or tribunal.

After the delegates left Philadelphia, each state was left to do whatever it wanted to do with the new proposal. It was taken for granted that each state would follow its own customs, practices, and procedures in deciding whether to consider or accept the new proposal. All thirteen states acted independently to debate and ratify the draft constitution in their own way. Twelve states elected delegates to attend individual state conventions. Rhode Island initially held a direct popular referendum, in which the proposed constitution was soundly defeated, then waited several years before convening its own state convention that narrowly adopted the new constitution.

The Constitution reflected the values and preferences of the elites who wrote it. Fortunately, the Framers believed in liberal democratic principles, with a limited but energetic and accountable government. Although the new constitution was the product of compromise, and suffered from some serious flaws (chief among them failing to abolish slavery and refusing to extend political rights to women), it secured unprecedented individual liberties and established the world's first federal constitutional republic. The American Constitution was a revolutionary document in a conservative world that, in time, became a conservative document in a revolutionary world.

International Civil Society

Civil society now extends internationally among the globalized bourgeoisie. Globalization has been a work in progress since the thirteenth century BC, when the Phoenicians first opened shop around the Mediterranean. Since then, as the boundaries of the known world expanded, advances in travel and communications made the planet smaller and more accessible. Almost every corner of the globe is now within easy reach, and almost everyone everywhere is incorporated into the global economy, whether they like it or not.

Over the last century, liberalism has become the dominant force driving globalization, with a broadly like-minded group of politicians, businesses, merchants, consumers, diplomats, scholars, and tourists forming the new global community. Members of this liberal whole-earth society routinely interact across national boundaries, confident that people everywhere are rational, reasonable, responsible, and will live up to their end of the bargain in all manner of international transactions. Anyone with broadband access can easily do business with complete strangers in other countries thousands of miles away, secure in the knowledge that the people on the other end will deliver as promised. All of this has made complex global artistic, commercial, cultural, scientific, social, and political interactions seem routine and unremarkable.

None of this would have surprised Karl Marx, who was among the first to see class as a global rather than a national phenomenon. Marx would have been astonished, however, to see the degree to which liberalism has become the dominant ideology of the age.

Culture

In 1787, John Jay thought that despite being a young, vulnerable, and quarrelsome country, America had one great advantage: it was a natural union based on a common culture. As Jay put it: "Providence has been pleased to give this one connected country to one united people – a people descended from the same ancestors, speaking the same language, professing the same religion, attached to the same principles of government, (and) very similar in their manners and customs."[18] In other words, the United States had a leg up on other emerging nation-states, thanks to its inhabitants' shared historical experiences, expectations, and interests. For all their differences, the people of the thirteen states had even more in common.

A shared culture is not necessary to establish a stable democratic state, but it helps. Jay, however, made the common mistake of confusing shared cultural values with cultural homogeneity. Although speaking the same language can be a significant advantage in establishing a stable nation-state, there is no inherent link between language, culture, and community. Many countries and confederations, including Switzerland and the EU, demonstrate that shared values are consistent with multiple cultures and languages, whereas the cultural differences among the various English-speaking countries (including Australia, Belize, Canada, Fiji, Hong Kong, India, Ireland, Jamaica, Kenya, New Zealand, Pakistan, Singapore, the United Kingdom, the United States, and Zimbabwe) show that a common tongue does not mean cultural homogeny.

Culture is too complex a variable to deal with comprehensively here. Of necessity, we will reduce culture to three core elements: class, ethnicity/tribalism,

---

[18] John Jay, *The Federalist Papers*, No. 2.

and religion. Each of these key cultural elements can serve to stabilize – or destabilize – emerging democracies.

Class

Although democracy does not require a classless society, limiting extreme differences of wealth and class reinforces important democratic values, including community building, equality, individual efficacy, and social solidarity. Class-based societies, in contrast, foster political hierarchy, authoritarianism, and perpetual social conflict.

Broadly speaking, there are three types of class societies: rigid class systems, fluid class systems, and egalitarian systems. The Indian caste and British class systems are examples of rigid class societies, where birth, custom, and law determine social status, and nothing much can be done to change the equation short of death and reincarnation. Rigid class systems corrupt both the ruling and subordinate classes, whether master and slave, baron and serf, Brahmin and Dalit, toff and yob, or daimyo and Burakumin.

American society represents a fluid class system, where social status is based primarily on wealth and education. Social mobility is possible, although it might prove more difficult as the economic gaps and barriers between the elite and underclass grow wider and less permeable. Since the 1980s, unprecedented wealth has concentrated in the top 1 percent of the population as the middle class has thinned, leaving society increasingly divided between haves and have-nots. This problem will continue to fester if the U.S. class system ossifies, upward mobility slows, and the vast wealth concentrated at the top remains in the same families for extended periods of time in the manner of aristocracies.

Norway and Denmark are examples of egalitarian democracies, where long-standing public preferences and policies limit social differences on the basis of birth, wealth, and legal status. This results in strong middle-class societies, characterized by a durable and resilient civil society, social solidarity, and long-standing political stability. It comes at a cost, however, in terms of an active and intrusive state, including heavy taxes, aggressive government-led wealth redistribution, and a highly regulated economy.

On the whole, the world is moving away from rigid class distinctions. Formal class distinctions have largely disappeared in the developed world, although vestiges of traditional class societies survive even in the determinedly egalitarian countries of Northern Europe, where all of the Scandinavian states, except Iceland, remain constitutional monarchies with hereditary royal families. Conversely, traditional notions about class and caste are fading in Britain, and to a lesser degree in India, although old habits of class identity and social hierarchy persist.

Ethnicity/Tribalism

Human history is the story of cooperation and conflict among rival groups. Ethnic and tribal clashes fill our history books and continue to trouble many parts of the world, where enduring clan loyalties promote xenophobia, discourage pluralism, and frustrate democratization.

In much of the developing world, ethnic and tribal loyalties still outweigh national allegiances. This is, in part, because in Africa, the Middle East, Asia, and Latin America, European colonial powers drew national borders to convenience themselves, rather than responding to indigenous political geography. It must be added, however, that if the colonial powers had instead grouped native populations into homogeneous ethnic or tribal enclaves, the result would not have been much better in terms of encouraging healthy democratic development.

In Rwanda, the problem is not just artificial borders but artificial tribes. Belgium, the former colonial power, perversely created the country's two main tribes by classifying taller and light-skinned locals as Tutsi, and shorter, dark-skinned natives as Hutu. This externally imposed construct had no organic kinship or cultural roots, yet it fundamentally reshaped Rwandan society and eventually led to the worst genocide since World War II.

Ethnicity is a somewhat broader and more inclusive concept than tribe. In ethnic communities, a shared culture, religion, and history are at least as important as genealogy and blood, although all of these elements are usually present. The Middle East provides the best example of this sort of complex cultural overlay, where superficially unitary Muslim populations subdivide into a maze of tribes, ethnicities, and sects: Sunni, Shi'a, Arabs, Persians, Pashtuns, Kurds, Alawites, Assyrians, Azeri, Druze, Turkmen, Salafis, Wahhabis, and countless other subgroups mingle and clash in an intricate and ever-changing political kaleidoscope.

Strong authoritarian rulers can suppress these destabilizing conflicts, sometimes for many years. In doing so, however, they aggravate the underlying problems, so that when the regime inevitably weakens, latent tensions erupt anew as rival groups reassert themselves and look to settle old scores. The sudden release of pent-up grievances is usually all the worse for having been repressed for so long.

Democracies, in contrast, prefer to resolve social conflicts through conventional political and legal channels. This can actually intensify sociopolitical instability in the short run, but in the long run only a pluralistic democracy can teach instinctively antagonistic factions how to negotiate, compromise, and eventually live in relative peace. In mature democracies, ethnic and tribal identities gradually fade into a cosmopolitan stew, where different cultures mix freely and cultural chauvinism softens into a benign nostalgia for the *auld sod*, with a shared appreciation for diverse ethnic customs, holidays, foods, and fashions.

Countries beset by seemingly intractable tribal and ethnic conflicts might need to take intermediate steps to defuse the situation, build trust, and find a mutually agreeable solution. Consociational democracy offers one possible way to calm troubled waters, by ensuring that each recognized group has a say in political decision making. Consociational democracy guarantees each group meaningful – usually proportional – political representation in government. This gives rival factions and potential troublemakers an incentive to play by the rules, offering the government some breathing room to seek a negotiated settlement.

Consociational democracy is not a panacea for resolving ethnic conflicts. Some groups are inevitably excluded from any grand social bargain, which can trigger ill will and blowback. Moreover, guaranteeing tribal or ethnic groups representation in government tends to reinforce, rather than resolve, the narrow, identity-based politics that caused the problems in the first place.

Religion

Samuel Huntington argues that some religions are compatible with democracy, some are incompatible, and the rest fall somewhere in between. Compatible religions embrace core democratic values, including individualism, reason, and tolerance. Incompatible religions freely mix matters of religion and state, stress dogmatic absolutes, promote faith over reason, demand unthinking submission to religious authorities, and incite intolerance of nonconforming beliefs. The rest combine these pro- and antidemocratic attitudes in various ways.

Protestantism tops Huntington's list of compatible religions; Islam, Buddhism, and Confucianism are among the major religions Huntington categorizes as antidemocratic. Islam is singled out as especially hostile to democracy for all the reasons listed previously, plus Huntington alleges that Islamic religious authorities actively seek to control all aspects of society, including public morality, politics, and law. We will return later to discuss the complex and controversial relationship between Islam and democracy.

Huntington cites Hinduism as a major religion with a mixed record on democracy. On the one hand, polytheistic Hindus are relatively tolerant of other gods and religions. On the other hand, Hinduism perpetuates India's caste system and promotes individual passivity and submission, especially among the lower castes. Although Huntington does not explicitly acknowledge it, one possible tiebreaker is that Hindu-dominated India has been the world's most populous stable democracy since it gained independence in 1947.

Finally, Huntington considers Catholicism to be a unique case – a religion that consciously changed categories. For most of the church's history, Catholic leaders were overtly hostile to democratic values and practices. This began to change with Vatican II, in the early 1960s, when church leaders repositioned the faith to embrace core democratic principles and supported Western democratic governments during the Cold War.

Although Huntington's article is masterful, his claim that three of the world's major religions are essentially irreconcilable with democracy might not be *halal*. His unabashed criticism of Buddhism, Confucianism, and especially Islam seems unfair, given that the basis for each of these three religions' alleged hostility to democratic government is not unique to those religions, but is widely shared among all global religions, including Christianity.

There is little in Christianity that is inherently democratic, and most traditional Christian narratives are explicitly antidemocratic. There is no biblical evidence that the Judeo-Christian God is now or ever has been a democrat, and there is considerable evidence to the contrary. God cast from heaven the only celestial being to challenge his absolute power and rebranded the rebel as Satan. A strict hierarchy of angels governs heaven itself. Jesus is the Lord and King of Kings, not the First Among Equals. To this day, earthly Christian leaders present themselves as shepherds of lost sheep. Until the Enlightenment, most Western theologians believed that the idea of a Christian democracy is an oxymoron, because Christianity demands obedience and humble submission to authority, and rejects the idea that active participation in public life is a virtue.

Despite Christianity's congenital antidemocratic message, with the Reformation and Enlightenment, mainstream Protestantism gradually developed attitudes and habits consistent with democratic values. The idea of salvation evolved into an acceptance of individual responsibility for one's own life and soul, which reinforced the importance of liberty, reason, and toleration. Even Jesus's hierarchical relationship with his disciples was retconned to justify the Anglo-American jury system of twelve men, good and true.

Just as no major religious belief system is inherently democratic, the converse is also true: all major religions contain some core beliefs and practices that are at least potentially compatible with self-government. Identifying and reinforcing these democratic tendencies can point the way for even the most rigidly authoritarian religions to reconcile faith with reason, and divinity with democracy.

For example, despite its tendency to promote social hierarchy, obedience, and passivity, much of Confucianism is readily compatible with democratic principles. Confucianism eschews coercive power, and advocates the restrained exercise of persuasive authority. It tacitly limits government power, by requiring officials to respect established customs, rituals, and morality. It encourages local autonomy and subsidiarity, rule by consensus, civic education, community spirit, social harmony, and the establishment of a strong civil society. It encourages everyone, whether rulers or citizens, to engage in self-education, self-reflection, and self-criticism.

Among the factors to consider in assessing a religion's potential compatibility with democracy are the extent to which: (1) it encourages individual reason and responsibility over faith and unthinking subservience to authority; (2) religious leaders use the state to promote their own religious agendas and impose their views on the rest of society, including nonbelievers; (3) religious leaders claim the right to govern or shape public policy; and (4) religious leaders treat other religions, as well as nonconformists and apostates, with ecumenical tolerance or aggressive hostility. It is worth remembering that a religion that fails any or all of these tests today might pass tomorrow with flying colors.

Why Dogmatic Societies Are Poor Soil for Democracy

Dogmatic societies stress unquestioning faith and obedience, with severe sanctions for those who do not toe the line with sufficient enthusiasm. In many cases, even peaceful dissent is punished as a combination of religious and secular crimes, including heresy, blasphemy, apostasy, sedition, and treason. Minor disagreements over obscure doctrine can provoke wildly disproportionate reactions, with the worst punishments often reserved for heretics and apostates – those who once believed, but changed their minds.[19]

In dogmatic societies, liberty is not a virtue to be encouraged, but an evil to be vigorously suppressed. It is revealing that the word "heretic" comes from the Greek *hairetikos*, meaning one who can make a free choice.

The explanation for this is simple. For those who believe in divine or objective Truth, once the Truth is known, there is no reason to tolerate dissent, because dissenters are not merely objectively wrong, they are at war with God. Once the Truth is known, all debate must end, and everyone needs only to shut up and fall in line. This approach does not encourage reason, tolerance, pluralism, liberty, freedom, or other democratic virtues.

Monotheistic societies are perhaps more prone to this sort of closed-minded behavior than polytheistic cultures. Polytheistic religions can afford to take a more relaxed view, because their divine universe contains diverse divinities with distinct divine views. Put another way, if a religion already has a dozen deities in the pantheon, no one is likely to get too upset about adding one more to the mix.

The Romans, despite their dark reputation in U.S. Sunday schools, were generally tolerant when it came to matters of religious belief. After conquering new territories, Roman priests routinely traveled to newly occupied lands to formally invite the local gods to move to Rome and live in peace with all the other gods. The priests always *seemed* pleased when the local deities invariably accepted their invitation. Judaism and Christianity puzzled the Romans, because they could not understand why the Judeo-Christian God was so violently jealous of all other gods.

Among modern global religions, Hinduism is perhaps the most inclined to accept religious pluralism with a shrug of Shiva's many shoulders. Hinduism

[19] The Iranian government considers the Baha'i to be apostates, and treats them accordingly. State and religious authorities have brutally persecuted Baha'i since the Iranian Revolution of 1979 – intimidating, imprisoning, torturing, and murdering hundreds, destroying their holy sites, and attempting forced conversions to Islam. Elsewhere in the Middle East, many Sunni consider Shi'a to be apostates, and Shi'a minorities have long been persecuted in Iraq and Saudi Arabia. In Saudi Arabia, the Wahhabis, a powerful Islamist sect, consider Ahmadis, Sufis, Druze, and other nonconforming sects to be heretics, whose beliefs are punishable by death.

suffers from the usual fits of religious intolerance and sectarian violence, but its comparatively relaxed attitude about religious coexistence has helped India to moderate and consolidate its democracy.

Blurring the line between state and religion poses a grave threat to democratic government. The American Founders dropped the ball on slavery, but they avoided untold other problems by strictly separating church and state. Even so, some American fundamentalists persist in latter-day attempts to breach the wall separating church and state, seeking to harness government power to promote their own religious beliefs and suppress competing views.

John Locke, the chief architect of the wall between church and state, was guardedly optimistic about the long-term compatibility of democracy and religion, so long as religious concerns are not allowed to interfere with state responsibilities. If matters of faith are left exclusively to individual conscience, and temporal matters left ultimately to the state, everyone wins.

History has largely vindicated Locke's views. In secular democracies, religious faith is less politicized, less oppressive, more tolerant, and more ecumenical than it is in countries with an established faith, or where there is no clear separation of church and state.[20] Even among the faithful, there is broad acceptance that a neutral, secular government is the best guarantor of individual rights, including the fundamental right of religious liberty.

Most organized religions now accept the idea of secular government. Islam is the last significant exception. In Islamist states, religion, morality, law, and politics are considered inseparable, and governed by overlapping networks of religious and political elites. Secular government and democracy are considered sinful, because it is arrogant and blasphemous for ordinary people to decide right and wrong. These matters should be left exclusively to God – who speaks, of course, solely through his self-appointed earthly clerics.

Finally, secular orthodoxy can be as dogmatic and oppressive as any theocracy. Plato's republic was a secular totalitarian state based on objective truth, where a handful of philosophers controlled every facet of community life. Lenin's theories about the dictatorship of the proletariat and democratic centralism (with the vanguard standing in for Plato's philosopher kings and "Marxist" theory replacing the Forms) gave rise to some of the most intolerant, violent, and repressive regimes in history.[21]

---

[20] One exception is the United Kingdom, which has two politically neutered established religions, one Presbyterian and the other Anglican.

[21] The term "Marxist" is in quotes because Lenin and his ideological successors departed significantly from Marx's original theories. Lenin's use of the word "democracy" probably deserves its own set of quotation marks; under Lenin's theory of democratic centralism, some initial public discussion and debate of pending policy might be permitted, but once the central authority makes its decision, no further debate or dissent is tolerated.

INSTITUTIONAL LEVEL

Stable democracies require sound government architecture – the institutions, rules, and procedures that determine how government will function. This is like creating political DNA from scratch; small differences in how the elements bond can determine whether government will fly like an eagle or a penguin.

There are eight institutional features common to all modern, stable democracies: an effective checks and balances system; the rule of law; an open, fair, and competitive electoral system; a professional civil service; government transparency; a secular state; a civilian state; and a commonwealth. We will examine each in turn.

Checks and Balances

An effective checks and balances system defines, divides, and disperses state power, so that ambition checks ambition and power checks power. This is done to protect individual rights, and to ensure that one faction does not permanently dominate government. It also aids political stability by slowing the decision-making process, encouraging greater deliberation, and making sure that different perspectives are fully considered before reaching a final decision.

Designing and institutionalizing the world's first comprehensive system of checks and balances was arguably America's most important contribution to political theory and practice. Yet although the U.S. system is noteworthy, it is not the only workable template.

There are three basic components in a comprehensive checks and balances system. First, *constitutionalism* requires an effective basic law that defines and limits state power, and guarantees fundamental rights against the government. Second, *separation of powers* divides national authority horizontally among different government departments. Third, *federalism* disperses sovereign power vertically between the central government and various regional governments.

Constitutionalism

A *constitution*, or *basic law*, is a foundational social contract that defines, organizes, and limits government power, establishes key institutions and procedures, and allocates rights and responsibilities. Because it is a fundamental law, ordinary laws and decrees cannot change its terms; it can only be modified through authoritative interpretation, amendment, suspension, or revocation procedures.[22]

---

[22] Constitutions are usually subject to authoritative interpretation by judges and other officials, which raises a whole series of issues, including whether or not a constitution is a living document that can be reinterpreted from time to time to fit current circumstances. Some argue that allowing reinterpretation gives judges necessary flexibility to keep a constitution up to date. Others argue that a living constitution is an oxymoron, and that laws need to have a fixed meaning or they are not really laws – only suggestions subject to judges' whims.

This debate aside, constitutional judgments that reinterpret constitutional guarantees in light of current circumstances might not breach the integrity of constitutional guarantees if the

A constitution can be formally written and ratified (the American model), or "unwritten" and built up over an extended period through a combination of special laws and convention (the British model).

Madison warned against relying too much on parchment promises, and noted that history is littered with constitutions that read well but delivered little or nothing in practice. It is not enough to write a fine document, wipe the ink from your hands, and congratulate everyone on a job well done. Constitutionalism presupposes the existence of effective institutions and procedures to enforce its terms.

Separation of Powers

Separation of powers involves dividing government responsibilities horizontally among different branches or departments. This channels and balances state power, placing it in multiple hands to prevent one person, faction, or branch of government from dominating the rest.

The American constitution divides government into three coequal branches: legislative, executive, and judicial. It further subdivides congressional power with a bicameral legislature. Each department has distinct, although overlapping, responsibilities. The legislature controls the purse and writes the laws; the executive enforces the laws, has a conditional veto over legislative acts, serves as commander-in-chief, speaks for the country in foreign relations, and controls the bureaucracy; and the judiciary claims the ultimate authority to say what the law is and apply general laws to individual cases.

Dividing government does not mean isolating each branch within a separate and unassailable fortress. The three departments are not autonomous; they are only partly insulated from each other and have overlapping responsibilities. This makes interactions among them complex and fluid, like a shifting Venn diagram.

What was once memorably said about British politics applies equally to U.S. government: it has the engine of a lawnmower and the brakes of a Rolls Royce.[23] Policy making is a ritualized struggle among the three coequal branches, where each department can modify, delay, or kill any government initiative it considers unacceptable.

The intent of a well-designed separation of power system is to establish a flexible, stable multipolar balance of power within government. It is a political

---

reinterpretation: (1) is allowed according to the terms of the constitution; (2) was intended by those who wrote, ratified, or promulgated the constitutional provisions in question; (3) is done to preserve founding constitutional principles or intent in the face of changed circumstances; (4) corrects a prior interpretive mistake; or (5) is necessary to decide an issue that was not anticipated at the time that the relevant constitutional provisions were written or ratified.

Regardless of any specific constitutional provisions concerning amendment, suspension, or repeal, basic laws are subject to reform or revocation by the people, as the ultimate sovereign authority, whether through conventional legal procedures, such as a public referendum or constitutional convention, or by extralegal means – revolution.

[23] Antony Jay and Jonathan Lynn, *The Complete Yes Prime Minister* (1988).

gyroscope, with a self-correcting equilibrium. Power ebbs and flows among the different departments, but overall the system maintains its dynamic stable state. Or think of it as a three-way tug of war: if one department manages to pull the flag too far in one direction, the other two can react to pull it back toward top dead center.

Tyranny exists, Madison wrote, when all power rests in the same hands, whether they belong to the one, the few, or the many, and whether they hold office by hereditary right, are appointed, or are elected.[24] According to Madison, to prevent a tyrannical concentration of power, each department should draw on different sources of power, and should answer to different constituencies. This divides the power flowing *to* each branch, as well as the powers emanating from each branch.[25]

At America's founding, only the House of Representatives answered directly to the people, and even then its members answered only to relatively small numbers of voters (30,000) in separate congressional districts. The president, vice president, and senators were indirectly elected,[26] and the president nominated federal judges and all major executive department heads, subject to Senate approval. These procedures were meant to ensure that each branch drew from a different fount of authority.

The United States established the gold standard for dividing government responsibilities, but the American model is not the only viable option. The British system, although it served as the main prototype for the United States, represents a different approach to the idea of checks and balances.

First, the American system divides government according to functions, whereas Britain divides government to accommodate different interests. The monarch represents the one, the House of Lords represents the few, and the House of Commons represents the many.

Second, the British system does not recognize the American principle of coequality; parliament is supreme.[27]

---

[24] "The accumulation of all power legislative, executive, and judiciary in the same hands, whether of one, a few, or many, and whether hereditary, self-appointed, or elective, may justly be pronounced the very definition of tyranny." James Madison, *The Federalist Papers* No. 47. Madison drew this definition from Montesquieu and Locke, and from Jefferson's *Notes on Virginia* ("[C]oncentrating these [powers] in the same hands is precisely the definition of despotic government."). Wills, *Explaining America*, at 112. This underlines Madison's conviction that America should not be a free or participatory democracy, because "pure" democracy places all power in the hands of the many, which is both tyrannical and destabilizing.

[25] Madison focused on tyranny, and never explicitly discussed separation of powers in the context of checks and balances. The only time Madison mentioned checks and balances was in his discussion of bicameralism, where each chamber serves as a check on the other. James Madison, *The Federalist* Papers Nos. 10 and 51.

[26] The Electoral College formally selects the president and vice president. State legislators controlled the selection of U.S. senators until the 17th Amendment changed the rules in 1913, to require direct popular elections.

[27] Most of the American Founders accepted, but worried about, the democratic principle of legislative supremacy. It is no coincidence that Article I concerns legislative power, Article II the

Third, Britain, like most parliamentary systems, blurs the lines between government departments far more freely than does America. Executive ministers, including the prime minister, are drawn from parliament, and usually belong to the political party that controls the legislature. Under most circumstances, this provides clear and undivided responsibility for government policy-making, which makes parliamentary governments more responsive, more efficient, and more clearly accountable than America's presidential system.[28]

Divided government, which is so common – and so vexing – in the United States is almost unheard of in Britain. Cabinet ministers, who are collectively referred to as "the Government," manage parliament, control the legislative agenda, and can dissolve parliament and call for new elections at any time and for any reason. This allows the executive branch to drive the national political agenda far more effectively than is usually the case in the United States. Conversely, parliament can call for a vote of confidence at any time, and if the Government loses the prime minister must either ask the sovereign to form a new Government, or must appeal to the country by calling a snap election.

Until recently, one official, the Lord Chancellor, played a major role in all three branches of government: as a senior government minister in the executive branch, as the presiding officer in the House of Lords, and as the head of the judiciary.[29] Such a thorough blurring of departmental lines would puzzle and alarm most Americans. Similarly, whereas Americans have always considered an independent judiciary to be an essential component of separation of powers theory, in Britain the judiciary remained part of the executive branch, and subject to the sovereign's will, until the Act of Settlement of 1701.[30] Even

---

executive, and Article III the judiciary. But the principle of coequality quickly became widely, if not universally, accepted as a fundamental principle of American constitutional theory.

[28] In most parliamentary systems, the same party or coalition controls both the legislative and executive branches, and members of the legislature dominate the executive cabinet. This makes ultimate responsibility for government decisions clear and unambiguous.

In presidential systems such as the United States, there is clear separation between the legislature and executive, and divided government is common. The legislative and executive branches routinely blame each other for any problems, and political responsibility is rarely clear. This is true even when the same party controls both branches of government, because neither branch answers to the other.

[29] Prime Minister Tony Blair significantly curtailed the Lord Chancellor's political and legal influence in 2007.

[30] The British judiciary was historically considered part of the executive branch, and judges served at the king's pleasure. This changed in 1701, when the Act of Settlement made the judiciary independent of the monarch's will by changing judicial tenure from "at pleasure" to "on good behavior," and requiring legislative consent before a judge could be removed from office.

Significantly, the Act of Settlement did not apply to British colonies in America, where judges continued to serve at the king's pleasure. Americans viewed colonial judges as instruments of tyranny and oppression. The absence of an independent colonial judiciary was one of the grievances that sparked the American Revolution, and the Declaration of Independence highlighted it as a main justification for war. In Jefferson's words: "*He has made judges dependent on his will alone, for the tenure of their offices, and the amount and payment of their salaries.*" The Constitutional Framers corrected this in Article III, which established the federal judiciary as an independent and (eventually) coequal department of government.

after this landmark declaration of judicial independence, the House of Lords retained substantial judicial responsibilities as Britain's highest court of appeal for another 300 years, until the creation of a new Supreme Court in 2009.

One of the costs of a checks and balances system is that government decision making is slower and less efficient than a consolidated authoritarian regime. Day-to-day governance is time-consuming, messy, wasteful, and frustrating, as the various departments try to pull the government in different directions.[31]

In real time, democracy is only beautiful in naïve anticipation or nostalgic retrospect. This is one reason why authoritarian states so often underestimate democracies. They mistake the day-to-day messiness of democratic governance for dissipation, when it is actually a source of democracy's resilience, adaptability, and strength.[32]

Although separation of powers complicates governance, it also forces government to be more consultative, deliberative, and transparent. Divided policy-making responsibilities require considerable thought, planning, discussion, negotiation, and compromise among different interests before an idea can become law. It also provides ample opportunities to revisit previous decisions, in order to make adjustments and correct mistakes.

Federalism

Federalism diffuses sovereign power by dividing government responsibilities vertically, between a central government and semiautonomous regional governments. In a true federal system, provincial, state, and/or local governments have a degree of independent legal and political authority – a share of sovereign power – so that the national government cannot coerce, commandeer, ignore, or dissolve the regional governments at will.[33]

Most political theorists agree with French political theorist Jean Bodin that sovereign authority is inherently indivisible. The United States challenged this conventional wisdom by placing ultimate political authority in the hands of the people, rather than vesting it in a monarch or legislature. The people then parceled out their power to different levels of government, effectively dividing sovereign power and responsibilities.[34]

---

[31] Even so, it would be misleading to call the U.S. government inefficient by design. The Framers did not set out to create a weak or do-nothing government. They sought to establish an active, efficient government within the framework of limited and accountable power. Of course, the Framers had to make many compromises to pass and ratify the proposed constitution, and some of these agreements made government less efficient than it might otherwise have been.

[32] It must be noted that democracies often *are* weak and/or decadent. The fundamental mistake that authoritarian governments make is that they rarely look beyond these obvious flaws to understand or appreciate the underlying and often subtle strengths of democratic societies.

[33] In unitary states, regional governments are subservient to the central government, and have no independent legal standing or authority. The central government is free to ignore, overrule, alter, coerce, co-opt, commandeer, or abolish any regional political subdivisions at will.

[34] Bernard Bailyn, *The Ideological Origins of the American Revolution*, at 198.

The relationship among the different levels of government in federal systems is often complex, with tensions common among governments that are at least occasionally rivals. Working out the details of U.S. federalism led to a civil war, and after more than 200 years it remains a work in progress.

Regional governments share sovereign authority with the central government, but this does not necessarily make them equal partners. The supremacy clause in the U.S. Constitution explicitly favors the federal government whenever a valid federal law conflicts with state law.

Federalism helps stabilize democracy in six ways. First, it adds another dimension to the checks and balances system, making it exponentially more difficult for one faction to dominate the government. In the United States, it is possible for one party to control all three branches of the federal government for a time, but inconceivable that one party could simultaneously control all three branches of all fifty state governments without destroying the republic in the process.

Second, federalism offers citizens an alternative safe harbor against government neglect and abuse. If the federal government is unresponsive or oppressive, the people can appeal to their regional governments for protection, or vice-versa. It is the two-parent principle – if one is behaving badly, hopefully the other will be more reasonable.

When Southern states proved relentlessly hostile to African-American demands for political equality, the National Association for the Advancement of Colored People (NAACP) turned to the federal government for relief.[35] Conversely, when the federal government refused to recognize equal rights for lesbians, gays, bisexuals, and transgendered persons, LGBT activists successfully petitioned sympathetic state governments to secure new privacy and status rights.

Third, as Montesquieu discovered and Madison elaborated, federalism allows modern democracies to overcome conventional size limitations without sacrificing core democratic principles of popular participation, consent, accountability, and subsidiarity. This revolutionary insight made democracy possible in the modern world of nation-states.

In 1816, Thomas Jefferson proposed reforming American federalism by replacing the original two levels of government with four semi-independent units: wards, counties, states, and the national government. The key to Jefferson's plan was the ward system. Each ward was to be twenty-five square miles in size – large enough to sustain a self-sufficient political community, but small enough to allow for full direct citizen participation.

Jefferson sought to institutionalize participatory democracy at the local level, and wanted to create a more effective check against tyranny. Citizens

---

[35] After Congress and the executive failed to act, the NAACP turned in desperation to the courts as a last resort. This illustrates that rather than having just two potential political safe harbors, Americans might have as many as six: the three branches at the federal level, and the three parallel branches at the state level.

of the various wards would elect representatives to each of the other levels of government, ensuring an organic, bottom-up approach to power and government. According to Hannah Arendt, Jefferson's ward-republic was "the only possible non-violent alternative to his earlier notions about the desirability of recurring revolutions."[36] Despite Jefferson's unsurpassed reputation, his idea sank without a bubble.[37]

As a result, America retains its original two-tier system of federal and state governments. County and local governments have no sovereign power or autonomous legal authority – they are legal creatures of the state, and subject to the state's will. In contrast to Jefferson's ward system, America's bifurcated system reinforces a top-down political model, where effective political power is concentrated in the federal and state capitals, rather than being dispersed among thousands of semiautonomous wards and counties.[38]

Fourth, federalism can simultaneously accommodate local customs and limit the undesirable side effects of narrow-minded parochialism. Federalism respects local traditions by allowing communities substantial leeway to do things their own way. It also reinforces nationalism, by allowing the central government to override local decisions when necessary and nudge the e pluribus toward the unum. Acting as a natural mediator, the federal government can manage local disputes while balancing local preferences against the national interest.

Fifth, federalism allows for political experimentation. Louis Brandeis called American states the great laboratories of democracy, because federalism allows individual states to "try novel social and economic experiments without risk to the rest of the country."[39]

Finally, because federal democracies are not limited in terms of size, nation-states can draw from a large and diverse pool of people and resources. This allows great economies of scale for defense, economic development, and other essential government endeavors.

On the down side, federal governments are susceptible to two contradictory but equally destructive tendencies. The first problem is creeping centralization. The political history of the United States is the story of the gradual migration of power from the states to the federal government.[40]

[36] Hannah Arendt, *On Revolution*.
[37] The Letters of Thomas Jefferson: 1743–1826, Letter to Joseph C. Cabell, February 2, 1816. Retrieved from *http://www.let.rug.nl/~usa/P/tj3/writings/brf/jefl241.html*. Cf., Arendt, *On Revolution*; Brian P. Janiskee, "Conservatives' Problems With Special Districts," The Claremont Institute, March 17, 2004; retrieved from *http://www.claremont.org/projects/pageid.2026/default.asp/*.
[38] Using Jefferson's figure of twenty-five square miles per ward, there would be approximately 140,000 wards in the United States today.
[39] *New State Ice Co. v. Liebmann*, 285 U.S. 262, 311 (1932), Brandeis, J., dissenting.
[40] American states still have significant autonomy with respect to state police powers (laws concerning the health, safety, and morals of state citizens), taxation, natural resources, physical infrastructure, business regulation, and education.

The second problem is that federal states are prone to fly apart because the central government is too weak to hold the country together. This is especially true of regional confederacies, such as the United States under the Articles of Confederation or the modern European Union, where effective sovereignty rests with the member-states, rather than with the central authority.[41]

Systemic failure because of lack of political gravity in the central government preys especially hard on weak federal states, such as the Soviet Union, Yugoslavia, and Czechoslovakia. Other proto-federal states currently toeing the abyss include Afghanistan, Iraq, Somalia, and Sudan. In Western Europe, Belgium appears to be most at risk of breaking apart, although it will likely avoid the worst consequences of a collapse, given Belgium's political and economic strengths, and its central importance to the EU.

There are some twenty-four federal states in the world today, including Argentina, Australia, Belgium, Brazil, Canada, India, Iraq, Mexico, Nigeria, Russia, Switzerland, and the United States. Some unitary states, including the United Kingdom and Spain, are moving toward establishing more decentralized, quasi-federal governments. It is unclear whether their trajectories will allow them to continue as unitary states with selectively devolved political powers granted to regional governments, or whether they will recreate themselves as true federal unions or break apart into weak confederacies of largely autonomous mini-states.[42]

The Rule of Law

Democracies are ultimately governed either by the rule of law or the law of the jungle. The former is a necessary precondition of a stable democracy; the latter is the hallmark of mob rule. Authoritarian regimes might occasionally respect the rule of law, but no democracy can survive for long without it.[43]

---

[41] Although the European Union leaves the balance of power between Brussels and member states purposefully vague, the individual states are in almost every respect more powerful than the central authority. The risks posed by a weak central authority might not be readily apparent in tranquil times, but will become obvious during an economic or political crisis. Madison and Hamilton discussed the problems posed by a weak central authority at length in *The Federalist Papers*, and concluded that a weak central authority is a far greater threat to republican government than a strong central authority.

[42] The United Kingdom is still trying to work out the details of devolution and define the evolving nature of the political union of England, Scotland, Wales, and Northern Ireland. Spain has been wrestling since the late 1970s to figure out how to divide power between the central government in Madrid and the regional governments of Cataluña, Barcelona, the Basque Country, Galicia, and Andalucía. The EU has, largely unintentionally, encouraged increased demands for subnational regional autonomy in Europe, even as it has pushed to make national borders obsolete and sought to transfer greater power to Brussels.

[43] It is important to note that China and other Confucianist countries dispute the claim that the rule of law is necessary for stable democratic government. The traditional Chinese view is that enlightened, moral leaders and virtuous, obedient citizens allow civilized countries to function

In a democracy, the rule of law means that society is governed by a set of norms duly enacted by the people or their representatives, faithfully administered by the executive, and fairly interpreted and applied by an independent judiciary. Government is a creature of law, not power; its behavior is constrained and guided by established rules, rather than being the blunt instrument by which the strong impose their will on the weak.

The rule of law sets boundaries on both states and individuals. Laws must be properly enacted, publicly disseminated, readily accessible, and reasonable. They must give fair notice of impermissible conduct and possible sanctions, must be generally applicable, and cannot discriminate for spurious or invidious reasons. The rule of law also requires rational, fair, and transparent procedures that yield rational, fair, and consistent results – where like cases are treated alike, and justice is not only done but is seen to be done.

Rule of law systems have three basic components: substantive rules, procedural rules, and an impartial judiciary. *Substantive rules* regulate, prohibit, or require specified actions. *Procedural rules* establish the steps required to determine whether substantive norms have been violated, to assign responsibility for violations, and to impose appropriate sanctions or remedies. Finally, an *impartial judiciary* is necessary to referee public and private disputes in a disinterested manner, by finding the facts, applying the rules, and doing justice in individual cases. There is considerable irony in the fact that democracies must rely so heavily on the least democratic branch of government to function properly.

Substantive Rules
Substantive rules regulate, prohibit, and sometimes require specified behaviors on the part of governments, individuals, and groups. These norms usually take the form of prohibitions – thou shalt not. Occasionally they require positive behavior – thou shalt – such as laws requiring government agencies to provide food stamps to the needy, obliging businesses to mitigate environmental damage, or compelling individuals to pay taxes.

Common substantive limits on government behavior include prohibitions against unreasonable searches and seizures, coerced confessions, torture or inhumane treatment, and prior restraints on speech. The precise limits on government power are open to debate, and vary considerably from country to country. Many democratic societies make these limits explicit through written

---

in the absence of law. From this perspective, the rule of law is a sign of disorder, arbitrary rule, and strife, rather than a fountain of peace, stability, and justice.

Marxists, on the other hand, view law as an instrument of class oppression, rather than as a source of dispassionate justice. For different reasons, they are as skeptical as Confucianists when it comes to embracing the idea that the rule of law is a necessary element of democratic governance.

constitutions, statutes, and regulations; other countries rely on informal custom and convention to determine what government can and cannot do.

Substantive rules to regulate individual behavior can be either criminal or civil in nature. Substantive criminal laws include injunctions against homicide, rape, and drunk driving. Civil laws include antitrust protections, workplace safety regulations, property law, contract law, and tort. The government's ability to regulate behavior through criminal laws must, at a minimum, respect the Roman maxim that there can be no crime without law (nulla crimen sine lege) and its common law corollary – that which is not forbidden is permitted. There are fewer constraints on civil laws, in part because civil remedies rarely involve imprisonment or other corporal punishment.

Procedural Rules

A rule of law system requires that the investigatory, trial, and appellate process be rational, reasonable, fair, and transparent. Procedural rules establish how to decide whether substantive rules have been violated, and if so, how to determine appropriate sanctions or remedies. As with substantive laws, the state must follow established rules, especially those that limit state discretion or prevent officials from tipping the scales to obtain an expedient or corrupt result.

Procedural rules are arguably even more important than substantive rules for institutionalizing the rule of law. It is possible, and perhaps desirable, to have a thin volume of substantive laws, but a thick and robust set of procedural rules.

The details of procedural justice are, like almost everything else in a democracy, open to debate. Five principles seem universally important, however, especially in criminal cases.

First, the government's power to investigate, prosecute, and punish must be clearly defined and limited, to guarantee fairness for the accused. Limits might include prohibitions against bills of attainder, ex post facto prosecutions, malicious or politically motivated prosecutions, and double jeopardy. These limits are usually more strict in criminal than civil cases; the injunction against ex post facto laws, for example, does not necessarily apply to civil law.

Second, during the investigatory and pretrial phases, essential procedural rights include, at a minimum, protection against punitive pretrial detention, involuntary confessions, torture, and inhumane or humiliating treatment. Positive rights should include a presumption of innocence, a right to effective counsel, reasonable bail, and reasonable discovery rights – including timely access to any evidence that might tend to exonerate the accused.

Third, during the trial phase, procedural due process requires additional rules to ensure fairness to the accused. These rules include a continuing presumption of innocence, with the burden of proof on the state at every step to prove guilt beyond a reasonable doubt. Other important trial rights include rights to effective counsel, a speedy and public trial, a competent and impartial judge, and vicinage rights, as well as the rights to confront one's accusers, present exculpatory evidence, and cross-examine witnesses. Finally, where there is a right to trial by jury, it must include the right to a fair jury drawn from a reasonable cross-section of the community.

Fourth, during the penalty phase of trial, any remedy, penalty, or punishment must be reasonable, proportional, and crafted to fit the individual case by taking into account relevant aggravating and mitigating factors. There can be no cruel and unusual or inhumane punishments, and judges should be required to justify their decisions publicly according to established legal principles.

Fifth, there must be a meaningful right of appeal. Appellate tribunals should be able to take a second look at the adequacy of fact finding, and review how the rules were interpreted and applied, to ensure the integrity of the investigatory and trial process.

An Independent Judiciary

An independent judiciary is indispensable to the rule of law. This is, in part, because the judicial branch is the only department of government designed to resist majoritarian power, rather than respond to it. In the normal course of justice, judges should be answerable only to law, conscience, and superior courts. Judges in some jurisdictions are subject to elections or some other form of public accountability, but this is controversial because it weakens the courts' counter-majoritarian function and challenges judicial independence.[44]

Whereas the legislative and executive branches ultimately answer to the people, judges can defy democratic gravity, because they are insulated from political pressure through constitutional safeguards such as tenure and salary guarantees.[45] Shielding judges from political pressure frees them to serve as

---

[44] Although judges are not directly answerable to legislatures or executive officials, they can be removed from office through impeachment, and can be checked indirectly through legislative control of judicial budgets and salaries. The judicial branch supervises its members through judicial rules and codes of ethical conduct, formal judicial disciplinary hearings, and other similar control mechanisms.

[45] This includes federal judges in the United States, as well as judges in most other democracies. Many American states, along with Japan and a handful of other democratic nations, subject their judges to periodic elections or some other form of popular referendum. Although this helps democratize the judiciary and makes it more responsive to popular will, it can also bring considerable political pressure to bear on the courts and individual judges, which can potentially distort the course of justice.

Although federal judges in the United States and judges in most other countries never have to face the electorate, the initial appointment process is highly political. In the United States, the confirmation process itself serves as something of a preemptive democratic check on the federal judiciary.

No amount of political insulation is sufficient to protect the courts from all social and political pressure. According to Robert Dahl, courts might resist the will of the majority for a time, but they rarely hold out for very long. Pressure to yield to public opinion can take many forms. The Southern judges charged with enforcing *Brown v. Board of Education* found themselves facing intense social pressure to defy the Supreme Court's desegregation orders and maintain segregation. They were expelled from their community organizations and country clubs, and socially ostracized. J. W. Peltason, *58 Lonely Men: Southern Federal Judges and School Desegregation* (University of Illinois Press 1971).

dispassionate defenders of the rule of law, protectors of minority and individual rights, and honest brokers in public and private disputes. That is the theory, at any rate.

Giving the least democratic branch of government such important responsibilities and exempting them from routine democratic oversight seems like a dangerous miscalculation, one that could invite judges to become tyrannical Platonic Guardians.

Alexander Hamilton thought such a scenario inconceivable. In *The Federalist* No. 78, he marked the judicial department as the least dangerous branch of government, and promised that judges never would – and never could – threaten individual liberties or become an oppressive political force independent of the other two branches.

Hamilton noted that judges have neither sword nor purse, nor force, nor will. Without a natural political constituency or a democratic power base, American judges have no independent coercive power. They must rely on the legislature for their budgets, and the executive to enforce their decisions.[46]

Judicial power ultimately depends on judges' perceived authority. Judges must rely on reason and persuasion to convince others to accept their rulings voluntarily, on the strength of their logic, judgment, and written opinions, popular respect for law, and public esteem for judicial integrity.

The greatest danger facing the judicial branch, Hamilton and Madison agreed, is not that the courts will grow oppressive, but that they will remain forever too weak to defend the rule of law and protect individual rights against willful states, powerful elites, and hostile majorities.

Although federal judges lack a popular mandate and independent coercive power, the U.S. Constitution formally establishes the judiciary as a coequal and independent branch of government.[47] Judges jealously guard their self-proclaimed authority to declare what the law is, and over the long term this has given U.S. judges considerable political influence. As de Tocqueville observed, few political questions arise in the United States that do not quickly turn into lawsuits. Judges seemingly decide political issues by accident, but by an accident that is repeated every day.

Perhaps the most important check on judicial authority is self-restraint. Judicial restraint begins with judges' pragmatic awareness of their personal

---

[46] The Constitution prohibits Congress from cutting judges' salaries, but this protection is not all that it seems to be. Congress is not required to increase judicial salaries, and has often pointedly withheld pay raises for judges to signal its displeasure with judicial rulings. Moreover, Congress can lower the starting salaries of newly appointed judges, cut the operational budgets of the federal courts, refuse to confirm judicial nominees, limit the jurisdiction of federal courts, and abolish or restructure the lower federal courts.

[47] Although nominally a coequal branch of the government, the federal judiciary receives less than 1 percent of the federal budget – about $7 billion – less than one-tenth the amount granted to the U.S. Department of Education each year. According to Chief Justice John Roberts, "For each citizen's tax dollar, only two-tenths of one penny go toward funding the entire third branch of government."

and institutional vulnerabilities. This institutional humility is reinforced by professional education and training that instill in judges an ethos of political neutrality and respect for law.[48]

Although judges are partially insulated from politics, they remain vulnerable to political passions and pressures, and are as prone as anyone to being swept up in the temper of the moment. Even in mature rule of law systems, judges can be stampeded into making bad decisions and perpetuating injustices.[49] In the long run, however, the courts' privileged position above the day-to-day political fray gives judges space for dispassionate reflection, repeated chances to revisit issues, and the ability to push – eventually – for the calm correction of past mistakes.

Aside from defending the rule of law and protecting minority rights, judges are expected to serve as honest brokers in all manner of public and private disputes. Madison saw the federal judiciary as the natural arbiter of government power and an indispensable intermediary in disputes between the federal government and the states. He expected judges to serve as a cooling, learned check on political passions, and to be dispassionate referees in private quarrels in which the state has no direct interest. De Tocqueville called judges and lawyers America's aristocracy, because they bring reason, education, experience, enlightenment, professionalism, judgment, moderation, and stability – in other words, a measure of excellence – to an otherwise anarchic political system.

An effective rule of law system also helps to keep the peace by ritualizing and pacifying conflict. People do not need to resort to violent self-help to defend their interests; they lawyer up and sue. In a rule of law system, people not only demand fairness and justice from the courts, they expect it. It is almost a cliché for aggrieved Americans to say that all they really want is their day in court, and a chance to plead their case to a judge or jury.

Although courts should strive to be apolitical, there is ample room for democratic checks and balances without violating the essential integrity of the rule of law. There is no inherent requirement that judges must be trained legal professionals, and the judiciary can be broadly defined to include juries. Athens had a rule of law system without professional lawyers or judges; judges were simply jurors selected at random from the jury, whose job was to make sure that everyone followed the rules. In the United States, until recently, many American jurisdictions did not require justices of the peace or other inferior judges to be lawyers, and there is still no requirement that Supreme Court Justices must be lawyers or have any legal or judicial experience. Japan reserves several positions on its supreme court for justices with nonjudicial backgrounds, including

---

[48] Justice Hugo Black took the idea of political neutrality to heart. After becoming a Supreme Court Justice, Black stopped voting in state and federal elections.

[49] Among the leading examples: *Dred Scott v. Sandford*, 60 U.S. 292 (1857); *Plessy v. Ferguson*, 163 U.S. 537 (1896); *Korematsu v. United States*, 323 U.S. 214 (1944); *District of Columbia v. Heller*, 554 U.S. 570 (2008); and *McDonald v. Chicago*, 561 U.S. 3025 (2010).

leading academics, diplomats and artists. More controversially, judges in most U.S. states, as well as in Japan and a few other countries, are either elected or subject to regular post-appointment public reviews.

In the United States, juries provide an important democratic counterweight to judges. In countries that do not have juries, lay judges sometimes serve as a check on professional judges, whether they sit in mixed panels[50] or independently.[51] Japan and the UK are among the countries that use both juries and lay judges in different courts.

Problems

Establishing the rule of law requires considerable time and effort. It is not a plug-and-play system that can be easily transferred from one country to another. Japan proved the exception during the Meiji era in the mid-nineteenth century, when it imported a largely prefabricated legal system, consisting of institutions, codes, and procedures borrowed whole from Britain, France, Germany, and the United States.[52] As a rule, however, building an effective rule of law system takes time, political will, and self-restraint on the part of ruling elites used to having their own way. It requires the creation of robust legal institutions, a professional legal class, an independent judiciary, and appropriate popular habits and expectations about law and justice. This is an accretive process that can take generations.

Some developing countries attempt to hasten the process by sending their aspiring lawyers and judges to established rule of law countries for formal legal education and training. This was a common practice during the nineteenth and twentieth centuries, when large numbers of students from colonial territories and newly independent states enrolled in law schools throughout Europe and North America. As a result, when the colonial system collapsed after World War II, many emerging countries in Africa and Asia already had in place a highly trained professional legal corps.

The practice was effective enough that in some troubled countries, such as Zimbabwe and Nigeria, the courts have been among the last redoubts of professional integrity in otherwise thoroughly corrupt regimes. But a handful of

---

[50] Italy uses mixed panels of lay and professional judges in some criminal trials, including the recent Amanda Knox trial. Mixed panels are also common in Central and Eastern European countries.

[51] In the lay magistrates courts in England and Wales, panels of three lay judges decide cases. They receive legal guidance from professional clerks, who are court administrators and take no formal part in the court's deliberations or judgments. Del Dickson, "The Selection and Appointment of Magistrates in England and Wales," 23 *University of Toledo Law Review* 697 (1992).

[52] In 1929–1930, China followed Japan's lead and adopted Western codes in an effort to escape foreign domination and the humiliating unequal treaties, which were justified on the grounds that Western powers and Japan considered China to be a lawless country. These codes were rarely enforced, however, and served as a façade to hide China's continued use of traditional Confucian social controls.

honest lawyers and judges cannot stand alone indefinitely against a tide of factional conflict and systemic corruption; the rule of law does not impose itself so much as insinuate itself in developing countries.

Foreign-trained lawyers and judges have helped institutionalize the rule of law in South Africa and Tanzania, and to a lesser extent in Kenya, Pakistan, and Indonesia. More recently, some of these countries have begun to establish their own domestic legal education programs designed to consolidate the rule of law at home and in neighboring states.

In institutionalized democracies, endemic corruption is less of a problem than in the developing world, but other problems, such as economic inequalities, distort their legal systems. In the United States, the best predictor of who will win a lawsuit is not the party with the facts, law, or justice on their side, but the party with the most resources to pour into the case.[53]

There are ways to limit the undue influence of wealth on the legal process. The right to free and effective counsel for indigents in criminal cases, a contingency fee system in civil cases, class-action lawsuits, transparent discovery procedures, a diverse professional judiciary, broadly representative and independent juries, and some combination of private and public legal aid are some of the ways that rule of law systems can level the playing field and encourage equal access to, and equal justice from, the courts.

Finally, some argue that the rule of law is an illusion. Anacharsis argued that laws are like spiders' webs – they catch the poor and weak, but allow the rich and powerful to fly right through.[54] Karl Marx went further, claiming that the rich and powerful are the spiders that spin the webs. He warned that the rule of law might seem fair and impartial, but the reality is that law is an instrument by which the dominant class imposes its will on society.

An Open, Fair, and Competitive Electoral System

According to Chinese tradition, it is bad luck to name a baby for at least a month after its birth. The custom began because high infant mortality rates led parents to avoid investing too much hope in a newborn's prospects, until the situation stabilized and its chances for survival improved.

Young democracies suffer from similarly high mortality rates, and cannot be considered safely institutionalized until there have been at least three consecutive peaceful and legal rotations of power between the party in charge and the opposition. At that point, a democracy's prospects for survival brighten considerably. The transition from fragile young democracy to mature institutionalized

---

[53] Wealth is always an advantage for the accused in criminal cases, but this advantage is partly offset by the right to appointed counsel, especially in jurisdictions where public defenders offices are institutionalized and relatively well financed.

[54] Plutarch, *Greek Lives*.

democracy is difficult, and one of the most daunting tasks is to create an open, fair, and competitive electoral system.

One problem that plagues young democracies is that the first party to gain power refuses to give it up when the time comes. This has been a persistent pattern in Africa, where liberation movements and founding political parties take power, often with the best of intentions, only to succumb to a combination of hubris and corruption. They begin to believe that they are indispensable to the country's survival, or grow accustomed to the trappings of power, and refuse to leave office, even when they lose their popular mandate. Many of these regimes continue to hold elections, but allow opposition parties no real chance to win.

Sham elections are a defining characteristic of illiberal democracy. Governments use any number of tricks to rig the results in favor of the ruling party. The state or ruling party often controls all important media outlets, or at least successfully muzzles the free press. Ballot boxes sometimes arrive at polling centers pre-marked. Government agents intimidate people into voting for the incumbent or not voting at all.

Perhaps most worrying, because it happens behind closed doors and out of the public eye, is that the vote-counting process is rigged, with the results predetermined. There is a saying, commonly attributed to Soviet leader Josef Stalin, that it does not matter who votes; all that matters is who counts the votes.

Mature democracies have their own problems maintaining a fair and competitive electoral system. Among the most serious difficulties are the corrupting influence of money, the advantages of incumbency, uncompetitive elections, and low turnover rates among elected officials.

Keeping a political system fair and competitive requires a level playing field, but two groups have particular advantages in mature democracies: wealthy (or well-financed) candidates, and incumbents. Both distort the electoral process and inhibit political competition. The former group has the resources to buy, rent, or influence the media, political elites, interest groups, government officials, party leaders, campaign advisors, consultants, pollsters, lawyers, and other assorted political fixers. Incumbents have significant advantages in soliciting campaign contributions, attracting media attention, writing self-interested election laws, and accessing public resources to pursue their personal agendas. And of course these two groups are not mutually exclusive.

Electoral systems in established democracies tend to grow less competitive over time, in part because of redistricting problems. Redistricting is intended to compensate for population shifts, by periodically rebalancing electoral districts. But the process is prone to ossify or become overly politicized. If little or no redistricting is done, demographic shifts can significantly distort voter strength over time, favoring lightly populated rural districts and penalizing urban voters. Another problem is that reapportionment and redistricting can become highly politicized, allowing a dominant political party to redraw district lines in its own favor.

In order to maintain a fair and competitive electoral system, democracies need to develop effective policies in these critical areas:

1. Guarantee near-universal adult suffrage and open contestation for offices.
2. Ensure broad association rights to organize political parties and interest groups.
3. Respect the principle of one person, one vote in at least one legislative house and for chief executives.
4. Limit partisan influence in the reapportionment and redistricting process.
5. Regulate political campaign financing by establishing reasonable limits on contributions and spending, and by requiring transparency with respect to donations and expenditures.
6. Provide sufficient trained and impartial officials to monitor and enforce election rules.
7. Develop a mechanism to ensure the prompt and peaceful transfer of power after elections.

A Professional Civil Service

Modern nation-states are too large and complex to put every decision to the people, or even to their elected representatives. Whether liberal or free, all democracies rely on professional civil administrators to do much of the day-to-day work of government.

Civil servants are career government employees who plan for and execute the will of the people. When they do good work we call them public servants, when they annoy us we call them bureaucrats.

Despite its dire reputation, a bureaucracy is only a human machine for communal work.[55] Its clockworks are rarely democratic, however; even in democratic regimes bureaucracies are invariably hierarchical. Bureaucrats are civil servants, and servants follow orders.[56]

Civil servants are akin to judges, in the sense that they are supposed to be dispassionate experts who follow the rules rather than their own personal preferences. So that they can do their jobs without undue political pressure, they are also customarily insulated from routine democratic accountability through tenure and salary protections.

Most liberal democrats reluctantly accept bureaucracy as another necessary evil of government. They do not like it, but in moments of candor they will grudgingly admit that it is an unavoidable part of modern life.

---

[55] Tom Wolfe, *The Right Stuff* (Farrar, Straus and Giroux 1979).
[56] It is rare, but possible, for a bureaucracy to be organized on democratic principles. The military is as hierarchical as any bureaucracy, but through the Civil War some U.S. military regiments elected their own officers. The same was true of anarchist militias during the Spanish Civil War.

Free democrats tend to react more strongly, and see bureaucracy as the antithesis of communitarian democracy. Rousseau rejected bureaucracy in the harshest terms, and forcefully railed against its establishment in any form. Bureaucracy corrupts democratic virtue, Rousseau warned, and he compared it to using mercenaries for national defense. Although Rousseau's views might seem unrealistic given the complex demands of modern society, he was equally severe in his assessment of modernity, and espoused a return to a simple, low-tech, highly localized lifestyle where bureaucracy would not be necessary.

Relying on a small army of professional administrators to run the government on a day-to-day basis threatens to undermine the core principles of people power. Civil servants have considerable collective influence, and they are not directly accountable to the electorate. This weakens democratic command and control, and encourages secrecy, cabals, and corruption.

The brilliant British duology, *Yes, Minister* and *Yes, Prime Minister*, satirizes the quiet war waged between politicians and civil servants to control the levers of power. Each side has its own distinct, and often conflicting, motives, methods, and goals.[57]

Elected politicians, including the books' protagonist, the Honorable Jim Hacker (Member of parliament, cabinet minister, and ultimately prime minister) are the people's elected representatives. Hacker sees himself as a political visionary, reformer, and statesman, with a popular mandate to implement his new ideas for the good of the country.

The civil service is a government within the government, often working in direct competition with elected politicians to shape public policy. The books' antagonist, Sir Humphrey Appleby, is the senior permanent secretary at the Department of Administrative Affairs – the bureaucrat in charge of the bureaucracy in charge of the bureaucracy.

Sir Humphrey is a civil servant who aspires to be a civil master. He is an administrative high-flyer, with an Oxford education, extensive professional training, considerable experience, the support of a vast network of like-minded colleagues, and a permanent government position with excellent pay, benefits, and guaranteed promotions. He views elected politicians as reckless amateurs, who pose a threat not only to good government but to civilization. It falls to Sir Humphrey to prevent Hacker from putting any of his half-baked schemes into effect. To that end, Sir Humphrey obfuscates, procrastinates, misdirects, dissembles, and does whatever is necessary, within the peculiar ethics of the civil service, to stymie his political master. Hacker looks to Sir Humphrey and the civil service for support and advice, not fully realizing that they are more interested in thwarting him than helping him. It is grist for two wry and insightful books.

[57] Antony Jay and Jonathan Lynn, *The Complete Yes Minister* (1984), and *The Complete Yes Prime Minister* (1988).

Three potentially serious problems associated with bureaucracy are red tape, corruption, and an inescapable iron cage. We will discuss each in turn.

Red Tape

Red tape is the mass of authoritative rules that define what government can and cannot do, and how. It is what most people think of when they think of bureaucracy: the inscrutable tangle of regulations that serve no apparent purpose except to make government more complex, inaccessible, inefficient, inflexible, inscrutable, and expensive than it should be.

In theory, red tape ensures that civil servants follow the rules, rather than their own personal preferences. But regulations often take on a life of their own, to make government slow, unresponsive, opaque, and frustrating. Whereas most bureaucracies develop informal practices to limit the undesirable effects of red tape, these shortcuts can defeat the point of holding civil servants to a rulebook in the first place. It is revealing that when public employees have job grievances, rather than going on strike they often choose to "work to rule," stopping government dead in its tracks simply by following regulations to the letter.

Sidebar 14: The Story of Red Tape[58]

Red tape originated in sixteenth-century Spain, when the government first used bright red ribbon to bind critical government documents requiring the Council of State's immediate attention. Red symbolized royal power and wealth (the dye was exorbitantly expensive). Routine administrative dossiers, in contrast, were bound with plain cloth ribbon.

Great Britain quickly adopted the practice of using red tape to mark important government documents. King Henry VIII sent Pope Clement VII eighty petitions to annul his marriage to Spanish-born Catherine of Aragon, all wrapped in bright red ribbon. Royal judges picked up on the idea, and used red tape to bind important legal documents. Author Charles Dickens is credited with the first modern use of the phrase in *David Copperfield*:

Britannia, that unfortunate female, is always before me, like a trussed fowl: skewered through and through with office-pens, and bound hand and foot with red tape.[59]

In the United States, Civil War veterans' records were bound with a red tape that made the files hard to open, sealing its dubious reputation for making life unnecessarily difficult.

---

[58] Herbert Kaufman, *Red Tape: Its Origins, Uses, and Abuses* (Brookings Institution Press 1977); John Herbert McCutcheon Craig, *A History of Red Tape: An Account of the Origins and Development of the Civil Service* (Macdonald & Evans 1955).

[59] Charles Dickens, *David Copperfield* ch.43 (Bradbury & Evans 1850).

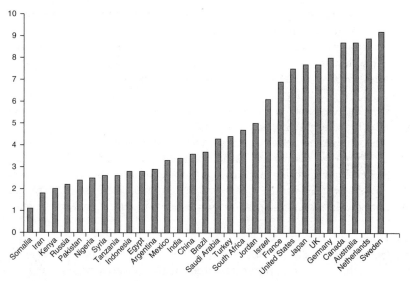

FIGURE 10.2 Corruption index for selected countries. Adapted from Transparency International, retrieved from *http://media.transparency.org/imaps/cpi2009/* (higher scores indicate less corruption).

Corruption

Corruption in the civil service can be more damaging than corruption among elected officials. Civil servants are permanent employees with considerable day-to-day authority and privileged access to government information and resources. They are powerful, well organized, and enjoy job and pay protections that make them difficult to remove absent serious misconduct.[60] Because they are not subject to routine democratic oversight, and usually work quietly out of the public eye, bad behavior can be difficult to discover and remedy. This creates a potentially fertile environment for entrenched, institutionalized corruption (Figure 10.2).

Emerging democracies can limit the damage by providing professional training programs to promote an ethos of personal ethics and self-restraint. If a country cannot offer adequate training for its civil servants, it should consider foreign education and exchange programs.

Another priority is bureaucratic transparency. Departments should be required to make – or at least explain – their decisions in public. It is one thing for agency heads to file obscure reports that no one will ever read; it is quite another to require them to submit to regular public questioning and independent audits. Making agency data, deliberations, and decision making readily accessible exposes government agencies to healthy public scrutiny. Ensuring open and competitive bidding for government contracts, protecting whistle-blowers,

---

[60] There is an apocryphal quote, attributed to American General George S. Patton, that civil servants are like broken cannons – they won't work and you can't fire them.

and regulating the revolving door between government and the private sector all encourage greater institutional transparency and integrity.

Civil servants inevitably face pressure to bend to the will of politicians, political majorities, and powerful special interests. They need tangible support, beyond professional and ethical training, to insulate them from undue political interference. Although salary and tenure guarantees are problematic in some respects, they are essential to insulate government workers from corrupting external influences, despite the acknowledged risks.

Finally, the single most effective measure to combat bureaucratic corruption might be as simple as decent pay. Much of the government corruption that exists in the developing world can be traced to unreasonably low compensation for public employees. Government workers are tempted, and in some instances virtually compelled, to seek illicit salary supplements just to make ends meet.

The Iron Cage

German sociologist Max Weber warned that bureaucracy is a Judas goat leading Western civilization into a trap that will ultimately destroy not just democracy but rational society. Weber's doomsday scenario is probably just social science fiction, but it is still worth considering, if only as a cautionary fable.

Weber notes that in a democracy, the many determine society's ultimate values. The government creates laws and policies that reflect those values, and civil servants faithfully execute their orders. As societies develop, however, the problems they face become increasingly complex, and require correspondingly more specialized expertise to find effective solutions. This leads to a growing dependence on experts, which marks the beginning of the end for democratic governance.

As social problems continue to multiply in scope and scale, professional politicians eventually lose their ability to govern, and gradually cede authority to the bureaucracy. Technocrats become more powerful, but soon find themselves increasingly isolated in ever-narrower subfields. At some point knowledge becomes hopelessly fragmented, and eventually even the experts lose the ability to shape public policy in a rational, holistic way.

Government responds by getting bigger and more powerful, but less effective. Like the sorcerer's apprentice, officials lose control of the situation as government and society become unmanageable. Regulations grow more prolix, burdensome, incomprehensible, and arbitrary. Government workers push out work they do not understand, according to rules they do not understand, to solve problems they do not understand. A rudderless, inertial bureaucracy takes over, trapping society in a despotic organizational nightmare with no clear exit. Or as Weber put it, an inescapable iron cage of our own making.[61]

Weber thought this to be an unavoidable consequence of modernity. Although his conclusion seems unduly grim and deterministic, if you are not at all worried about the possibility of something like this happening, there might be something wrong with you.

---

[61] This scenario was the theme of Terry Gilliam's tar-black comedy, *Brazil*.

Government Transparency

Our city is thrown open to the world. ... [W]e never expel a foreigner and prevent him from seeing or learning anything of which the secret, if revealed to an enemy, might profit him. We rely not upon management or trickery, but upon our own hearts and hands.[62]

– Pericles

When Americans know things, it just leads to trouble.[63]

– Stephen Colbert

Sunshine is not only the best disinfectant; it also makes the best reading light. The free flow of information in an open society provides citizens with the intelligence they need to make informed decisions, and exposes incompetence, corruption, conspiracies, and cabals. This is why all healthy democracies share the view that government transparency is (almost) always preferable to secrecy.[64]

For a variety of reasons both good and bad, government officials do not always want the public to know what they are up to. Knowledge is power, and whoever controls the former will eventually control the latter. This is why secrecy is the cornerstone of authoritarian rule: it empowers the state and privileged insiders to the exclusion of everyone else.

---

[62] Thucidides, *Pericles' Funeral Oration.*

[63] Stephen Colbert, *The Colbert Report,* Oct. 27, 2010.

[64] The only exceptions to the rule of disclosure involve a handful of compelling – and temporary – circumstances where secrecy is necessary to serve a vital state interest, such as diplomatic negotiations, or troop movements during military operations. In such cases, there is a high risk of grievous and irreparable harm from disclosure that might justify a narrow, temporary injunction against the publication of especially sensitive information. But even these limited exceptions are susceptible to abuse. In many instances, following government claims of irreparable harm to national security should information be disclosed, later revelations through Freedom of Information Act requests or unauthorized leaks reveal that classified information was often kept secret not to protect lives or property, but to protect government officials from embarrassment, government from possible legal liability, or because secrecy was inertial and the information was classified for no real reason at all.

The litigation that gave birth to the state secrets doctrine, *United States v. Reynolds,* 345 U.S. 1 (1953), is a case in point. After the 1948 crash of a B-29 Superfortress bomber, killing all aboard, the widows of three crew members sought access to the crash reports for their lawsuit against the government. The federal courts refused to allow the widows to read the reports, based the government's unsupported claim that the documents contained secret information that might threaten national security. More than fifty years later, a Freedom of Information Act filing revealed that the government's national security claim was phony, and that officials only wanted to cover up evidence of shoddy maintenance and other facts indicating that the plane was in poor mechanical condition prior the crash.

The United Kingdom has the highly restrictive State Secrets Act, giving the government broad powers to censor information and prevent the publication of books and other materials that the government deems a potential threat to national security. Such a law would be unconstitutional in the United States.

In democracies, knowledge is diffused throughout society. No one controls it, or perhaps more accurately, everyone does. Everyone has the fundamental right to gather and disseminate information, and the public has the right to know whatever individual privacy rights or fundamental legal privileges do not protect. The free flow of information promotes liberty, freedom, inclusion, equality, and transparency, and it also strengthens public confidence in government.

In America, the public's right to know dates from colonial days. A free press has been considered a fundamental right since *Zenger's Case*.[65] Other related rights, including free speech and the right to a public trial, are even older. In colonial New England, the town meeting system was premised on open government and the free flow of information. The Founders' obsession with establishing a national postal system was rooted in their desire to facilitate the uninhibited exchange of ideas.

Today, modern sunshine laws, such as the federal Freedom of Information Act and California's Brown Act encourage open government and make it difficult for officials to make backroom deals or obscure how policy decisions are made.[66] Comprehensive campaign reporting requirements, notably the Federal Election Campaign Act of 1974, open the books on election financing.

The most important, and most dangerous, claimed exception to the rule of government transparency in the United States is national security. The final arbiter in these cases is the Supreme Court. In balancing the public's right to know against claimed national security interests, the Court's record has been decidedly mixed. In most cases, the Court quietly defers to executive judgment, as happened in 1953, when the justices created the state secrets doctrine in *United States v. Reynolds*.[67] Occasionally, however, the Court has rejected government attempts to suppress allegedly sensitive information, as it did in the *Pentagon Papers* case.[68]

---

[65] John Peter Zenger was a New York newspaper publisher who was arrested and charged with seditious libel in 1734. He had published articles critical of William Cosby, the corrupt royal governor of New York, and refused to reveal the authors' names to British authorities. In seditious libel cases, the truth is not a defense, and the judge in the case, Chief Justice Delancey, assumed that the trial would result in a quick conviction. Noted Philadelphia lawyer Andrew Hamilton defended Zenger, urging the jury to ignore the judge's instructions and acquit Zenger in the name of liberty and freedom of the press. The jury agreed and quickly acquitted Zenger. The case emboldened American publishers to print more articles critical of government officials, and solidified American opinion about the importance of a free press. For a first-hand account of the case, see Andrew Hamilton, *A Brief Narrative of the Case and Tryal of John Peter Zenger* (1736). Livingston Rutherford, *John Peter Zenger; His Press, His Trial, and a Bibliography of Zenger Imprints... Also a Reprint of the First Edition of the Trial* (Dodd, Mead & Co. 1904).

[66] The fact that General Electric raked in $14.2 billion in profits in 2010, and yet paid no corporate taxes, despite making a $5.1 billion profit from its U.S. operations, was a huge scandal at the time, and a political embarrassment for G.E. But the damage would have been far worse had no one known about it except for General Electric and a few complicit government officials. Retrieved from http://www.nytimes.com/2011/03/25/business/economy/25tax.html?_r=2&hp.

[67] *United States v. Reynolds*, 345 U.S. 1 (1953). Cf. footnote 64.

[68] *New York Times v. United States*, 403 U.S. 713 (1971).

Sidebar 15: I've Got a Secret[69]

The Supreme Court's traditional deference to the executive and legislative branches on national security issues sometimes causes the justices to make strange legal contortions to avoid ordering the government to disclose allegedly sensitive information.

In 2013, the Supreme Court ruled 5–4 that no one had standing to challenge the constitutionality of a top-secret federal anti-terror surveillance program because, as it is a secret program, no one could prove that they were specifically targeted or had suffered any specific damages.[70]

Justice Samuel Alito, writing for the majority, explained that because the plaintiffs "have no actual knowledge of the government's targeted practices," they could only speculate about whether their rights were violated, which fails to meet the Constitution's case or controversy requirement. Alito admitted, with uncommon frankness, that the Court's decision was to prevent judges from "usurping the powers of the political branches" in national security matters.

One of the losing parties, Peter Godwin of the PEN American Center, complained that "in order to challenge the legality of the program ... you have to show that you're being monitored. You can't show this, of course, because the program is a secret." The ACLU's Jameel Jaffer added that the Court's decision "insulates the statute from meaningful judicial review, and leaves Americans' privacy rights to the mercy of the political branches."

At a minimum, government transparency means guaranteeing the uninhibited flow of information, not only through effective speech and press rights, but also by ensuring that all public records are preserved and made readily available to the public in a timely manner.[71] Thomas Jefferson's idea for the Library of Congress reflected a related but even more ambitious goal – that the government should serve as an open repository of all the world's knowledge. Today, the Library of Congress, National Archives, hundreds of official Federal Repositories scattered across the country, and countless government Web sites give Americans unparalleled access to comprehensive official information on almost any subject.

---

[69] Excerpted and adapted from David Savage, "Supreme Court Rules Out Secret Surveillance Lawsuits," *Los Angeles Times*, February 26, 2013.

[70] *Clapper v. Amnesty International*, 133 S.Ct. 1138 (2013).

[71] In 2010, a major scandal hit the small blue-collar city of Bell, California. City officials had for years managed to keep their salaries secret, and when reporters Ruben Vives and Jeff Gottlieb of the *Los Angeles Times* investigated, they discovered that Bell officials were among the highest paid city officials in the country. The mayor, Robert Rizzo, had a base salary of $1.5 million to govern a city of 38,000 people. City officials had also quietly awarded themselves multimillion-dollar pensions, and had siphoned off nearly $7 million of additional city funds into their own pockets. The scandal led to new online reporting requirements for all California cities.

Other countries in Scandinavia and elsewhere appoint special government officials – ombudsmen – to serve as official watchdogs and guarantors of open and responsive government.

Since 2008, Mexico has undertaken ambitious reforms to make its notoriously opaque legal system more transparent. The government is trying to replace its secretive inquisitorial criminal justice system, in which trials are conducted mostly behind closed doors and out of public view, with a new adversarial system where cases are tried in open court.

Another way to promote government transparency is to subject government offices and officials to periodic public audits. In ancient Athens, public officials were routinely required to give a formal accounting of their actions while in office. Modern democracies might benefit from their example.[72]

The Internet has revolutionized government transparency, by making it possible for government records to be instantly and universally disseminated at little or no cost. Up-to-the-minute information about government business, lobbying activities, and campaign financing can now be made readily available to everyone with basic broadband access. The Internet has also led to the creation of alternative news media, as well as social media and other new avenues of public communication and comment, that have frustrated government efforts to restrict the free flow of information.[73]

A Secular State

Separating government from religion is necessary to build a healthy, stable, pluralistic democracy. Sectarian regimes are fundamentally incompatible with free or liberal democratic government, no matter how benign and inclusive the dominant religion claims to be.

A secular state does not mean a secular society. The United States is a highly religious society, but has a constitutionally mandated secular government.

---

[72] Athenian officials were routinely sued on leaving office, and required to give a formal public accounting in open court of their actions while in office.

[73] The technology to do this is readily available; all that is lacking is the political will to make it happen. Government data is often hidden in files stored in isolated locations with limited access. Some governments are quick to put public information online and make it readily available, but others resist transparency for various reasons. In many jurisdictions, even if public records are technically available for public inspection, they are often literally under lock and key. The Internet makes the cause of government secrecy significantly more difficult to maintain. The Net is a cheap, effective, and often anonymous way to disseminate information globally, and a host of would-be whistleblowers, leakers, bloggers, and reporters rely on the web to investigate and report government (mis)behavior. Two recent examples of massive leaks of sensitive government records include the WikiLeaks scandal, and the Edward Snowden affair, respectively involving the unauthorized disclosure of thousands of classified U.S. State Department and National Security Agency (NSA) documents. The effect of the Internet on government transparency is most obvious in authoritarian states and illiberal democracies – countries such as China and Iran – where massive government efforts to regulate the Internet and control the public flow of information have proved only partially effective.

Separating state and religion means that religion is a matter of private belief, not a public political force. Religious faith is a question of liberty, not freedom, and just as government cannot rightly interfere in matters of individual conscience, religion has no legitimate role to play in government.

There are three major theories regarding separation of church and state. John Locke argued for a wall between church and state, to protect the state from religious intolerance.[74] Roger Williams advocated a wall for the opposite reason – to protect the integrity of religion from state interference. James Madison favored a third view, that some reasonable state accommodation of religion might be permissible under strictly limited circumstances. The modern version of Madison's theory allows for limited state accommodation of religion, if and only if: (1) the law has a secular purpose; (2) it does not tend to establish, endorse, or favor any religion over another religion, or favor religion over nonreligious belief; and (3) it does not tend to compromise the state's secular responsibilities.[75]

Secular states take different approaches to separate religion from government. The United States and Turkey both have constitutionally mandated secular governments, but sharply disagree about what this means.

The United States vacillates between Locke's wall theory and Madison's principle of limited accommodation. The former defines the Constitution's Establishment Clause broadly to prohibit any step toward state endorsement of a religious belief. The latter approach argues that official acknowledgement of the country's religious traditions is permissible, and the Free Exercise Clause permits some limited accommodations of religious beliefs and practices.

The U.S. government offers religious organizations significant tax benefits as charitable organizations, but the government does not discriminate among religions and treats all religious charities in precisely the same way that it treats secular charities. Choosing to register as a tax-exempt charitable organization comes at some cost in terms of free speech rights: religious and secular charities are limited in their ability to participate in partisan political activities and lobbying or risk losing their tax-exempt status.[76]

There are some small but vocal groups of fundamentalist Christians who challenge America's constitutional secularism. They claim that the United States is a Christian nation, and that federal and state governments should

---

[74] In a letter to Richard Price on October 9, 1780, Benjamin Franklin wrote, "When a religion is good, I conceive it will support itself; and, when it does not support itself, and God does not take care to support it, so that its professors are obliged to call for the help of the civil power, it is a sign, I apprehend, of its being a bad one." Thomas S. Kidd, *God of Liberty: A Religious History of the American Revolution*, 169–170 (Basic Books 2012).

[75] Madison distanced himself from this position later in his life, and adopted Locke and Jefferson's position. As a member of the first Congress, Madison initially voted to appoint a congressional chaplain. He later changed his mind and decided that using federal money to support an official chaplain was clearly unconstitutional, but by then it was too late, and the congressional chaplain's office is still alive and well.

[76] Section 501 (c)(3) of the Internal Revenue Code.

favor Christian groups, promote Christian values, display Christian symbols in public places, offer direct public support to Christian organizations, and discriminate against non-Christian religious and secular groups.

Despite cyclical sectarian pressures and occasional government missteps, the United States has been remarkably successful in maintaining its constitutionally mandated secularism, and with few exceptions this has been done amicably. Because of the relatively clean separation between church and state, and strict government neutrality in matters of religious belief, America has largely avoided the sectarian conflicts that have plagued other countries. There is remarkably little tension among different religions, between religious and secular groups, or between the state and organized religions.

Turkey's secularism, in contrast, tends to validate Roger Williams's fear of a state that seeks to control and subsume religion. The aim of Turkey's secularism is not so much to confine matters of faith and religion to the private realm, but to keep religious beliefs and practices under strict state supervision and control. The Turkish government oversees all religious education, supervises all mosques, approves the content of weekly sermons, and pays all imams' wages. As a consequence, organized religion in Turkey is subservient to the state, rather than serving as an independent social force. [77]

Some secular states, including Turkey and France, limit religion by restricting individual demonstrations of religious faith in public spaces. Both countries bar individuals from wearing proscribed religious symbols, including crucifixes, stars of David, or hijabs, in schools and in other public buildings – restrictions that would be almost unthinkable in the United States.

In Germany, religious groups must apply to the state for official recognition as public corporations – roughly analogous to nonprofit charitable organizations in the United States. Although direct state subsidies to religious groups are no longer common in Germany, the government still collects "church taxes" from registered members of each recognized religion, then passes the money on to the appropriate religious organizations, minus an administrative fee. In 2011, the federal government collected $6.3 billion for the Roman Catholic Church, and a combined $5.5 billion for all Protestant churches. In addition, most German public schools offer religion courses, and although the state hires the instructors, the appropriate religious authorities must certify their fitness to teach.

[77] The situation has changed somewhat under Prime Minister Recep Tayyip Erdogan's moderate Islamist government. Unlike previous administrations, which strictly enforced Mustafa Kemal Ataturk's secularist ideology, Mr. Erdogan has actively promoted Islamic values in government, and strengthened the hand of religious forces in Turkish society. Mr. Erdogan's critics accuse him of dangerously blurring the line between mosque and state, undermining Turkish democracy, and increasing tensions between the country's secular and religious factions.

This illustrates another danger of placing religion under state supervision and control: policies and practices intended to ensure official secularism and state supervision of religious practices can be flipped, to allow religious authorities to guide government policy and the state to promote a preferred religion. When religion becomes an extension of government, it is often an open question whether the dog will wag its tail or the tail will wag its dog.

Germany protects individual belief under Article 4 of the Basic Law, but the federal constitution distinguishes between individual liberty of conscience and the collective right to organize and operate as a religion. Special laws deny official recognition or support for "cults," "sects," "psychic groups," or other "new religions," and forbid the public display of religious symbols associated with the Nazi Party, including the swastika and Celtic cross.

Three religions have had particular difficulties securing official approval from German authorities: Jehovah's Witnesses, Islam, and Scientology. For more than fifty years, the German government has refused to recognize Jehovah's Witnesses or allow the group to register as a public religious organization. Recently, Berlin and a few other local jurisdictions offered the Witnesses limited official recognition for the first time. Germany has also long refused to recognize Muslim congregations as public religious organizations, despite, or perhaps because of, the large numbers of Muslims who have immigrated to Germany since the 1960s. In a sign that German attitudes toward Islam might be shifting, three states moved to recognize Islam as an official religion by late 2013. Finally, the federal government has repeatedly ruled that the Church of Scientology is a commercial operation and cannot register as a religious corporation.

Elsewhere in Europe, the Austrian, Swiss, and Swedish governments also collect taxes on behalf of recognized religious organizations. Spain and Italy allow taxpayers to choose whether a portion of their taxes will go to a recognized religious organization or to other state-administered projects. Norway, Belgium, and Greece still directly subsidize officially recognized religions.[78]

In the United Kingdom, religious liberty is well protected, but like almost everything else is regulated by convention and parliament. The UK has two established churches, the Church of England (Anglican) and the Church of Scotland (Presbyterian).[79] Commencing with Henry VIII, the British monarch is the Supreme Governor of the Church of England; the Church of Scotland is formally independent. Convention prohibits British monarchs from marrying Catholics, and because of complex unwritten rules concerning senior state officials who profess nonconformist beliefs, politicians tread softly when it comes to publicizing their personal religious preferences. Former Prime Minister Tony Blair felt compelled to wait until he left office before officially converting to Catholicism in 2007. Despite these problems, Britain has a well-deserved reputation for ecclesiastical tolerance and secular governance. The two established churches have no real political power or ambition, and seem content to remain passive wards of the state.[80]

---

[78] *New York Times*, p. A5, October 7, 2012.

[79] Parliament disestablished the Church of Ireland in 1869, and the Church of Wales in 1914.

[80] Aldous Huxley mocked this British proclivity in *Brave New World*, with the character of the arch-community songster, a banal pop entertainer with superficial religious duties. It is technically a religious office, with all meaningful religious content removed – "Christianity without tears."

In the satirical political novel, *Yes Prime Minister*, the story of "The Bishop's Gambit" deals with Prime Minister Jim Hacker's appointment of a new bishop for Bury St. Edmunds. Hacker

In Latin America, Mexico is officially a secular state, although the government's efforts to put principle into practice have not always gone to plan. Until the mid-nineteenth century, the Catholic Church was intimately involved in domestic politics at all levels. This changed in 1859, when the government enacted the Ley Lerdo, authorizing the state to seize church property and abolish all monastic orders. In 1929, the dominant political party, the Institutional Revolutionary Party promulgated the Ley Calles, authorizing the state to seize all church-owned private property and shutter unregistered churches. The church has vigorously resisted these laws, and actively supports the main opposition party, the conservative National Action Party.

A Civilian State

In many developing countries, a politically engaged military is as dangerous to democratic government as a sectarian state; and just as the best way to avoid a sectarian government is to separate state and religion, the best way to avoid a martial state is to separate the military from politics. This means, at a minimum, asserting effective civilian command and control over all military, paramilitary, internal security, and law enforcement organizations.

A politicized military poses a triple threat to emerging democracies. First, it will short-circuit domestic democratization efforts. Second, it will distort government decision making and national budgets, to the detriment of long-term economic development. Third, it will use security concerns as an excuse to expand state power and limit individual liberties, subverting the idea of a limited, balanced, and accountable government.

The Roman Republic was justifiably paranoid about the potential danger that its own armies posed to its civilian government. During the republican era, all popular assemblies convened to discuss military matters (*comitia centuriata*), including the election of military leaders and declarations of war, were considered armies, and by law were required to convene outside the city limits.

Roman generals were not allowed to bring their troops into the Republic under any circumstances, under pain of death for everyone involved. In 49 BC, Julius Caesar willfully disobeyed the law and crossed the Rubicon River with his troops, intending to march on Rome. Caesar fully understood the significance of the moment, declaring, *alea iacta est* ("the die is cast"). His actions sparked a bloody civil war, and his victory marked the effective end of the Republic.

is shocked to discover that of the two candidates that the Church of England proposes, one is an atheist and the other is a disestablishmentarian. Arguing in favor of appointing the atheist, the prime minister's permanent secretary, Sir Humphrey Appleby, explains that theology does not matter to the Church of England, because the Church is a social organization, not a religious congregation. God's role in the Church is optional, but the Queen's role is essential. Sir Humphrey reassures Hacker by noting that Church leaders are careful to ensure a proper balance among bishops who believe in God and those who do not.

There are some plausible reasons why a developing country's armed forces might be tempted to intervene in domestic politics. Developing countries suffer from a multitude of problems, including political and economic instability, corruption, and violent factional conflict. In many cases, the military is the most – and sometimes the only – effective political institution available to deal with these difficulties. Moreover, military officers in many underdeveloped countries are better educated, more cosmopolitan, more experienced, more disciplined, and less corrupt than the civilian political class.

All of this might tempt military leaders to conclude that they are best qualified to run the country. Especially when civilian governments struggle to deal with the myriad problems that plague them, the military might feel emboldened to leave the barracks and seize control "for the good of the nation." During the 2013 Egyptian military coup that overthrew President Mohammed Morsi, one senior officer sought to justify military intervention by noting, "We are disciplined, and we have the weapons. ... That's what's on the market right now. Do you see any other solid institution on the scene?"[81] Although understandable at some level, military intervention is invariably a mistake.

At best, a military government might serve as a form of developmental dictatorship – enhancing security, imposing order, and making the trains run on time. But even in this best-case scenario, military intervention only results in a more efficiently oppressive authoritarian state.

Whatever the short-term benefits of military rule might be, it is counterproductive in the long run. For starters, military discipline and competence are often greatly exaggerated. Military leaders rarely want for confidence, but often lack the ability to solve complex political, economic, and social problems. Turning warriors into nation-builders is far more difficult than most military leaders imagine.

Moreover, military rule is inherently destabilizing. It stunts the development of civil society and undermines domestic democratization efforts. On occasion, military intervention is specifically and perhaps even sincerely intended to protect democratic rule, but these interventions rarely work, and they always have serious unintended consequences. Military rule is the antithesis of people power, and little good can come of it.

The most successful military-led democratization project began in Turkey in 1922, when Mustafa Kemal Ataturk and the Turkish National Army put the last remnants of the Ottoman Sultanate out of its misery and established the Turkish Republic. Although many of Ataturk's reforms were admirable – separating mosque and state, establishing a progressive educational system, emancipating women, and transforming the ruins of empire into a modern democratic nation-state – the negative side effects have been serious and enduring.

---

[81] Ben Hubbard, "Military Reasserts Its Allegiance to Its Privileges," *New York Times*, July 4, 2013.

More than eighty years later, the Turkish military remains the self-appointed guardian of Ataturk's legacy. The armed forces have intervened repeatedly in domestic politics, with coups in 1960, 1971, and 1980, and another intervention in 1997 to force moderate Islamist Prime Minister Necmettin Erbakan to resign (see Sidebar 16). Turkey's military has routinely banned Islamist political parties, barred individual candidates from seeking office, and vetoed legislation that the military considers unacceptable. In 2010, forty senior officers were arrested and charged with plotting yet another coup, under the code name of Sledgehammer. The military considers itself to be a progressive, modernizing, and democratizing force, but its net effect in terms of protecting and promoting republican government is debatable.

Military intervention is like a political stroke; the first one makes a second more likely. If the military leaves its barracks once, even if it promptly restores civilian rule, it is more likely to intervene a second time with less cause or restraint, setting up a destructive vacillation between civilian and military rule. In 2013, for the first time in its seventy-year history, Pakistan saw a civilian government serve out its full term and peacefully hand power to a rival civilian political party without an intervening military coup.

Sidebar 16: Destroying Democracy in Order to Save It (Part I): A Very Turkish Coup[82]

Between 1923 and 1990, Turkey suffered three military coups, in 1960, 1971, and 1980. The military justified each intervention by citing its role as the ultimate guardian of Turkish democracy and secularism.

Something different happened in 1997. Speaking to the American-Turkish Council at its annual convention in Washington, DC, senior Turkish General Cevik Bir told his audience:

In Turkey we have a marriage of Islam and democracy. ... The child of this marriage is secularism. Now this child gets sick from time to time. The Turkish Armed Forces is the doctor who saves the child. Depending on how sick the kid is, we administer the necessary medicine to make sure the child recuperates.

A few days later, General Bir and other top military officers moved against moderate Islamist Prime Minister Necmettin Erbakan. Unlike previous interventions, the generals did not dissolve parliament, suspend the constitution, or impose direct military rule. Instead, they forced Mr. Erbakan to sign a series of declarations designed to protect Turkey's secular democracy, including executive orders to abolish the *tarikats* (Sufi schools)

---

[82] Ugur Akinci, "Turkey and the US in 1997: Different Voices, Same Chord," *Hurriyet Daily News*, January 18, 1998. Retrieved from *http://www.hurriyetdailynews.com/turkey-and-the-us-in-1997different-voices-same-chord.aspx?pageID=438&n=turkey-and-the-us-in-1997different-voices-same-chord-1998-01-18*.

and other Islamist education centers, impose a headscarf ban at Turkish universities, and assert state control over media organizations that had criticized the military's practice of discharging overtly religious soldiers. The generals then forced Mr. Erbakan to resign, barred him from politics for five years, and abolished his political organization, the Welfare Party. The episode became known as the "silent coup," or "the first postmodern coup."

Mr. Erbakan died in 2011. In April 2012, General Bir and thirty other current and former senior officers were arrested and charged with organizing the 1997 intervention.

Relentless military interference in domestic politics thwarted democratization efforts in Latin America for more than a century after the region's independence from colonial rule. In Africa and Asia, highly politicized militaries continue to hobble democratization efforts in Pakistan, Burma, Nigeria, Egypt, and other countries where the armed forces are often the de facto fourth branch of government. The democracy that emerged from the Egyptian Arab Spring of 2012 lasted less than a year before being crushed in a coup, foreshadowing an uncertain future for Egyptian democracy.

The great irony is that in most developing countries the armed forces do little to protect the nation from external enemies; their main function is to repress their own people. Costa Rica's audacious answer to this problem was to abolish its national army in 1948, and it has been a stable and prosperous democracy ever since.

Costa Rica's solution has not caught on elsewhere. Other emerging democracies dismiss its success as unique and irreproducible, and continue to finance their platinum militaries with tin economies. Even Costa Rica's immediate neighbors stubbornly ignore its example, and have repeatedly welcomed military rule, in the false hope that martial law might lead to clean government, economic development, and progressive social reforms.

Western democracies are not immune from military interference in domestic politics. In the immediate aftermath of the American Revolution, Alexander Hamilton wanted to use the Continental Army to install George Washington as the country's supreme leader. Washington rejected Hamilton's idea and disbanded his army. Sometime later, when the Framers debated whether to establish a standing army, opponents feared that a permanent, institutionalized military would lead inexorably to tyranny. After much debate, the Framers left the issue unresolved, but adopted several important constitutional provisions to guarantee civilian command and control of all military forces, making the president commander in chief, imposing budgetary constraints on military expenditures (including a maximum two year military funding cycle), and instituting other formal and informal checks designed to nullify the military's political influence.

Despite America's long tradition of civilian command and control of all military and paramilitary forces, military personnel have played an important part in U.S. politics. Several retired generals have been elected president, including George Washington, Andrew Jackson, Ulysses S. Grant, and Dwight Eisenhower. Active-duty officers hold important government posts, especially those dealing with national security. Almost half of all CIA directors have been active-duty military officers. Most recently, General David Petraeus served as CIA director in 2011, although unlike some of his predecessors he resigned his commission immediately before taking office.[83] The current head of the National Security Agency (NSA) is Army General Keith Alexander. Each branch of the military, including the Coast Guard, operates its own stand-alone intelligence organization, and the Defense Intelligence Agency serves as the main inter-service spy agency, also under direct military control.

A long series of military conflicts since World War II has led to the gradual militarization of the national budget. Military spending now accounts for nearly 25 percent of all federal spending. The United States spends more on defense than the next thirteen countries combined. Most European countries spend less than 2 percent of their national budgets on defense. The U.S. military actively lobbies government on issues it considers crucial to its mission, from funding new weapons systems to exempting the armed forces from environmental regulations.

Despite these problems, there is an enduring consensus against military interference in domestic politics, and the principle of civilian command and control has never been seriously questioned. To its credit, the U.S. military has not shown any inclination to intervene in domestic politics beyond conventional lobbying efforts, and the possibility of a military coup remains inconceivable outside of novelists' imaginations.[84]

A Commonwealth

Democracy is not wedded to any specific economic system, although it tends to gravitate toward a limited number of readily compatible economic models. The first economic priority for any emerging democracy is growth; a country that cannot sustain economic development will not be democratic for long. But a democracy must do more than that – it must build a commonwealth.

---

[83] General Petraeus resigned as CIA director in November 2012, because of publicity about a personal sex scandal. General Michael Hayden is a more recent example of an active military officer who served in various national security posts, including director of the NSA from 1999–2002, and Director of the CIA from 2006–2009. General Hayden retired from active military duty in 2008.

[84] Among the best novels that center on hypothetical American military coups: Sinclair Lewis, *It Can't Happen Here* (1935); Fletcher Knebel and Charles W. Bailey II, *Seven Days In May* (1962); and Tom De Haven, *Top Secret USSA* (1987).

A commonwealth means that the economy benefits the many individually, and simultaneously serves the interests of the whole. A commonwealth encourages the pursuit of individual interest within the context of a shared enterprise – offering each person a stake in the economic system, backed by mutual promises of aid and support.

Some democratic societies take a deliberate approach to creating a commonwealth. In eighteenth-century America, the colonies of Virginia, Massachusetts, Pennsylvania, and Kentucky made explicit their promise of a commonwealth, and today they are still officially known as commonwealths, not states.

Despite some latter-day myths to the contrary, the American Founders were not laissez-faire capitalists. They saw government as an indispensable engine of economic growth, harnessed to serve the public good. Even Alexander Hamilton, the patron saint of New York financiers, pushed the federal government to take the lead in developing the national economy and building a commonwealth.[85]

From the beginning, federal and state governments helped create and manage the country's infrastructure – opening new lands, building new roads, bridges, and canals, and establishing a navy specifically designed to protect America's global economic interests.[86] Federal and state governments actively promoted a middle-class society by giving ordinary people the opportunity to stake a claim in the country, including millions of individual land grants in the western territories.

The idea of consciously promoting a middle-class commonwealth began to waver after the Civil War, as a new class of wealthy industrialists began to drive the national economy.[87] A new economic theory emerged, holding that the government should promote the interests of the richest Americans, with secondary benefits trickling down to the middle and lower classes. These two theories of economic development – whether to build the economy from the top down or the middle class outward – have been at the heart of all subsequent arguments about the proper role of government in shaping national economic policy.

Other developed democracies have focused more consistently on maintaining a broadly egalitarian economy. Northern European countries such as the Netherlands, Germany, Denmark, Norway, Sweden, and Finland have been particularly successful in this regard.

Commonwealths also exist, however tenuously, on an international scale. One modern attempt to build an international commonwealth is the Commonwealth of Nations, formerly known as the British Commonwealth and now often referred to simply as "the Commonwealth." The Commonwealth is a

---

[85] Alexander Hamilton, *The Federalist Papers* No. 11.

[86] Initially, the American navy was designed to protect American merchants and economic interests from rival European countries and Barbary pirates.

[87] De Tocqueville noted that the rough economic equality of a middle-class society was an essential condition of U.S. life, and one of the main reasons why U.S. democracy was successful.

loosely aligned league of fifty-four countries, most with historical ties to the old British Empire. It is less an economic commonwealth than an attempt to promote shared values, interests, and goals among its member states. It has been successful enough to attract applications from Francophone countries in Africa that have no historical ties to the United Kingdom, including Mozambique in 1995 and Rwanda in 2009. Perhaps the most positive contribution of the Commonwealth is that it has actively sought to support emerging democracies in Africa, Asia, Central America, and the Caribbean.

The most ambitious modern international commonwealth is the EU, formerly known as the European Commonwealth. The EU seeks to forge an ever-closer economic and political commonwealth on a continental scale. It has the advantage of having a core membership of mature democracies, and has had some notable successes in managing economic development, limiting economic inequalities, and stabilizing democracy in Spain, Portugal, and Greece.

The EU faces multiple challenges, including what to do with emerging democracies in central Europe, how to deal with longstanding rivalries among its members, how to reconcile its members' divergent economic and political interests, how to prop up the continent's weakest economies, and how to answer the thorny question of Turkey's place in Europe.

With these and other problems, the EU's fate remains unsettled. The alliance has always been premised on top-down bureaucratic rule making rather than organic, bottom-up democratic governance. It is a confederation of states, not people, and its primary responsibility is to protect state interests. Because the individual member-states, rather than the European people, empower and control Brussels, the central government has always been feeble, subject to the whims of its members, and detached from lives and concerns of ordinary Europeans. Despite its flaws and uncertain future, the EU represents the world's most ambitious attempt to build a stable, integrated international commonwealth

11

Three Misconceptions about Democratization

Political scientists are at our best explaining why what just happened was inevitable. We are less good at ex ante predictions, so most of us quickly learn to make vague oracular prophecies that will seem to come true no matter what.

In his article *Will Countries Become More Democratic?* Samuel Huntington was characteristically bolder than most. First, he asked an important question that still begs to be answered: which developing countries are most – or least – likely to democratize? He proved his place in the discipline's pantheon yet again, by proposing detailed predictive criteria and specifying which states were the best and worst bets. With the benefit of hindsight, Huntington's predictions proved to be hit or miss, but he went down swinging.

Here we briefly examine three common, but erroneous, claims that Huntington and other leading political scientists make about democratization.

CLAIM #1: POOR COUNTRIES WILL NOT BECOME DEMOCRATIC

Can poor countries become democratic? Two giants of political science, Huntington and Hannah Arendt, say no.

Arendt argued that democracy is a beautiful choice limited to relatively wealthy societies. Self-government requires surplus resources to support democratic institutions and processes. Poor countries, where people struggle to survive, cannot afford such luxury.

Huntington cited simple but compelling data to support his claim that poor countries will not become democratic. He found that only two of thirty-six low-income countries were democratic, and eighteen of twenty-four advanced industrial countries were stable democracies. Huntington hypothesized that states must first reach a certain level of economic prosperity, which he called the *transition zone*, before democracy becomes a realistic possibility.

The transition zone is critical, because the decisions that a country makes during this phase of development will tend to lock it onto either a democratic or authoritarian path for the long run. Focusing aid and attention on countries in the transition zone might decisively nudge them toward the democratic path. Showering foreign aid on poorer countries might be justifiable on humanitarian or geopolitical grounds, but pouring resources into countries such as Bangladesh or Niger in the hope of transforming them into stable democracies is wishful thinking.

A related view, widely held among political scientists and economists, is that the level of economic development necessary to reach the transition zone requires strong authoritarian leadership – a developmental dictatorship – to create the conditions necessary for sustained economic growth. Democracies are thought to be too inefficient, chaotic, and contentious to build a robust and sustainable economy; only a powerful and decisive central authority can provide the organization, discipline, resources, and will necessary to enable a fledgling economy to take off.

Is democracy a luxury reserved exclusively for economically privileged societies? Although poverty is the bane of developing countries, it does not necessarily preclude democratization. Ancient Athens was poor by modern standards, yet gave rise to one of history's greatest democracies. The European Dark Ages were defined by want, ignorance, and suffering, but served as the nursery for modern democratic institutions, including town meetings and juries. In the New World, the Iroquois confederacy thrived in a Stone Age economy. The original American colonies solidified their democratic traditions more than 200 years before they managed to forge a prosperous national economy. Iceland and Costa Rica were mired in poverty for centuries before they made the transition to republican government in the 1940s, and only afterward did their economies begin to take off.

Those who argue that economic development is a necessary precondition of democracy usually cite Africa as Exhibit A. After indigenous nationalist movements liberated the continent in the 1950s and 1960s, democracy struggled everywhere to take root. Although all African states now claim to be democratic, since 1950 there have only been a small handful of occasions when a ruling party has peacefully and promptly yielded power to an opposition party following free and fair elections.[1]

Much of the continent remains in seemingly permanent crisis, dominated by a motley assortment of authoritarian regimes, illiberal democracies, and

---

[1] Staffan Lindberg, *Democracy and Elections in Africa* (The Johns Hopkins University Press 2006). The peaceful transfer of power to an opposition party following an election has occurred at least once in Senegal, Zambia, Ghana, Kenya, Malawi, and South Africa. South Africa's peaceful transition from apartheid to an inclusive democracy was unexpected, but the real test for South Africa will come when the ANC loses an election, and must decide whether to keep power or yield to the opposition.

unstable liberal democracies. The region is plagued by extreme poverty, high unemployment, endemic corruption, tribalism, gross economic inequality, dire living conditions, brutal exploitation, political violence, insurgency, terrorism, militarism, civil war, and chronic underdevelopment. Half of the population lives on less than $1 a day, and even in relatively wealthy South Africa, nearly 40 percent of the population lives on less than $2 per day.

Yet if the African example proves anything, it gives the lie to the false hope of developmental dictatorships. Authoritarian governments have been standard issue in Africa since independence, with little to show for it. For more than fifty years, these regimes have utterly failed to improve the lot of ordinary Africans.

The good news is that Africa has indigenous democratic traditions that state-centered theorists often overlook. Before the colonial era, the Kikuyu – inhabitants of what later became Kenya – established the Gikuyu system, a village-based democratic government that prospered until the British dismantled it.[2]

In the modern era, traditional democratic decision making remains common at the village level, most notably among the Igbo of Nigeria, but also among the Ga (Ghana), Ashante (Ghana), Yoruba (West Africa), Abesheini (Kenya) and Kalahari (Southern Africa).[3] Even where kings, chiefs, tribal elders, or other traditional authoritarian leaders predominate there are proto-democratic, participatory, and consensual elements built into the system. The best known of these are the local public assemblies where residents gather in "village meetings under the big tree" to discuss and decide matters of common concern.[4]

South Africa's national democratization efforts have unexpectedly strengthened indigenous democratic tendencies.[5] Elsewhere, Benin, Botswana, Ghana, and Namibia have recently become conditional success stories, and to a lesser degree countries such as Ivory Coast, Kenya, Liberia, Nigeria, Rwanda, Senegal, Sierra Leone, Tanzania, and Uganda have made significant progress toward democratization. In much of Africa, however, democracy has failed to gain a secure foothold, hamstrung by the stubborn legacy of colonialism, authoritarian rule, institutionalized corruption, and kleptocratic elites.

Still, there is little evidence that poverty precludes democratization, nor is there any reason to believe that developmental dictatorship is the answer to

---

[2] Apollos O. Nwauwa, "Concepts of Democracy and Democratization in Africa Revisited," Paper presented at the Fourth Annual Kent State University Symposium on Democracy (Kent State University Press 2005).

[3] George B. Ayittey, *Indigenous African Institutions* (Transnational Publishers 1991). Many of these tribes are led by kings that have adopted various democratic practices and institutions, including representative parliaments and participatory village assemblies.

[4] Id. Mwakikagile, Godfrey *Africa and the West* (Nova Science Publishers 2000) at 33.

[5] J. Michael Williams, "Leading from Behind: Democratic Consolidation and the Chieftaincy in South Africa," 42 *The Journal of Modern African Studies* 113 (2004); and *Chieftaincy, the State, and Democracy* (Indiana University Press 2009). Maxwell Owusu, "Democracy and Africa – a View from the Village," 30 *The Journal of Modern African Studies* 369 (Sept. 1992).

Africa's problems. Poverty is not the disease that causes democracy to wither and die; it is merely a painful symptom of a constellation of other problems that constrain developing countries in Africa and elsewhere.

There is no reason why ordinary Africans must live in poverty. It is a wealthy continent in terms of its natural and human resources. The gross maldistribution of wealth is the real barrier to sustainable development and democratization. Extreme economic inequalities perpetuate class rule, and condemn the many to live in poverty and ignorance. The poor lack access to education and economic opportunities, and have no obvious way to escape their situation except crime, emigration, or death. The absence of a strong African middle class short-circuits economic and political development, reinforces the unacceptable status quo, and leaves society without an effective counterweight to state power and the ruling elite.

Democracy might require some minimal level of economic development. Free democracy, in particular, demands a significant investment of time and treasure, and might be an impractical choice for a society that is perpetually on the edge of starvation. But participatory democracy is more dependent on time than treasure, and people who live in traditional agrarian societies often have more free time than those who live in wealthy urbanized societies. Moreover, people who live in rural areas often form exceptionally close-knit communities out of necessity, because they depend on each other to survive far more than do people in industrial and postindustrial societies. If there is a threshold level of development necessary to sustain democracy, it would seem to be significantly lower than Huntington and Arendt assume.

Just as there is no inherent reason why poor countries cannot be democratic, there is nothing to suggest that democratic governments are incapable of creating sustained economic growth. The idea that it is necessary to suffer authoritarian rule in order to create a healthy national economy is a self-interested fable fostered by elites to justify their rule. The myth of developmental dictatorship exaggerates authoritarian virtues and underestimates the positive democratic qualities of initiative, responsibility, mutual support, optimism, and restless energy. Most importantly, it ignores democracy's proven ability to align self-interest and the common good, and promote the greatest good for the greatest number.

CLAIM #2: SOCIETIES WITHOUT DEMOCRATIC TRADITIONS
WILL NOT BECOME DEMOCRATIC

This is a common argument and an uncommonly silly one. The idea that a people with little or no experience with democratic government are incapable of building or maintaining a democracy is tautological nonsense. There are enough modern examples of countries with little or no prior democratic experience that have made a successful transition to refute this canard, including Japan,

South Korea, the Philippines, Mexico, Costa Rica, most of South America and the Caribbean, South Africa, Spain, Portugal, the Baltic Republics, and much of central Europe.

Nonetheless, this theory has lately been resurrected to reinforce conventional pessimism about the prospects for democracy in the Middle East. Although countries such as Tunisia, Morocco, Libya, Egypt, Iran, and Iraq all face daunting challenges, and their efforts to democratize might fail for any number of reasons, to write them off at square one merely because they somehow lack democratic DNA in their cultural genes is simplistic political determinism, if not simple prejudice.

CLAIM # 3: ISLAM IS FUNDAMENTALLY INCOMPATIBLE WITH DEMOCRACY.

Huntington singled out Islam as an irredeemably antidemocratic religion. Two lines of argument suggest that he is wrong.

First, Islam is not unique in its antidemocratic tendencies. All major religions have issues to work through before they can embrace democratic values. Islam is no exception, but it has sometimes been unfairly singled out on this count.

Most religions are based on divine wisdom received long ago. They are by nature conservative, dogmatic, and authoritarian, in part because this was how the world was organized until well into the modern era. And because religion revolves around revealed deific truth, it has a natural tendency to be intolerant of those who perceive a different truth.

Some of the most troubling characteristics cited to prove Islam's supposed incompatibility with democracy are not religious principles at all, but mutable cultural traditions. The status of women in the Muslim world is based far more on cultural norms than on Koranic text, and as these customs evolve, Muslim women are slowly gaining ground. Progress has been uneven, but the pace of reform will likely quicken as female literacy and educational levels rise, and a critical mass of Muslim women refuse to remain silent and submissive.

The tendency of Islamist regimes to conflate religious and secular crimes is appalling, but not unique. The Iranian practice of treating peaceful political dissent as a capital offense ("being at war against God," or *moharebeh* in Farsi) and executing nonviolent protesters as enemies of God (*mohareb*) is a generic form of brutal despotism masquerading as religious piety.

Such injustices are not peculiar to Islam; they are peculiar to theocracies. Confusing crimes against the state and crimes against religion was common practice in Europe for centuries, where the mildest criticism of political or religious leaders was considered both treason and blasphemy, and punished in the most gruesome ways imaginable.

Some critics concede that Islam might be compatible with democracy, but only if its adherents constitute a small minority in a diverse pluralistic democracy. Of course, the same can be said of any religion, or any secular faction for that matter. All factions are more inclined to mind their manners when they are vulnerable minorities in a pluralistic society, their options safely constrained by competing factions. Conversely, even the most reasonable, tolerant, and ecumenical religion can become a casual oppressor when it becomes part of a cohesive majority.

Religious discrimination against minority sects is often so pervasive and casual that the oppressors refuse to acknowledge it, and might not even perceive it. In the United States, some fundamentalist Christian groups aggressively promote government-funded religious displays, such as placing large Easter crosses on public lands. By custom, these monuments are prominently displayed on hilltops, visible for miles around. When these displays are challenged in court for violating the Establishment Clause, their defenders often resort to legal subterfuge to skirt constitutional requirements and preserve their unique privileges.

Christian groups and their allies suddenly declare an Easter cross to be a "war memorial," and deny the religious symbolism of the display. Or they might rig a phony sale of the small bits of land directly under the cross to a favored private party who has already vowed to preserve the religious display. The groups defending these crosses usually couch their claims in terms of religious liberty, but their sole concern is to promote their own religion over all others.

In one recent case involving a large cross planted on public land as a war memorial in California's Mojave Desert, Supreme Court Justice Antonin Scalia insisted during oral argument that the cross is not a Christian symbol, but a memorial to represent all war dead.[6] While interrogating the lawyer representing religious and secular groups challenging the cross's legality, Scalia stated that, "It's erected as a war memorial. I assume it is erected in honor of all of the war dead." The lawyer responded that he had visited many Jewish cemeteries and, "There is never a cross on a tombstone of a Jew." Scalia angrily shot back, "I don't think you can leap from that to the conclusion that the only war dead that that cross honors are the Christian war dead. I think that is an outrageous conclusion." The most significant aspect of this exchange is that Scalia, an educated man of reason and faith – Locke's ideal citizen – could not even conceive that people of other faiths might feel subordinated by state-sponsored

---

[6] *Salazar v. Buono*, 559 U.S. 700 (2010). In this case, the claim that the cross was originally erected as a war memorial was credible, although that did not necessarily resolve the underlying constitutional issues. Litigation began when the federal government refused to give a Buddhist group permission to place its own war memorial next to the Christian cross.

This case is distinguishable from the Easter Cross cases, where publicly funded crosses on public land suddenly become ersatz "war memorials" after litigation appears likely. For an example of this type of case, see *Jewish War Veterans v. City of San Diego*, 629 F.3d 1099 (2011).

sectarian displays that explicitly and exclusively promote the country's dominant religion.

Half way around the world, Israel is a shining example of a liberal democracy in the world's toughest neighborhood. It is at its best when it stays true to its roots as a pluralistic, secular democracy that respects the equal rights of all its citizens. It is less admirable when it acts as an ethnic Jewish state to promote Jewish interests over those of other groups,[7] and at its worst when it behaves as a sectarian state and systematically favors one orthodoxy over all other competing Jewish, Muslim, Christian, and secular interests.

Of course Islamist states such as Saudi Arabia and Iran are much worse in terms of systematic religious discrimination and oppression. Saudi Arabia officially prohibits the practice of any religion other than Islam, bars non-Muslims from visiting Mecca and other holy cities, and refuses to allow non-Muslims to be buried on Saudi soil. The government insists that 100 percent of its citizens are Muslim, and just in case anyone gets any ideas, apostasy, heresy, and witchcraft are all capital offenses. The Saudi government still executes individuals convicted of sorcery.[8] Iran treats religious dissent even more harshly than it punishes political dissent, especially when it comes to atheists, apostates, and those who belong to religious sects that authorities consider heretical, such as the Baha'i.

Once more, however, Islam is not the root cause of oppression in either Saudi Arabia or Iran. Religion is merely a convenient instrument by which one dominant faction seeks to eliminate its rivals, with the harshest treatment often reserved for competing Islamic factions. These two countries do not demonstrate the unique or inherent brutality of Islam; they are simply modern reminders of how dogmatic and despotic regimes have always treated nonconformists. Given the chance, elements within any religion will be sorely tempted to use the state to impose their will on the rest of society, through acts of symbolic and substantive domination.

The second line of argument regarding Islam and democracy is that there is room for cautious optimism about its potential to reconcile itself with

---

[7] As an officially Jewish state, Israel has taken extraordinary measures to ensure that Jews remain an unassailable majority within its borders. Yet the grand prize for this sort of strategic ethnic engineering goes to Burma, which recently enacted a law limiting Muslim families to two children, in an attempt to protect the majority Buddhist population from the country's rapidly growing Rohingya Muslim population, which currently accounts for just 4 percent of the country's population.

[8] Saudi Arabia beheaded Amina bint Abdel Halim Nassar in 2011, after she was convicted of witchcraft and sorcery. Ms. Nassar was accused of selling magic potions and spells, and was alleged to have kept books on magic in her home. In another recent sorcery case, Ali Hussain Sibat, a former TV host, was arrested and charged with sorcery in 2008. Convicted and sentenced to death in 2009, he remains in prison. See, Mohammed Jamjoom and Saad Abedine, "Saudi Woman Beheaded for 'Witchcraft and Sorcery,'" retrieved from *http://www.cnn.com/2011/12/13/world/meast/saudi-arabia-beheading*, Dec. 14, 2011.

democratic values. Islam has no single leader of the faith, no global hierarchy, and no dominant central institution that wields plenary power over all believers. Religious authority is decentralized, and the faithful are generally free to choose their own leaders. Some Islamic schools of thought, notably the Najaf School, actively seek to separate religion and politics, because they believe that politics inevitably corrupts religion.[9] These proto-democratic elements leave sufficient room to promote individual autonomy, reason, responsibility, choice, and diversity.

Islam has a long history of promoting education, reason, science, and toleration. The first word that God spoke to Mohammed was, "Read." During the Dark Ages, while European Christians were busy burning books, witches, and apostates, Muslim, Jewish, and Christian scholars worked side by side in the Islamic world to advance the frontiers of science, medicine, law, philosophy, and political theory. Great Muslim libraries preserved the classical knowledge that later made the European Renaissance possible.

Today, this traditional strain of liberal, enlightened Islam is under siege by violently intolerant Islamists. They might not realize it yet, but Islamist groups such as al Qaeda, Boko Haram, and al-Shabaab, who terrorize and murder innocent people in the name of Allah, have already lost the Islamic culture wars.

There are unmistakable signs of nascent liberalization in the Muslim world, if not the first stirrings of a full-blown Islamic Reformation. In Iran, there is a growing reformist belief that Shi'a Muslims can have an individual relationship with God, rather than having to rely on clerical intermediaries, with all the political consequences that implies.[10]

Turkey long ago proved that liberal democracy is possible in an observant Islamic society. Bangladesh, a self-proclaimed Islamic republic, recently announced its intention to transform itself gradually into a secular democracy. Bosnia, Indonesia, Kuwait, Lebanon, Malaysia, Morocco, Pakistan, Tunisia, and Zanzibar have all demonstrated considerable potential as emerging democracies.[11] Afghanistan, Algeria, Egypt, Iran, Iraq, Libya, the Palestinian Authority, and Syria all show more tentative early signs of democratization, although sustained progress has so far proved elusive.

---

[9] The Najaf School is a Shi'a sect centered in Iraq. The Qom School, a rival Iranian Shi'a sect, takes the opposing view; its adherents believe that establishing a "perfect" Islamist state on Earth will invite the second coming of the Mahdi, or Guided One – the Islamic redeemer who will rid the world of evil.

[10] Thomas Erdbrink, "Two Candidates Shake Up Iran's Presidential Race," *New York Times*, May 12, 2013. When announced presidential candidate Esfandiar Rahim Mashaei explicitly adhered to this view, Iranian clerics declared his views to be "deviant," and the Council of Guardians rejected his candidacy.

[11] Zanzibar is the Muslim-dominated part of Tanzania, where 90 percent of the population is Muslim.

Sidebar 17: Street Justice in Iran[12]

When some Iranian shoppers caught a pickpocket red-handed near Tehran University in March 2013, a small group of passers-by spontaneously assembled to decide what to do with him. Crime is a serious problem in Tehran, and residents feel increasingly frustrated and afraid. As the ad hoc jury of fifteen men debated the pickpocket's fate, a number of women hovered nearby, but did not try to intervene.

If the men decided to hand the suspect over to the police, he would probably be treated harshly. Two young muggers had recently been hanged from nearby construction cranes, their bodies left to dangle in the wind as a warning to others.

One juror acted as a prosecutor, and argued that criminals deserved to be treated harshly. Others urged restraint. The pickpocket begged to be released, claiming that he was only a poor man desperate to feed his family.

After a lengthy debate, the jury voted 10–5 to let him go. The majority saw the decision as an act of mercy, in the spirit of the Persian New Year (*Nowruz*), the country's most important public holiday.

The lucky pickpocket immediately ran off, while the jurors lingered to discuss what to do about the city's growing crime wave.

In Afghanistan, arguably the least promising test case for democracy in the Islamic world, there is tantalizing evidence of an emerging democratic culture. The difficulties Afghans face are formidable: economic underdevelopment, poverty, a feeble and thoroughly corrupt central authority,[13] terrible infrastructure, a dysfunctional educational system, high illiteracy rates, often willful ignorance and intolerance, a weak civil society, a decades-long civil war, warlordism, xenophobia and cultural isolationism, a war and poppy-based economy, a resurgent Taliban, and the often-brutal subjugation of women. Yet despite this disheartening litany of problems, many of the basic elements needed to build a democratic society are already in place. Afghanistan is a federal nation, with a longstanding tradition of local autonomy and community-based political participation. It has organic, indigenous democratic customs and institutions, such as the *loya jirga* (grand jirga) and the *wolesi jirga* (people's jirga) that can potentially serve as the foundation for greater citizen participation in government decision making. Despite the country's many problems, the idea of democracy in Afghanistan is perhaps not as far-fetched as conventional wisdom might suggest.

---

[12] Adapted from Ramin Mostaghim, "Tolstoy, the Equinox, and a Cry for Mercy in Iran," *Los Angeles Times*, March 17, 2013.

[13] The current Afghan president, Hamid Karzai, is sometimes mockingly called the Mayor of Kabul, owing to his inability to assert his authority outside the capital city.

There are other reasons to be guardedly optimistic about the ability of Islamic societies to democratize. There is genuine enthusiasm for democracy in many parts of the Muslim world. Turkey, Lebanon, and Indonesia all have relatively developed democratic traditions, and although these societies remain troubled in some respects, they are useful role models for other Islamic states struggling to make the transition from authoritarianism to democracy. Countries such as Tunisia and Morocco show tantalizing signs of democratization. Finally, expatriate Muslim populations currently thriving in Western democracies seem ready and willing to encourage democratization efforts in their former homelands.

Among the depressingly large number of authoritarian states in the Islamic world, those with strong secular traditions, including Tunisia, Egypt, and Syria, are more likely to make the transition to democracy sooner than states with strong sectarian governments, such as Saudi Arabia and Iran. Even so, Iran has a highly educated middle class that might move quickly to demand democratic reforms, once the country's autocratic religious leaders begin to lose their grip on power.

As the Islamic world struggles to reconcile faith and reason, it is worth remembering that it took Christianity 2,000 years to come to terms with the idea of secular democracy. In that sense, it is perhaps not surprising that Islamic countries have had to suffer through a similar adjustment process.

12

How Democracies Die

St. Augustine observed that all political systems, no matter how virtuous, eventually degenerate and disappear. As a rule, democracies die in any of three ways: external crisis, internal crisis, and/or gradual decay owing to apathy, corruption, and creeping authoritarianism.

EXTERNAL CRISIS

Democracies are as vulnerable to external attack as any other political system. Mature democracies, however, are perhaps more resilient in the face of external threats than nondemocratic states. Outsiders often mistake the naturally contentious democratic process for weakness, and underestimate democracies' singular ability to pull themselves together and present a united front against an external threat.

Democracy's unique virtue of offering ordinary citizens a tangible stake in society gives them compelling personal reasons to pledge their lives, fortunes, and sacred honor to protect their investment. This is *rational patriotism* – the public virtú that makes healthy democracies difficult to conquer and almost impossible to pacify. Rational patriotism helps mature democracies weather all manner of regional or global crises, whether man-made or natural.

INTERNAL CRISIS

Democracies are generally more susceptible to domestic than external crises. Emerging democracies are especially prone to implode before democratic habits can be fully realized and institutionalized. But internal social, economic, and political crises can also threaten mature democracies, which remain vulnerable to the self-destructive effects of selfishness and faction. Left unchecked, domestic factional disputes can quickly escalate into uncontrolled violence, civil war, and catastrophic system failure.

Conversely, established democracies are sometimes victims of their own success, undone by hubris and overreach. Democracy can be an incredible engine of growth, innovation, wealth, and national power, and countries that grow especially strong and prosperous begin to harbor greater ambitions. This tendency is reinforced by democracy's natural preferences for liberty, pluralism, free markets, and free trade – all of which encourage democratic states to extend their reach, if they can, beyond their own borders.

Successful democracies tend to think big, and they see the world as it is – interconnected. Like any country, they will take reasonable steps to protect their interests, and as their interests expand a successful democracy will gradually assume greater international responsibilities. Unchecked, these entanglements can become a sticky trap that leaves the country economically, militarily, and politically exhausted.

Athens' expanding regional ambitions and her resulting rivalry with Sparta led directly to her untimely collapse. Some see modern parallels with the United States, which over the last century has incrementally assumed ever-more burdensome responsibilities as the world's sole effective police force and global superpower. This has come at a considerable – and perhaps unsustainable – cost in terms of American blood, treasure, and prestige.

APATHETIC DECAY, CORRUPTION, AND CREEPING AUTHORITARIANISM

Aristotle thought that democracies naturally degenerate into anarchy and mob rule. Modern democracies, however, are more likely to drift toward authoritarianism, in a leisurely death spiral of cumulative decay – the ignoble rot of incremental centralization, corruption, partisan gridlock, bureaucratization, and public apathy. Federalism fails by degrees, checks and balances degrade, political turnover slows, the rule of law gradually breaks down, and government transparency and accountability wither away.

One leading indicator of this process is the accretive centralization of power. Healthy federal democracies respect the principle of subsidiarity. As democracies age, however, power tends to move from the periphery to the center.[1]

The second sign of democratic decay is systemic corruption. Corruption itself is not a sign of impending doom. All political systems are corrupt, and democracies are no exception. The body politic, however, is like the human

---

[1] The opposite problem is also common, especially among developing democracies, when the center loses power and regional governments assume greater effective authority and autonomy. In this case, democratic deterioration takes the form of centrifugal decay, as regional squabbles cause the country to break down into its component parts, with different regional government going their own ways.

body, in that corruption and other political pathogens are usually kept in check by a healthy immune system: checks and balances, government transparency, the rule of law, and a free and fair electoral system that encourages a salutary circulation of political elites. These limit the corrosive effects of corruption by denying it a safe place to hide and metastasize.

Sidebar 18: Getting Fat at the Public Trough[2]

Each year in the English town of High Wycombe, the mayor, the town's twenty Charter Trustees, and thirty other city officials parade before the public to be weighed on a large antique scale. The custom began in 1678, fell out of use for a time, and was revived in 1892.

Standing before the assembled townspeople, the Macebearer weighs each official in turn. If he or she has not gained weight since the previous year's ceremony, the Macebearer cries, "... *and no more!*" as the crowd cheers.

But if the official has gained weight, the Macebearer shouts, "... *and some more!*" as the crowd loudly jeers and boos. As bad as it seems, it used to be worse. Not long ago, the crowd threw rotten fruits and vegetables at any official who dared to gain weight at taxpayer expense.

FIGURE 12.1 ... and no more! Mayor Trevor Snaith triumphant at the 2013 weighing-in ceremony. Photo courtesy of the Mayor's Office, High Wycombe.

[2] Retrieved from *http://mayorofwycombe.co.uk/mayor-making/*. A special thanks to Mrs. Jenny Howe, Secretary to the Mayor of High Wycombe, for her kind assistance.

Corruption becomes an existential threat when the political immune system begins to fail. Power becomes concentrated in fewer hands, the same people and factions stay in power for too long, and government grows increasingly opaque and unresponsive. This allows corruption to become institutionalized and corrosive.

In the United States, this occurs when circumstances allow one political party to dominate a state or local government for an extended period of time, largely exempt from the constraints of checks and balances. The two most notorious examples of this are the Tammany Hall political machine in New York during the nineteenth century, and the unholy alliance between Chicago's Democratic party and the Chicago Mob during Prohibition in the 1920s and 1930s.[3]

The third cause of democratic decay is bureaucratic strangulation. Death by bureaucracy is a unique product of the modern age – it is Max Weber's iron cage. Weber claimed that all rational political systems, including democracies, will inevitably grow more complex, unresponsive, and ineffective over time. In response, governments must increasingly rely on bureaucratic experts to solve their problems, but this only reinforces the downward spiral. The political system eventually becomes so complex and unwieldy that it becomes unmanageable, and cannot be fixed through conventional political means. The only possible solution is to blow everything up and start over again.[4] Although Weber probably exaggerated the severity and inevitability of death by bureaucratization, anyone who has had to deal at length with a government agency will likely see some merit in his argument.

The fourth horseman of the democratic apocalypse, and the most dangerous, is public apathy. A democracy's fate ultimately rests with its people, and if citizens withdraw from public life to focus exclusively on their private interests rather than the common good, democracy will struggle and ultimately fail.

The real trouble begins when people not only lose interest in politics, but begin to believe that government itself is the source of their problems. This sets in motion destructive reverberations that become a self-fulfilling prophecy. As citizens disengage from politics and alienate themselves from the people's government, public officials will become correspondingly autonomous

---

[3] Chicago columnist Mike Royko wanted the city's motto to be changed from *Urbs in Horto* ("City in a Garden") to *Ubi Est Mea* ("Where's Mine?"). Ben Joravsky, "The Radical Royko," *Chicago Reader*, July 15, 1999.

[4] There has been a similar and instructive co-evolution with modern technology. In a single generation, automobiles have gone from being simple machines that average high school students could easily repair, to extraordinarily complex beasts that are all but immune to do-it-yourself solutions. Even inherently simple machines, such as bicycles, are affected; robots now build bicycle shifters in such a complex and intricate way that no mere human being can rebuild them. Like Humpty Dumpty, they cannot be put back together again; the only option is to throw them out and start over.

and powerful, and a new ruling class will emerge to rule in its own interests. Through this gradual process of mutual disengagement, democracy slowly fades away until, like the Cheshire cat, only a toothy smile remains.

BOWLING ALONE AND THE BIG SPLIT

One symptom of apathetic decay is the decline of voluntary associations, the basic building blocks of civil society. This happens as people withdraw into their own private lives, and stop joining with others to pursue common interests. Civic disengagement is often attributed to selfishness, but another major factor is population mobility and the resulting breakdown of stable, cohesive communities. In highly transitory populations, people lose their communal sense of belonging, which causes their elemental social relationships to fray, as neighborhoods become disaggregated collections of relative strangers. As people disconnect from one another, they become atomized, and no longer freely bond together to form social and civic organizations.

Robert Putnam wrote about this phenomenon in his book, *Bowling Alone*. Putnam argues that the breakdown of civil society can be glimpsed in the seemingly trivial fact that Americans are choosing in ever-greater numbers to bowl as individuals, rather than participating in organized leagues.[5]

Assuming that Putnam's hypothesis is correct, this would worry free democrats more than liberal democrats. Free democrats place a high value on community building and participation, whereas liberal democrats are inclined to view the ebb and flow of voluntary associations as an unremarkable by-product of liberty and individual choice. There are lots of reasons why people might prefer to bowl alone, and the fate of American democracy does not necessarily hang in the balance because league nights at the local alley are less popular than they used to be.

Another bowling metaphor describes a second alleged symptom of democratic decay: *the big split*. This theory holds that Americans are currently in the process of self-segregating – choosing to live in relatively homogeneous communities of like-minded people, on the basis of the common identity of race, ethnicity, religion, and/or ideology.[6] Although the United States is a diverse country, the argument goes, individual neighborhoods are once more becoming increasingly monochromatic and insular.

There is some controversy as to whether this is happening, and if it is occurring, what it means. In the nineteenth and twentieth centuries, racial segregation in America was perfectly obvious, especially in the South where it was backed by the force of law. The federal government finally dismantled de jure

---

[5] Robert D. Putnam, *Bowling Alone: The Collapse and Revival of American Community* (Simon & Schuster 2001).

[6] Bill Bishop and Robert G. Cushing, *The Big Sort: Why the Clustering of Like-Minded America Is Tearing Us Apart* (Houghton Mifflin Harcourt 2008).

segregation by the early 1970s, but this process inadvertently hastened the breakdown of many traditional ethnic neighborhoods, as well. As it turned out, most Americans did not necessarily want to live in homogeneous ethnic neighborhoods, and once desegregation began in earnest, many traditional ethnic communities also dispersed.

At the same time, there were reactionary movements to resegregate, this time on the basis of private individual choices rather than government policies. De facto segregation gained momentum in the late 1960s, with so-called white flight out of urban centers and into the surrounding suburbs. White families abandoned inner-city areas in droves, leaving downtown Detroit, Cleveland, Philadelphia, and other cities almost exclusively black and poor. There was a joke at the time that racial integration was the brief interval between the time that the first black family moved into a neighborhood and the last white family moved out.

Before long, however, most suburbs also diversified. Without government help to enforce private exclusive covenants, and with new civil rights legislation such as the Fair Housing Act, neighborhoods and landlords could no longer casually discriminate on the basis of race, ethnicity, religion, or for any other invidious reason.

Today, it is difficult for any one demographic group to monopolize a neighborhood that is in any way a desirable place to live. Ethnic and other factional clusters can, however, establish a political majority in particular neighborhoods or districts, which can have significant political and social advantages for the dominant group.

It is sometimes tempting to think of the United States as hyper-partisan and segregated on the basis of ideology – Red America versus Blue America. There is little evidence, however, that Americans consciously choose in large numbers to live in ideologically segregated ghettoes, isolated from those with different political views. People choose where to live for all sorts of different reasons – jobs, schools, weather, neighborhood environment, nearby amenities, infrastructure, family, geography, or simple inertia. There is no evidence that large numbers of people choose where to live on the basis of a desire to live in an ideological bubble.

The real big split in America is based on wealth, and it is hardly a new phenomenon. The rich live in one part of town, the poor in another, and the middle classes are scattered in between. One relatively new trend is that gated communities, once the exclusive privilege of the rich, have trickled down to middle-class neighborhoods. But even these shining gated communities on a hill are usually diverse in every way except economic status.

Assuming for the moment that the big split is real, and American neighborhoods are becoming like-minded, homogeneous enclaves, the question remains as to what the consequences of this might be. There are some tangible benefits to living in relatively homogeneous communities. Orchestras are strictly segregated by instrument, yet that does not prevent them from making beautiful music together. Neighborhoods where people have a lot in common are more likely to create cohesive and stable communities, echoing the communal feeling of the old ethnic enclaves. The resulting sense of unity, identity, and purpose might strengthen civil society, and reinvigorate private associations and civic groups, which would reassure those who worry about Americans who bowl alone.

13

How Democratic Is the United States?

Despite free democracy's roots in colonial New England, America's Founders – apart from Jefferson and Paine – did not want the new nation to be a free or participatory republic. Their prejudices were openly admitted and well documented, although their anti-populist views are often exaggerated today to make them appear more narrow-minded and elitist than they were.

With few exceptions, the Founders and Framers believed in progressive Enlightenment principles. Yet despite their common attachment to liberty and liberal democracy, they were deeply divided as to the best course for the new republic.

They papered over their differences during the Revolution and established a loose confederacy under the Articles of Confederation, leaving the balance of power with the individual states, and most of the important underlying issues unresolved. When the republic began to founder, every state except Rhode Island sent delegates to Philadelphia in the summer of 1787 to strike a new deal. Once there, the delegates quickly agreed that the Articles were beyond salvation, and that the deteriorating political and economic situation demanded a new approach and a more robust federal republic.

The Framers loved liberty, but they craved stability. This led them to mistrust freedom and participatory democracy. In trying to explain the country's new direction in *The Federalist Papers*, Hamilton, Madison, and Jay drew on their knowledge of political history and the new science of politics. They thought that they understood empirically why earlier democracies had all failed so quickly and miserably, and they were determined not to repeat past mistakes. As they saw it, free democracy's fatal flaw is that it grants the majority a blank check, leading inevitably to majoritarian bullying, the suppression of minority rights and individual liberties, and uncontrolled factional conflict. These problems trap free and participatory democracies in a state of perpetual vibration between chaos and tyranny, making them inherently unstable.[1]

Accordingly, the Framers sought to establish a new form of government that would be broadly representative and accountable, but also stable and enduring. They called the United States a democracy and a republic, following the fashionable vocabulary of the day, but it looked like nothing the world had seen before.

From day one, the United States was a bold experiment in popular government and a work in progress. Almost before the ink was dry on the new constitution, the Framers were already busy tinkering with the clockworks, quickly adding a bill of rights and arguing about what everything meant. Those arguments and adjustments continue today.

How democratic was the Framers' Constitution, and how democratic is the contemporary United States? To answer these questions, we will use the same criteria established at the beginning of this book: freedom, liberty, rights and duties, participation and representation, inclusion, equality, and power.

FREEDOM

The Constitution was conspicuously silent about freedom. It did not limit or destroy existing free institutions and practices, but it did nothing to acknowledge, strengthen, or preserve them. The Constitution failed to guarantee – or even mention – town meetings or other freedoms, apart from recognizing limited voting rights, an undefined right to republican government, and a narrow right to trial by jury in criminal cases.

The new constitution barely mentioned individual voting rights, leaving the details to the states and to Congress.[2] It significantly limited electoral freedom by establishing indirect elections for senators and the president, and exempting federal judges from any form of popular review. The only significant change to this original blueprint came in 1913, when the 17th Amendment mandated the direct election of Senators. The Constitution has never provided for any sort of national referendum, initiative, or proposition.

Today, although limited in scope (only the House and Senate are directly elected), the right to vote in federal elections remains secure and meaningful. The United States has never missed a federal election in more than 200 years, including one civil war, two world wars, two British invasions (one martial, one musical), and countless other political and economic crises.

---

[1] Alexander Hamilton, *The Federalist Papers*, No. 9.
[2] In *Minor v. Happersett*, 88 U.S. 162 (1875), the Supreme Court denied women the franchise, ruling that there is no federal constitutional right to vote.

The constitutional right to a republican form of government has not fared as well. Whatever the Framers meant by this phrase, they left it undefined, and today it remains a hollow right.[3]

Article III only briefly mentions the third freedom, the right to trial by jury in criminal cases. It took the 6th and 7th Amendments to secure a comprehensive constitutional right to jury trials in criminal and civil cases. Almost immediately afterward, the Supreme Court acted to limit jury rights, tying the right to a jury trial to the due process rights of criminal defendants and civil litigants, rather than recognizing a broad positive right for citizens to participate in government as jurors.

Following these precedents, the Supreme Court based its later landmark decisions to open the jury box to women and racial minorities on litigants' rights to a fair trial and a representative jury pool, rather than recognizing a positive right for women and minorities to serve as jurors. As a consequence, Americans have a due process right to a jury trial if they are accused of a crime or are a party to a civil suit, but they do not have a right to be jurors.

The government can compel eligible persons to serve on juries. In this sense, Americans can be forced to be free— an idea that might have pleased Rousseau. Mandatory service is required, however, to vindicate litigants' rights to a jury pool drawn from a fair cross section of the community, not to encourage broad popular participation in government decision making.

The jury system is America's last great bastion of freedom, and offers a unique, hands-on civic education. De Tocqueville described juries as a "public school, ever open." But it is an institution under siege. Despite the jury's unique status as America's only national free institution, and its essential role in shaping American society, there has been a quiet war waged to limit or eliminate juries – civil juries, in particular.

Even as the jury box opened to include racial minorities and women, the right to a jury trial in civil cases has been curtailed, and jury independence and discretion limited. This has been the result of sustained attacks by hostile commercial interests, which see juries as reflexively anticorporate.

Railroad companies led the initial assault on civil juries in the mid-nineteenth century, followed by a second wave of attacks spearheaded by insurance companies and allied interests in the twentieth and early twenty-first centuries.

During the nineteenth century, railroad companies won a series of landmark court decisions limiting jury discretion to impose liability and award damages, thanks to novel legal doctrines such as proximate cause and other new judicial rules designed to limit compensatory and punitive damages.[4] Business interests

---

[3] The Supreme Court has written off the Guarantee Clause as a nonjusticiable "political question," meaning that the clause is not subject to ordinary judicial review. *Luther v. Borden*, 48 U.S. 1 (1849); *Baker v. Carr*, 369 U.S. 186 (1962).

[4] *Palsgraf v. Long Island RR Co.*, 248 NY 339, 163 N.E. 99 (1928).

have consistently pushed to limit the scope of the 7th Amendment, and the courts have dutifully restricted the right to jury trial to common law cases and refused to extend jury rights to cases brought under the courts' equity jurisdiction.

Today, insurance companies and their allies continue the attack under the banner of "tort reform" – code for limiting jury discretion, capping jury awards, and shielding corporations from legal liability. Multinational businesses are fighting to create a complex litigation exception to the 7th Amendment, which would eliminate jury trials in difficult civil cases, in favor of trials before judges, who are presumably more sympathetic to business interests.[5]

Although the American jury enjoys constitutional protection and is in no immediate danger of extinction, there is precedent for a quick and unexpected erosion of jury rights in other common law countries. With little warning or public fanfare, the British government abolished most civil juries in the 1960s, and restricted the right to trial by jury in criminal cases by exempting entire categories of crimes, including misdemeanors and a broad swath of crimes loosely related to terrorism.

The United States seems to be drifting in a similar direction. Since the 1970s, the federal government has placed significant new limits on juries, restricting general verdicts, giving judges greater power to guide, alter, or reverse jury verdicts, permitting majority verdicts, and cutting the required number of jurors from twelve to as few as six. Many states have followed the federal government's lead in curbing jury autonomy and power. The federal government has limited the right to jury trial in terrorism cases by funneling suspects to Guantanamo Bay, where they are largely beyond the reach of civilian courts, and are either tried before special military tribunals, or are held indefinitely without trial.

In their cumulative effect, these restrictions are worrying. The jury is America's last great free institution, and as the jury goes so goes American freedom, if not democracy.

Despite these problems, there is at least some room for optimism about American freedom. The Constitution does not actively prohibit or suppress freedom; it merely does not guarantee or promote it. The sin is one of omission, not commission, and as a consequence it would be relatively easy to remedy, if the American people ever muster the collective will to try.

[5] The basic theory is that some civil cases are too complex for ordinary people to understand, and in these cases fair trial rights should trump the right to trial by jury. The idea first gained traction in a footnote in a 1970 Supreme Court case, in which the majority hinted that "the practical abilities and limitations of juries may affect the right to a trial by jury in civil cases." *Ross v. Bernard*, 396 U.S. 531 n.10 (1970). The leading federal cases on the matter are contradictory. *In re Japanese Electronic Products Antitrust Litigation*, 631 F.2d 1069 (3rd Cir. 1980) held that the 5th Amendment's due process right might outweigh the 7th Amendment's right to a civil jury trial in some complex cases. *In re United States Financial Securities Litigation*, 609 F.2d 411 (9th Cir. 1979) ruled that no civil case is too complex to justify abrogating the 7th Amendment right to a civil jury trial. There has not been a definitive Supreme Court ruling on the issue.

The Constitution begins with a simple phrase that embodies the idea of freedom as well as any ever uttered: *We the People*. Was this artful turn of a phrase just empty rhetoric? It must have meant *something*. If states' rights or individual liberties were the Framers' primary concerns, the Constitution would have begun with *We the States*, or perhaps *We the Rugged Individualists*. The words that the Framers chose must have some significance.

There is nothing to prevent Americans from expanding freedom at any time. With minimal fuss, the government, or the people, could resurrect Jefferson's ward system proposal, or create a new national referendum and initiative process. With each passing year, however, it seems less likely that American freedom will ever be enhanced in any meaningful way. The more pressing question is whether anything can or will be done to stop the erosion of the few freedoms that Americans still enjoy.

Perhaps the best hope for American freedom lies with the states. All fifty states currently provide their citizens with considerably more freedom than does the federal government. All states provide for the direct election of all legislators and governors, and most states either elect or democratically confirm judges. All states guarantee the right to trial by jury. More than half of the states allow popular initiatives, propositions, and/or referenda. A few states still have township systems with regular town hall meetings, although these residual examples of direct democracy are less powerful than they used to be, even in New England. On the down side, even these limited state freedoms are under attack, often by the same commercial interests that want to limit jury rights, although there are vocal criticisms of state-level direct democracy coming from the populist left, as well.[6]

The original failure of the Constitution to guarantee town meetings and other free institutions profoundly affected the subsequent course of U.S. history. This constitutional silence went a long way toward making freedom the forgotten right. The United States today is the home of the brave, but it is no longer the land of the free (Figure 13.1).

Freedom
Free Institutions: C
Free Participation Rights: C-
Direct Democracy: D (Federal) B (States)

---

[6] For a sampling of right- and left-wing critiques of direct democracy, see, e.g., Thomas Carlyle, *Latter-Day Pamphlets* (1850); Thomas E. Cronin, *Direct Democracy: The Politics of Initiative, Referendum, and Recall* (Harvard University Press 1989). Direct democracy, especially as practiced in California, is subject to two contradictory criticisms: that corporations are unfairly singled out and punished by populist initiatives; and that corporations and powerful special interests have co-opted the initiative system to further elite interests. The empirical evidence does not support either assertion. John G. Matsusaka, *For the Many or the Few: The Initiative, Public Policy, and American Democracy* (University of Chicago 2005).

FIGURE 13.1 Who Stole the Freedom Bell? Original illustration by Ian Zell.

LIBERTY

Whereas the Constitution all but ignores freedom, liberty is its leitmotif. It is America's siren song, the beacon that lights the way for the huddled masses, oppressed on foreign shores, yearning to breathe *libere*. (Had Emma Lazarus been a citizen of the Roman republic, she would have known that breathing is a liberty, not a freedom).

Despite its longstanding dedication to individual autonomy and independence, the American government restricts liberty from time to time, sometimes with good reason and other times for less noble purposes. The most common justifications for limiting popular liberties involve traditional police powers: public order, morals, and safety.

More controversially, beginning in the early 20th century, the United States has significantly curtailed liberty in the name of national security, triggered by a domino line of international crises: World War I, World War II, the Cold War, the Korean War, the Vietnam War, the war on drugs, the war on illegal immigration, the war on terror, and a host of other threats real and imagined. This has led to a steady erosion of individual liberties, and the corresponding rise of an increasingly strong and intrusive surveillance state.

America's singular attachment to liberty has had some unintended social consequences. The American ideal of rugged individualism gave rise to a society that instinctively favors competition over cooperation, and self-interest over the common good. This has fostered a tendency toward selfishness that occasionally betrays an indifference toward others, especially the weak, poor, and unfortunate.

The country's periodic infatuation with laissez-faire capitalism and libertarian economics has led to an unprecedented concentration of wealth in relatively few hands, a long-term trend that has accelerated since the 1980s. The American wealth curve now consists of a small, hyper-rich elite, a distressed and shrinking middle class, and a burgeoning underclass. The wealthiest 1 percent of Americans claims 34 percent of national income, and has more financial wealth than the bottom 95 percent of the population. The top 10 percent controls two-thirds of the country's wealth, and the richest 400 Americans control more capital than the bottom 50 percent of the population.[7] Many accept this unprecedented economic inequality as the fair and just result of individual initiative, responsibility, and liberty, although such claims are controversial.

Despite these and other difficulties, liberty remains *the* defining American right. It is the essence of the country, and forms the core of its national identity. Liberty resonates so profoundly in the American psyche that if it comes at considerable cost in terms of equality, community, and social justice, it is a price that most Americans seem quite willing to pay.

Liberty: A-

Sidebar 19: Individualism and Social Responsibility[8]

In a 2013 speech, President Obama urged Americans to support his new gun-control proposal by appealing to the common good:

We don't live in isolation. We live in a society, a government of and by and for the people. We are responsible for each other.

[7] Joseph E. Stiglitz, *The Price of Inequality: How Today's Divided Society Endangers Our Future* (W. W. Norton 2012).
http://www.census.gov/hhes/www/income/data/inequality/index.html.
http://www.politifact.com/wisconsin/statements/2011/mar/10/michael-moore/michael-moore-says-400-americans-have-more-wealth-/.
http://motherjones.com/politics/2011/02/income-inequality-in-america-chart-graph.
According to *Forbes* magazine and Edward Wolff, an economist at New York University and Bard College, the richest 400 Americans were worth $1.27 trillion in 2009, whereas the poorest 60 percent of U.S. households together were worth $1.22 trillion, or 2.3 percent of the country's total net worth in 2009. In 2010, the figures were $1.37 trillion for the richest 400 Americans, and $1.26 trillion for the poorest 60 percent of U.S. households. This means that the United States' richest 400 people possess more wealth than 60 million American households, out of a total of approximately 100 million households in the country.
[8] Excerpted and adapted from http://www.npr.org/2013/03/19/174708597/when-pitching-the-common-good-is-bad?sc=emaf#commentBlock. MarYam G. Hamidani, Hazel Rose Markus, and Alyssa S. Fu , "In the Land of the Free, Interdependent Action Undermines Motivation," 24 *Psychological Science* 189 (2013).

One recent study, however, suggests that encouraging Americans to think about others is not a good idea. Stanford psychologist MarYam Hamidani found that most Americans are confused and demotivated by such appeals.

When encouraged to work toward a common goal, Americans do not work as hard, and are not as effective at solving problems, as when they are encouraged to work for themselves. The exception is Asian Americans, who are equally motivated by appeals to independence or interdependence, possibly because they are exposed to both the American preference for individualism and the Asian cultural emphasis on communal interdependence.

As for President Obama's appeal to the common good to sell gun control, NPR correspondent Shankar Vedantam is skeptical:

Americans, in general, are not receptive to being told they have to control anything. And, in fact, the gun lobby, very smartly, has focused its message on individual rights and [liberties]. Basically, what the bottom line is, in America, when you make an appeal that goes against individual liberty, in the long run, almost always, you're going to lose.

RIGHTS AND DUTIES

There has always been an American consensus about rights and duties. Americans continue to embrace traditional Enlightenment thought when it comes to individual rights, although there is considerable disagreement about the fine print.

First, Americans favor natural rights over positivism. In the eighteenth century, natural rights theory gave disgruntled colonists an excuse to disregard British laws that they considered unjust. The apotheosis of natural rights came with Jefferson's Declaration of Independence, and since then Americans have never seriously questioned the mystical origins of natural rights, or had cause to reexamine their conviction that natural rights trump positive law if and when the two conflict.

Americans have cited natural rights and natural law to justify both sides of every important civil rights issue since the seventeenth century. Natural rights theory rationalized slavery and segregation, but at the same time promoted racial equality and integration. It justified the exclusion of women from public life, and also vindicated female suffrage and feminism. Today, it supports legal discrimination against homosexuals, and simultaneously champions equal rights for lesbians and gays to marry. Americans love the idea of numinous rights that supersede positive law, even when they disagree about the content of those rights.

Second, Americans have always emphasized rights over duties. The litany of express and implied constitutional rights is long, whereas the list of constitutionally mandated duties is quite short.

Americans are especially wary of positive duties – those that require them to do something, rather than merely refraining from doing something. Although

American law recognizes many statutory and regulatory duties, most of these laws take the form of negative injunctions (thou shalt not), or are conditional and linked to voluntary choices (if thou chooseth to do A, then thou shalt also do B).[9] It is rare that a law flatly imposes a positive universal obligation on individuals (thou shalt).

The Constitution contains just three positive individual duties, all merely implied: to obey valid laws, pay taxes, and serve as a juror when summoned.[10] One other significant positive duty is worth noting, although it is statutory and currently imposed only on men: the requirement to register for the military draft, and to serve if called.[11]

Third, most Americans favor negative rights and positive political-legal rights. They are ambivalent, at best, about positive socioeconomic rights.

Negative rights limit the government's authority to infringe on individual liberty and private choice. They include the fundamental constitutional rights of speech, assembly, association, press, religion, and privacy. Positive political-legal rights include the right to vote, petition the government, and the right of indigents to appointed counsel in criminal cases.

Americans are more dubious about positive social and economic rights. Since the Great Depression, however, there has been a growing acceptance of certain entitlements, including rights to education, public safety, working conditions, social welfare, social security, and health care.

Finally, Americans strongly favor individual rights over group rights. The United States has a highly individualistic culture, and its laws rarely grant or recognize group rights. With few exceptions, it is up to individuals to claim and enforce constitutional and statutory rights. Even class action lawsuits are

---

[9] Examples of conditional duties include the obligation of oil companies to mitigate environmental damage, or the duty of tuna fishermen to ensure that dolphins are not killed while harvesting yellowtail.

[10] The Constitution does not explicitly require individuals to obey the law or pay taxes or serve on juries – it leaves these questions to the federal government and the states. There are two other positive constitutional duties worth mentioning. The first is *imminent domain*, which is the forced sale of private property for the public good. Because the 5th Amendment requires just compensation for imminent domain seizures, the Constitution actually limits government power to confiscate private property, and gives people positive rights against the government, rather than imposing a new, positive burden on individuals. Second, the 13th Amendment obligated slave owners to release their slaves, and so added a new positive burden regarding private behavior, although this provision was rendered moot 150 years ago.

[11] Although there has not been an active draft since the 1970's, young men must register when they turn eighteen, to give Congress a fast track option to restore the draft, if necessary. Another significant positive statutory duty is the federal mandate to buy medical insurance under the Patient Protection and Affordable Care Act (PPACA) of 2010, also known as Obamacare. In terms of severity, it does not compare to being compelled to join the military, but many Americans nonetheless consider the health care mandate an unprecedented, if not tyrannical, burden. Finally, there are periodic calls to establish a national public service requirement for young adults. Proponents claim that it would promote the common good, encourage civic engagement, and produce more responsible citizens, but to date nothing has ever come of it.

treated as aggregated individual claims, rather than as a means to vindicate group rights. Rights that at first glance seem to be group rights, such as assembly and association, merely protect individuals' rights to create and join groups; the groups themselves have no rights beyond those of their individual members. In American law, the whole is rarely worth more than the sum of its parts.

There are some exceptions to the rule against group rights. First, state, national, and foreign governments have considerable latitude to sue on behalf of their citizens. Similarly, Indian tribes are treated as semi-sovereign governments, and enjoy federally recognized group rights.

Second, early affirmative action laws, designed to remedy past discrimination against historically disfavored groups, sometimes recognized group rights and entitlements. But these laws have always been controversial, and it did not take long before lawmakers and judges began to roll back affirmative action programs and reconvert group rights into individual rights. Under most current affirmative action laws, mere membership in a protected group or class is no longer sufficient to seek legal redress; individuals must prove that they were actual victims of past discrimination.

Finally, the most important modern exception to the rule against group rights involves corporations. After more than two centuries of consistently resisting the idea of group rights, in 2010 the Supreme Court suddenly reversed course and embraced the idea of group rights for limited liability companies in the *Citizens United* case.[12] In choosing to treat corporations persons and as special favorites of the law, the Roberts Court radically changed the discourse of American rights theory, by transforming free speech rights into group rights – for corporations only.

Rights and Duties
Natural Rights: A
Positivism: D
Negative Rights: A
Positive Political and Legal Rights: B
Positive Social and Economic Rights: C-
Duties: C
Individual Rights: A
Group Rights: D

PARTICIPATION AND REPRESENTATION

America is a representative democracy, with direct elections for both House and Senate, indirect presidential elections, and no popular approval or review of federal judges or civil servants. Federal elections are first-past-the-post in single-member districts, resulting in a stable two-party system. All state

---

[12] *Citizens United v. FEC*, 558 U.S. 50 (2010).

governments require direct elections for all legislative and gubernatorial seats. Most state judges are either elected or subject to some meaningful form of post-appointment public review.

One significant recent development is that the two major national political parties are less powerful than they used to be, because of the explosive growth of independent campaign fundraising since the 1970s. Previously, most candidates relied on political parties for their campaign resources, which allowed party leaders to dictate terms and enforce party discipline. Many candidates now bypass party leaders entirely and appeal directly to private donors for support, and Political Action Committees (PACs) threaten to supplant political parties as the most powerful aggregators of campaign funds and expenditures.

Another factor contributing to the decline of political parties has been the overhaul of the presidential nomination process. After Richard Nixon's 1968 election victory, both parties changed their nomination procedures to rely more heavily on state-run primary elections to select presidential candidates. This undercut the power of party bosses, who had controlled the nomination process. Party officials still retain considerable influence through the selection of "at large" delegates, but primary voters now elect the majority of delegates for both party-nominating conventions.

All of this has weakened party influence, with mixed consequences. As the power of political parties and party leaders ebbs, more independent candidates are able to compete for elective office. But the huge influx of independent campaign money has led to growing concerns about corruption and influence peddling. Weakened party leadership has eroded party discipline in Congress, causing government to grow less organized, disciplined, and civil. In order to finance increasingly expensive campaigns, most legislators now spend more time fundraising than governing.

Another persistent problem is low voter turnout. In the 2012 presidential election, 57.5 percent of the eligible population cast ballots – higher than average for a U.S. election, but lower than the voting rates in most other institutionalized democracies. Voter turnout is significantly less in non-presidential election years, and still less in primary elections. In the 2010 mid-term elections, only 38 percent of eligible adults bothered to vote.[13]

Although some democracies attempt to remedy declining participation rates by requiring citizens to vote, this is not the American way. Some state governments encourage greater citizen participation through a range of positive inducements, including election lotteries and raffles. A few states have even considered paying citizens to vote.

For the most part, however, any "get out the vote" efforts are left to political parties, candidates, and the private sector. Political candidates are ultimately

[13] United States Elections Project, retrieved from http://elections.gmu.edu/Turnout_2008G.html; cf., http://elections.gmu.edu/Turnout_2010G.html.

responsible for making sure that their supporters vote. One increasingly popular way to do this is to hire political consultants and use targeted political advertising. João Santana, a Brazilian political consultant, describes his role in this way: "Just as psychoanalysts help people to have sex without guilt, we help people to like politics without remorse."[14]

Participation and Representation
Representation: B
Voter Turnout: C-

INCLUSION

At inception, the U.S. political system was closed and exclusive, except in comparison to every other country in the world. Relative to its contemporaries, the United States has always been among the most open, diverse, and inclusive of all political systems – even factoring in the long-term formal exclusion of slaves and women, and the informal disenfranchisement of Southern blacks between the end of Reconstruction and the mid-1960s.

The Constitution left most voter qualifications to the states. Propertyless white males were initially barred from voting in some jurisdictions, but universal white male suffrage quickly became the rule. Free black males had the right to vote in some states but not in others,[15] whereas women and slaves had no political rights that white men were bound to respect.

For a brief moment after the Civil War, it looked like there might be a relatively quick incorporation of black males into American political life. During Reconstruction, Southern freedmen used their new voting rights to elect African-American representatives to Congress and a variety of state and local offices.

The promise of peaceful racial inclusion and conciliation came to an abrupt halt with the end of Reconstruction. Left unsupervised, Southern states quickly disenfranchised black voters and nullified other hard-won political rights through a mix of law, custom, intimidation, and terror. Southern governments passed new laws requiring racial segregation and marginalizing racial minorities. The Supreme Court gave its blessing to de jure segregation in *Plessy v. Ferguson*, ushering in the Jim Crow era of separate and unequal rights.[16]

---

[14] "As Brazil's Influence Expands, So Does a Campaign Strategist's Success," *New York Times*, April 6, 2013.

[15] Among the states that formally recognized voting rights for free black males prior to 1800: Delaware, Maryland, Massachusetts, New Hampshire, New Jersey, New York, North Carolina, and Pennsylvania. South Carolina was the only state to explicitly exclude free blacks from voting, although other states made it difficult or impossible for black voters to exercise their rights. It was only after 1820, with the Founders mostly dead, and a new generation of more aggressively antagonistic politicians in power, that Southern states moved aggressively to disenfranchise free blacks.

[16] *Plessy v. Ferguson*, 163 U.S. 536 (1896).

In 1954, the Supreme Court partially healed this self-inflicted wound with *Brown v. Board of Education*, prohibiting de jure racial segregation in public education.[17] Ten years later, the other two branches of the federal government belatedly joined the Court to end segregation and reopen the political process to racial minorities. The Civil Rights Act of 1964 and Voting Rights Act of 1965 marked the end of state-sanctioned racial exclusion, although de facto discrimination remains a problem.

Women were the other great exclusion from American politics. With the exception of New Jersey, where women had the right to vote from 1776 until 1807, women had few effective political rights until the 19th Amendment extended the franchise to both sexes in 1919. Even then, women in some states had to wait until the 1970s to secure full and equal political rights.[18]

Today, the American political process is broadly inclusive by any measure. With few exceptions, all adult citizens enjoy full political rights, including near-universal adult suffrage and open contestation for offices.[19] There are no invidious barriers to political participation, and wealth remains the only spurious obstacle to seeking federal office.[20]

Inclusion
Voting/Franchise Rights: A
Open Contestation Rights: A-

POLITICAL AND LEGAL EQUALITY

The original American promise was that all men are created equal. U.S. history has been the story of trying to live up to that promise, as well as redefining "all men" to include all women.

[17] *Brown v. Board of Education*, 347 U.S. 483 (1954).
[18] One contemporary example of denying American women equal political rights was the practice of requiring women to volunteer and register for jury service (men were automatically included once they reached legal voting age). This practice was especially common among Southern states, and justified on the grounds that it allowed women to remain at home with their children. The Supreme Court initially gave its blessing to the practice in *Hoyt v. Florida*, 368 U.S. 57 (1961), but later changed its mind and overruled *Hoyt* in *Taylor v. Louisiana*, 419 U.S. 522 (1975).
[19] The only significant groups that presently cannot legally vote are minors, incarcerated felons, and foreign residents. The mentally ill and insane have the right to vote in most, but not all, states. Even among the states restricting the rights of mentally handicapped and insane citizens to vote, there is considerable uncertainty as to how to determine and apply an appropriate standard. Maine technically bars the mentally ill and the insane from voting, and in 2001, Maine courts ruled that adult citizens have the right to vote only if they understand the nature and effect of voting and can make a choice. This standard has become a model for other states, but it has proven exceptionally difficult to operationalize. Maine officials have not been able to provide election officials with further guidance, and as a consequence the law is not being enforced. Pam Belluck, "States Face Decisions on Who Is Mentally Fit to Vote," *New York Times*, June 19, 2007.
[20] The fees required to run for federal office vary significantly among the states. In South Carolina there is a $10,000 filing fee to run for the U.S. Senate, whereas in Vermont there is no filing fee.

For a country that places such a high value on political equality, the U.S. political system remains surprisingly unequal at the federal level. Political equality at the state level is significantly better, ironically thanks to the U.S. Supreme Court.

The two best measures of political equality are whether every person's vote and voice carry the same weight as all others. The United States fares badly on both counts. At the federal level, only the House of Representatives respects the principle of one person, one vote. Even this limited promise of political equality was slow to materialize, as urbanization and redistricting problems led to gross malapportionment among congressional districts that lasted for more than 100 years in many parts of the country. Owing to extreme population differences among congressional districts, one rural vote was often worth up to ten times more than an urban vote, giving rural voters a disproportionate representational advantage.

The Supreme Court finally resolved this situation in *Wesberry v. Sanders* (1964),[21] requiring congressional district lines to be drawn according to the principle of one person, one vote. *Wesberry* applies only to the House of Representatives, however, and does not affect either Senate or presidential elections.

Senate representation is on the basis of the equality of states, not people. California's two Senators represent 37 million residents, whereas Wyoming's two Senators represent barely a half-million people, making one Wyoming vote worth seventy-four California votes. Wyoming and other small and sparsely populated states see nothing wrong with this.

This inequality makes a difference in ways big and small. Visitors to Washington, DC, will find that senators representing smaller states are far more accessible to their constituents than senators who represent large states. Every January, the University of San Diego political science department takes a group of undergraduates to the capital as part of an American politics seminar. When California students try to visit their senators, they invariably fail to meet them in person, and usually receive an indifferent reception from uninterested staff. Students from smaller states, such as Hawaii and Vermont, stand a much better chance of meeting their senators, and are often treated as visiting royalty. The stark difference in access and treatment offers a valuable practical lesson about political equality.[22]

In some states candidates are required to gather thousands of signatures for nominating petitions, which can be expensive. In many states, it is tougher for third-party candidates to qualify for the ballot than it is for candidates representing one of the two major parties. Aside from filing fees and other state-imposed costs, it is exorbitantly expensive to run for federal office, whether for the House, Senate, or presidency. Congressional campaigns now cost an average of more than $1,400,000, and Senate campaigns cost an average of nearly $10 million. In presidential elections, winning candidate Barack Obama spent $730 million in 2010. These figures do not include independent expenditures from PACs or SuperPACs. Retrieved from http://www.opensecrets.org/bigpicture/elec_stats.php?cycle=2010.

[21] *Wesberry v. Sanders*, 376 U.S. 1 (1964).

[22] In January 2009, a group of USD students and faculty were in Washington to witness President Obama's inauguration. The group visited Senator Barbara Boxer's office in the Hart Building

Presidential elections are similarly weighted in favor of less-populated states. The number of each state's electors is determined by adding the number of representatives to the number of senators. This means that even the most sparsely populated state is guaranteed three electoral votes.

California has 55 electoral votes (one elector per 672,727 persons) versus Wyoming's 3 electoral votes (one elector per 166,666 persons). Although the raw numbers favor California, each Wyoming voter has more than four times the voting strength of a California voter in presidential elections. This is one reason why presidential candidates spend a disproportionate amount of time campaigning in small rural states – something no rational candidate would do if every vote counted equally. It is also why small states fight to preserve the Electoral College, despite its archaic irrationality and the significant political inequalities it perpetuates.

State governments have greater respect for the principle of voter equality, thanks to the U.S. Supreme Court. All state legislative chambers must be apportioned on a one person, one vote basis.[23] In addition, the governors of all fifty states are directly elected, as are many state judges.

The second dimension of political equality is whether everyone has an equal voice in elections and political decision making. The United States also fares badly here, trending toward even greater disparities on the basis of wealth and related factors. As it turns out, money not only can buy love, it can also buy media access, lawyers, consultants, lobbyists, political candidates, and sometimes government officials. All of these things are of fundamental importance to political candidates and their sponsors.

It would be difficult to exaggerate the distortional effects that money has on U.S. politics. Unlike political campaigns in other countries, which begin as little as six weeks prior to a regularly scheduled election, American politicians, especially members of Congress, are now locked into a more or less permanent campaign cycle – an endless series of fundraising, political advertising, and electioneering with no off season. All of this costs – and generates – tremendous amounts of money, which warps the political system to the advantage of those with the deepest pockets.

As campaigning grows more demanding and expensive, only wealthy candidates, or those backed by affluent sponsors, stand a realistic chance of winning a federal election. Not that the rich have it easy; thanks to the political system's bottomless appetite for campaign cash, no one political organization or

---

to ask the staff (the senator was unavailable, as always) whether they could help find tickets to a preinaugural event – anything would do. Bored staffers told the group that they only had tickets to one event, The People's Party. Without a trace of irony, they added that we could not have any tickets to that event, because The People's Party was by special invitation only. In the meantime, a student from Montana went a few doors down to talk to her Senator, Max Baucus, who invited everyone to attend the official Montana Big Sky inaugural party.

[23] *Reynolds v. Sims*, 377 U.S. 533 (1964).

candidate, no matter how well off, can lightly afford to alienate their wealthiest core supporters by challenging their vested interests.

In contrast with the Warren Court's efforts to equalize voter strength in the 1960s, the Roberts Court has rejected most federal and state efforts to level the playing field with respect to campaign financing and political speech.

The Court's role in the matter began obliquely more than a century ago, in *Santa Clara County v. Southern Pacific Railroad*,[24] an otherwise obscure case with a literally unprecedented dictum: that corporations are legal persons for some purposes under the 14th Amendment.[25] In 2010, the Roberts Court exhumed the *Santa Clara County* case and used it to overrule a century's worth of precedents, ruling for the first time that corporations are persons for constitutional purposes, and granting them broad new free speech rights.

In *Citizens United v. FEC*,[26] a 5–4 majority struck down a key provision of the McCain-Feingold campaign reform law (also known as the Bipartisan Campaign Reform Act, or BCRA), which prohibited corporations and labor unions from using their general funds to pay for electioneering media (e.g., commercials, television shows, movies) less than thirty days before a primary election or sixty days before a general election. In voiding that part of the BCRA, the Court declared that corporations have the same free speech rights as natural persons, and may spend unlimited amounts of money to influence elections, as long as their efforts are not actively coordinated with political campaigns.

In the *Citizens United* case, the majority transmogrified individual rights into group rights for corporations. Corporations have two significant advantages over natural persons: there is no limit to their size, and they are potentially immortal. These advantages allow corporations to concentrate vast amounts of wealth indefinitely, giving them powers and abilities far beyond those of mortal men. The Court's ruling means that some "people" are more equal than others in terms of their ability to influence the political process.[27]

The Roberts Court has shown equal care and concern for wealthy individuals, ruling that money and speech are interchangeable commodities for affluent

[24] 118 U.S. 394 (1886).

[25] Although the case is often cited as precedent that corporations are people for some purposes under the 14th Amendment, there is nothing in the court's opinion to that effect. The claim was part of a headnote, written and inserted after the case was decided by the court reporter, J. C. Bancroft Davis, the former president of the Newburgh and New York Railroad Company. In the headnote, Mr. Davis claimed that the Justices had refused to allow the Southern Pacific Railroad Company to argue that corporations are persons under the 14th Amendment because, according to Davis, all of the Justices agreed that they are.

[26] *Citizens United v. FEC*, 558 U.S. 50 (2010).

[27] Justice John Paul Stevens, who dissented in *Citizens United*, compared the Court's decision to allocating presidential candidates different amounts of time to speak during televised debates on the basis of how much money they had and how much time they were willing to buy.

citizens, as well as for corporations. The bellwether cases here are *Davis v. FEC* (2008),[28] and *Arizona Free Enterprise Club's Free Enterprise PAC v. Bennett* (2011).[29]

In *Davis*, a 5–4 Court struck down the so-called Millionaire's Amendment of the BCRA, which sought to narrow spending inequalities between wealthy self-funded candidates, and candidates who rely on public campaign contributions. The law raised the limits that candidates could seek from contributors if they faced an opponent who spent disproportionate amounts of their own money campaigning for office. A sharply divided Court ruled that this amounted to an unconstitutional penalty on rich, self-financed candidates.

The *Arizona Free Enterprise* case involved a state law intended to equalize campaign spending in state and local elections. A matching funds provision of the law allowed publicly financed candidates to apply for additional state funds to offset inordinate expenditures by self-financed opponents. Two months before the 2010 state primary election, the Supreme Court issued a provisional ruling that stayed an Arizona court decision upholding the law, and enjoined the state from enforcing its matching funds provisions.[30] The following year, the Supreme Court struck down the law on First Amendment grounds in another 5–4 ruling.[31]

These two decisions are especially interesting, because neither law limited or regulated speech in any way. By equalizing campaign spending, without placing any limits on the private expenditures of wealthy candidates, both laws actually guaranteed both more speech and more equal speech.

The bottom line is that it takes a lot of money to be competitive in federal elections. The average congressional campaign now costs more than $1.4 million dollars, with individual expenses of more than $100,000 per day.[32] Senate campaigns cost more than $9.8 million each, on average.[33]

All of that is small beer compared to what it takes to run a successful presidential campaign. In 2008, political newcomer Barack Obama spent $730 million during his successful bid for the White House.[34] In 2012, Mr. Obama and his Republican challenger, Mitt Romney, spent more than $1 billion each, with various PACs, SuperPACs, and other private interest groups tossing in another $600 million in independent expenditures.

Not only is it exorbitantly expensive to run for federal office; most elections are surprisingly uncompetitive. Among federal legislators seeking reelection

---

[28] 554 U.S. 724 (2008).

[29] *Arizona Free Enterprise Club's Free Enterprise PAC v. Bennett*, 131 S. Ct. 2806 (2011).

[30] *McComish v. Bennett*, 131 S. Ct. 644 (2010). This case was later combined with the *Arizona Free Enterprise* case.

[31] *Arizona Free Enterprise Club's Free Enterprise PAC v. Bennett*, 131 S. Ct. 2806 (2011).

[32] Retrieved from http://www.opensecrets.org/bigpicture/elec_stats.php?cycle=2010.

[33] Retrieved from http://www.opensecrets.org/bigpicture/elec_stats.php?cycle=2010; http://www.opensecrets.org/bigpicture/stats.php?cycle=2008&Display=A&Type=A.

[34] Retrieved from http://www.opensecrets.org/pres08/summary.php?cycle=2008&cid=N00009638.

over the last ten years, 96 percent of House incumbents and 86 percent of Senate incumbents kept their seats.[35] Between high campaign costs and low turnover, ordinary citizens no longer have a realistic chance to compete for federal office.

There have been some positive developments in federal elections, notably the creation of the Federal Election Commission, increased campaign finance transparency, the democratization of the presidential party nomination process, and the addition of the public campaign financing option in presidential elections. It still takes deep pockets to run a competitive presidential campaign, but the process is significantly more transparent and democratic than it used to be, and the public financing option gives candidates with relatively modest financial backing a fighting chance to run a competitive campaign – if they can qualify for matching funds during the primary season, and can secure their party's nomination for the general election.[36]

In contrast to political equality, legal equality is generally well established at both the federal and state levels, with one major – and familiar – exception: wealth. The principle of equal justice before the law is a cornerstone of American jurisprudence, although there are some significant gaps between theory and practice.

In civil cases, equal access to justice is secured primarily through the use of contingency fees. In contingency fee cases, plaintiffs do not pay their attorneys' fees up front; lawyers earn a percentage of the award if they win or negotiate a favorable settlement. This allows plaintiffs access to "free" legal representation, if the prospects for victory make economic sense for a lawyer to take the case.

In criminal cases, several fundamental rights designed to equalize the legal process were secure at the birth of the republic, including privileges against self-incrimination and involuntary confessions, and the right to reasonable bail. More recently, courts have taken additional steps to equalize criminal justice,[37] perhaps most importantly by establishing the modern right to free and effective legal counsel for indigent defendants.[38]

Many states still struggle to provide adequate legal representation to poor defendants. Twenty-six states still do not have full-time public defender offices, and where they do exist they are often grossly underfunded and overworked.

---

[35] Retrieved from http://www.opensecrets.org/bigpicture/reelect.php.

[36] Under the current system, candidates receive matching grants during the primaries. If they are successful in securing their party's nomination, however, for the general election cycle they receive outright grants, with no matching funds requirement.

[37] In *Powell v. Alabama*, 287 U.S. 45 (1932), the Court recognized a limited due process right that indigent defendants, in capital cases, who could not adequately defend themselves because of ignorance, illiteracy, feeblemindedness, or other similar disabilities, had a constitutional right of effective access to counsel. The government had the corollary duty to assign counsel in a timely manner before and during trial.

[38] *Gideon v. Wainright*, 372 U.S. 335 (1963).

Most states with established public defender offices leave the financing to county governments, leading to significant inequalities between relatively well-funded urban counties and chronically underfunded rural counties. Most jurisdictions must contract with private lawyers to represent at least some indigent defendants, with mixed results.

No matter how well-funded and effective state-run public defender programs are, wealthy defendants still have significant advantages over indigent and middle-class defendants, including access to better lawyers, investigators, and expert witnesses. Rich defendants evade trial more often than indigent defendants, are acquitted more often, and if convicted are more likely to receive lenient sentences or have their convictions limited or overturned on appeal.[39] The harshest punishment, the death penalty, is reserved almost exclusively for the poorest defendants.[40]

SOCIAL AND ECONOMIC EQUALITY

The United States considers itself to be a classless, egalitarian, middle-class society, but the reality is more complicated than the myth. Beginning in the late 1960s, inflation, recession, globalization, economic dislocations, new government economic and tax policies, and skyrocketing education and health care costs have all conspired to squeeze the middle class and open an unprecedented gap between the richest and poorest Americans. These trends accelerated in the 1980s, with the apotheosis of trickle-down economic policies that consciously promoted the interests of the wealthiest Americans – "job creators" – as the main engine of economic growth. As a result, the United States now has the most unequal wealth distribution curve among developed countries, on a par with many third-world nations – a situation that is not likely to improve anytime soon.[41]

There has been surprisingly little public pressure to address income and wealth inequality. Most Americans, even those on the losing side of the economic bell curve, take a dim view of government attempts to redistribute private wealth. Americans continue to believe that upward mobility is easier in the

[39] After actress Hedy Lamarr was arrested for shoplifting, columnist Drew Pearson wrote a sympathetic article that excused her behavior as a symptom of a disease. Chief Justice Earl Warren retorted, "When poor people are afflicted with the disease they are jailed. Richer people are given a chance to return the property." Ed Cray, *Chief Justice*, p. 459.

[40] This inequity is not universal. In China, party membership and political connections are more important than wealth. All else being equal, it is safer to be a poor party member than a wealthy private citizen when faced with the prospect of serious criminal charges. *The Economist*, February 2012, p. 45. In many countries, belonging to an unpopular religious or ethnic minority significantly increases the chances of harsher treatment, including the ultimate penalty in capital cases. In the United States, there is a racial bias in the application of the death penalty, but it is the victim's race, not the defendant's, that matters most.

[41] As billionaire Warren Buffett wryly observed, "[I]f it's class warfare, my class is winning." Warren Buffett, Interview with Ted Koppel, ABC News, *Nightline*, May 21, 2003.

United States than in other countries, and they are willing to accept extreme economic inequalities today largely because they aspire to be rich themselves one day. Many Americans also suspect that any expansion of state entitlements represents an unwelcome step toward socialism, which will result in a more powerful government and a corresponding loss of liberty.

Equality
Political: D (Federal) B (States)
Legal: A-
Socio-economic: D

POWER: CHECKS AND BALANCES, SEPARATION OF POWERS,
AND FEDERALISM

The U.S. political system was designed to define, divide, and diffuse government power. On the whole, this arrangement still works well. The checks and balances system is vigorous and effective; it is difficult for any one faction to control the entire federal government, and impossible to control all fifty state governments simultaneously.

There are two especially significant problems worth noting. First, presidential power has increased significantly since the Great Depression, and in many respects the presidency has replaced Congress as the most powerful branch of government. Congress has, either voluntarily or through inaction, relinquished much of its authority to the executive in domestic matters, including most of its budget responsibilities, control over the legislative agenda, and the growth of executive agencies. Congress has ceded even more power to the executive in foreign affairs, including plenary power in diplomatic and foreign relations, the power to fight undeclared wars, and comprehensive but ill-defined national security powers.

Despite the resulting emergence of the so-called imperial presidency, the U.S. political system has managed to maintain a rough political equilibrium. This is, in large part, because even as Congress has relinquished its responsibilities, the judiciary has become more assertive in protecting the core elements of the Constitution's separation of powers architecture.[42]

---

[42] In his concurrence in the Steel Seizure Case, *Youngstown Sheet & Tube Co. v. Sawyer*, 343 U.S. 579 (1952), Justice Robert Jackson wrote:

I cannot be brought to believe that this country will suffer if the Court refuses further to aggrandize the presidential office, already so potent and so relatively immune from judicial review, at the expense of Congress.

But I have no illusion that any decision by this Court can keep power in the hands of Congress if it is not wise and timely in meeting its problems. ... If not good law, there was worldly wisdom in the maxim attributed to Napoleon that "The tools belong to the man who can use them." We may say that power to legislate for emergencies belongs in the hands of Congress, but only Congress itself can prevent power from slipping through its fingers.

The second problem is that virulent partisanship and chronic political gridlock have become a defining characteristic of modern American politics. For a variety of reasons, Republicans and Democrats today are less likely to work together or to compromise than they used to be, although no one should be fooled into thinking that the United States ever had a golden age when politicians routinely put aside partisan differences to cooperate for the common good. Combative partisanship has always been a fact of life in American politics, but the relationship between the two major parties today is even more contentious than usual. The population is sharply divided on a broad range of political, social, and economic issues, and the political system reflects these fundamental disagreements.

American federalism is also healthy and vigorous, although the central government is vastly more powerful today than it was in 1787. Once again, the Supreme Court has played a crucial role in this process, facilitating and legitimizing the flow of power from the states to the central government with its open-ended interpretations of the Commerce Clause and the Tax and Spend Clause. For more than 200 years, the Supreme Court has consistently favored federal authority over states' rights, enabling Congress to expand, by several orders of magnitude, the central government's authority in areas formerly left to the states.

States retain significant autonomy with respect to their traditional police powers (matters involving public health, safety, education, welfare, and morals), and they continue to serve as potential counterweights to federal overreach. Individual states still occasionally assert claims of residual sovereign authority, and latent tensions between the federal and state governments remain an important part of American constitutionalism.

In matters reserved to the states under the Constitution, the federal government cannot simply order, coerce, or dragoon states into complying with federal mandates. It can, however, encourage states to comply, by offering federal money and other resources as a positive inducement, or by threatening to cut federal subsidies for popular state programs as a negative incentive.[43] The Supreme Court has taken it upon itself to draw the line between legitimate persuasion and impermissible coercion, and over the last decade or so it has begun to side more often with the states, especially in cases involving unfunded federal mandates.

With all its defects, delays and inconveniences, men have discovered no technique for long preserving free government except that the Executive be under the law, and that the law be made by parliamentary deliberations.

Such institutions may be destined to pass away. But it is the duty of the Court to be last, not first, to give them up.

[43] To encourage states to increase the legal drinking age from eighteen to twenty-one, the federal government threatened to cut federal funding for state roads and highways by five percent in states that did not raise their minimum legal drinking age to the federal standard. The Supreme Court upheld the law, ruling that it was persuasive, not coercive. *Dole v. South Dakota*, 483 U.S. 203 (1987).

POWER: THE RULE OF LAW

Despite some problems during the colonial period, including a shortage of formally trained legal professionals and the absence of an independent judiciary, the original thirteen American colonies already had relatively stable, institutionalized rule of law systems before the Revolutionary era.[44] Respect for law is deeply ingrained in American beliefs, habits, and expectations. As de Tocqueville noted, Americans have always been attached to law as a primary means to vindicate their rights, and they have always shared the conviction that government must be based on law rather than will.

The American government generally respects the rule of law. Judges are highly educated and have a strong professional ethos, and if not politically neutral they are formally nonpartisan, and sensitive to the need for judicial self-restraint.

The main threat to the rule of law is wealth inequality. The gap between rich and poor distorts the course of justice, giving the rich access to a better quality of justice than the middle and lower classes can reasonably expect.

Racial and ethnic discrimination continues to be a problem, especially in the criminal justice system. In cities like New York, with active stop and frisk programs, racial minorities are more likely to be stopped, questioned, and frisked by police officers than whites. Minorities are also more likely to end up in prison: African Americans and Hispanics currently constitute 60 percent of the prison population, but comprise only 30 percent of the American population. Most social scientists see these data as evidence of residual racism in the legal system. Some argue, however, that other factors can explain much of the discrepancy, including higher rates of poverty, drug use and trafficking, and the prevalence of violent gang culture among some urban minority populations.

Corruption levels in America are relatively low compared to most other countries, and what corruption there is does not threaten system stability. Transparency International's 2010 Corruption Perceptions Index (CPI) ranked the United States twenty-second among all countries, although it scored toward the low end of the CPI among developed democracies.

Transparency International, 2010 Corruption Perceptions Index (selected countries).
Scored on a scale from 0 (highly corrupt) to 10 (very clean):
New Zealand: 9.3
Sweden: 9.2
Canada: 8.9

---

[44] This was despite the lack of professionally trained judges and lawyers throughout the colonies, and the Crown's constant meddling and heavy-handed attempts to control the course of colonial justice.

Netherlands: 8.8
Australia: 8.7
Norway: 8.6
Ireland: 8.0
Germany: 7.9
Japan: 7.8
UK: 7.6
US: 7.1
France: 6.8
Italy: 3.9

Sidebar 20: Destroying Democracy in Order to Save It (Part II): Detroit[45]

Detroit is a deeply troubled city. It has a current budget deficit of $300 million, and is burdened by $14 billion in long-term debt. Municipal finances are a mess, the tax base is dwindling rapidly, and a host of current and former city officials stand accused of corruption and malfeasance.

In February 2013, Republican Governor Rick Snyder declared a financial emergency, sidelined the city's elected officials, and appointed Kevyn Orr, a political outsider, to serve as the city's emergency manager.

Emergency managers are unelected czars, with sweeping and virtually unchecked authority to stabilize municipal finances and restore government services. Mr. Orr has broad unilateral powers to fire city employees, break public contracts, slash government services, sell city property, and cut the city's pension obligations. He can declare bankruptcy and liquidate public assets on his own authority, without any local accountability or institutional checks. In late 2013, Mr. Orr did just that, making Detroit the largest city in U.S. history to declare bankruptcy.

In nearby Pontiac, three successive emergency managers slashed that city's municipal workforce from 600 to 50, outsourced all essential services, including the police and fire departments, and put almost every publicly owned asset – including City Hall – up for sale. "It's not really a city anymore," one resident noted, "There's nothing left now." The Pontiac city

---

[45] Sarah Cwiek, "Will Emergency Manager Help or Hurt Detroit?" *Morning Edition*, NPR, March 4, 2013, retrieved from *http://www.npr.org/2013/03/04/173393681/will-emergency-manager-help-or-hurt-detroit*; Sarah Hulett, "Can Detroit Be Saved?" *Weekend Edition Saturday*, NPR, March 2, 2013, retrieved from *http://www.npr.org/2013/03/02/173295986/can-detroit-be-saved*; Quinn Klenefelter, "Michigan Officials Take Control of Detroit's Empty Wallet," *All Things Considered*, NPR March 1, 2013, retrieved from *http://www.npr.org/2013/03/01/173241269/michigan-officials-take-control-of-detroits-empty-wallet*; "Lessons For Detroit in Pontiac's Years of Emergency Oversight" *New York Times*, March 14, 2013, retrieved from *http://www.nytimes.com/2013/03/14/us/lessons-for-detroit-in-pontiacs-years-of-emergency-oversight.html?hpw&_r=0*.

council and mayor still hold office, but they are no longer actively involved in city governance.

Back in Detroit, state legislator Rashida Tlaib worries that suspending democracy there will only make a bad situation worse:

You know, emergency managers should not be coming in and moving around our taxpayer dollars without any kind of accountability or transparency. I don't understand how we can really truly change things if we're not self-governing.

The rule of law includes government transparency. The people's business must not only be done, it must be seen to be done. In most respects, the American government is open and accountable to its people. Several constitutional provisions reinforce the principle of transparency, notably near-absolute free speech, free press, and public trial rights. Modern statutory trends also favor greater transparency, including federal sunshine laws like the Freedom of Information Act. The Internet has revolutionized the cause of transparency, by making the instantaneous dissemination of information possible, usually with government cooperation, but sometimes in the face of government efforts to stop, limit, or control disclosure.

The main ongoing threat to government transparency is the federal government's longstanding preoccupation with national security. It has become the government's go-to excuse to exempt itself from established rules and to block public access to any information that it unilaterally deems sensitive.

The government's claimed power to classify information and create secret institutions and procedures has expanded exponentially since World War I. During two world wars and the Cold War the government created a succession of covert spy organizations with secret, "black" budgets. It also restricted the routine flow of information by creating an immense cache of classified information.[46] In the aftermath of 9/11, Congress authorized broad covert intelligence gathering, approved indefinite detention without legal process for "unlawful combatants" captured during the war on terror, allowed the government to employ harsh interrogation methods, loosened or abandoned legal restrictions regarding the gathering and use of hearsay testimony and other

[46] The number of classified documents is classified. The Moynihan Commission on Government Secrecy estimated in 1997 that 400,000 new "Top Secret" documents are created annually. These documents have the highest level of secrecy available, based on the standard that information contained in these documents would, if revealed, cause "exceptionally grave damage to national security."

According to the *Christian Science Monitor*, a total of 55 million documents were classified as secret or top secret in 2009. Each document averaged about 10 pages, for a total of 560 million pages of classified information. WikiLeaks' Trove is a Mere Drop in Ocean of U.S. Classified Documents," *Christian Science Monitor*, December 21, 2010, *http://www.csmonitor.com/USA/Politics/DC-Decoder/2010/1221/WikiLeaks-trove-is-a-mere-drop-in-ocean-of-US-classified-documents/*.

forms of previously inadmissible evidence, established secret courts (including the FISA court and special military tribunals) with broad powers to authorize spying on Americans and foreigners, and placed terror detainees beyond public scrutiny and ordinary judicial review. Congress passed additional legislation, including the USA PATRIOT Act, granting the executive branch broad and vaguely defined powers to conduct warrantless surveillance without having to inform the public or the courts. President Obama has further claimed unilateral authority to order extraordinary rendition, and to authorize the targeted killing of suspected terrorists, including American citizens, without notice, trial, or normal due process, if they cannot reasonably be arrested or detained through other means.

The NSA and other surveillance agencies now routinely engage in warrantless searches to gather massive amounts of data on Americans, by keeping track of all phone numbers called, all Web sites visited, and the postal addresses of all mail correspondence. Most of the time this information, called metadata, identifies who is communicating with whom, but does not involve accessing the content of those communications, which would presumably still require a search warrant. Such large-scale data mining allows the government to track social relationships on a global scale, which the government claims is essential to investigate, track, and disrupt terrorist groups.

The Supreme Court has also facilitated government secrecy, by refusing to second-guess the other two branches on matters involving national security. The Court has created or sanctioned new legal doctrines, such as the state secrets privilege, to allow the executive branch to suppress evidence or dismiss lawsuits by merely asserting – usually without having to produce any supporting evidence – that public disclosure of allegedly sensitive information in court might possibly tend to compromise national security.

Government Power
Constitutionalism: A
Limited Government: B
Checks and Balances: A-
Separation of Powers: A
Federalism: B
Rule of Law: A-
Transparency: B-

THE FINAL SCORECARD

The United States does not always get the respect it deserves as the world's first modern democracy. The ancient Athenians would have scoffed at the idea that it is a democracy at all, and would have called it an aristocracy. Modern Europeans routinely criticize American democracy, out of a combination of traditional Old World condescension and a desire to divert public attention from their problems.

The rest of the world considers the French Revolution, not the American Revolution, to be the touchstone of democratization. America's enemies dismiss the United States as a decadent neo-imperialist power on the verge of collapse, and even America's staunchest allies consider her a unique case whose virtues cannot be replicated. As a result, most aspiring democracies look elsewhere for their inspiration. This is a mistake, because the world has much to learn from the United States about how to build and maintain a vibrant, stable democratic government.

Americans, in turn, are too quick to regard other democracies as inferior copies of the American original, and stubbornly refuse to look elsewhere for alternative solutions to common problems.[47] This is also a mistake, because there is much that the United States can learn from the rest of the world about different approaches to self-government.

The United States has a mature, practical, and interesting perspective on democracy. The American Founders and Framers were ambivalent about popular rule, and rejected out of hand the idea that the United States should be a free or participatory democracy. They were pragmatic revolutionaries, who wanted a republican government that would be limited, balanced, stable, energetic, and accountable. They were navigating uncharted waters; previous experiments with democratic government had all failed miserably for lack of one or more of these qualities, and there was no guarantee that their efforts would fare any better.[48]

---

[47] Antonin Scalia endorses the idea of American exceptionalism, and vigorously rejects the use of comparative jurisprudence in constitutional interpretation. Scalia argues that what foreigners think is irrelevant to U.S. constitutional law, and Americans rightly do not want to be governed by the views of foreigners. *U.S. Association of Constitutional Law Discussion: The Constitutional Relevance of Foreign Court Decisions*, January 13, 2005. Scalia calls the use of foreign cases in U.S. constitutional jurisprudence "dangerous dicta," and rejects the idea of considering "foreign moods, fads, or fashions" in American constitutional jurisprudence. *Lawrence v. Texas*, 539 U.S. 553, 598 (2003). In that case, a 6–3 majority struck down Texas's antisodomy law that had outlawed all forms of homosexual sexual conduct. Justice Kennedy, writing for the majority, discussed other country's practices, leading Justice Scalia to issue a strong dissent.

Scalia later added that "the practices of the 'world community'" are irrelevant to U.S. law, noting that foreigners' "notions of justice are (thankfully) not always those of our people," and that their views "cannot be imposed on Americans through the Constitution." *Atkins v. Virginia*, 536 U.S. 304 (2002). In this case, the Court ruled 6–3 that executing mentally retarded defendants violates the 8th Amendment's prohibition of cruel and unusual punishment. Justice Stevens, writing for the majority, discussed other countries' practices at length, and Justice Scalia again vigorously dissented.

[48] Switzerland, a loose but stable democratic confederacy in Madison's time, was a potentially fatal counterpoint to Madison's argument about the comparative virtues of free and liberal democracy. Madison tried to avoid the issue, arguing that Switzerland was not a suitable model for democratic governments in the New World or anywhere else. He noted that Switzerland was not a modern federal nation-state, and was such a weak confederacy that it could scarcely be considered a nation at all. Moreover, it was isolated, small, politically and economically inconsequential, and the product of a unique set of historic and cultural circumstances that, in Madison's opinion, were not replicable elsewhere. James Madison, *The Federalist Papers*, Nos. 19, 42–43.

Although Madison, Hamilton, and others adopted the Enlightenment political vocabulary that was in vogue at the time, using words such as "democracy,"
"republic," "liberty," and "freedom" to describe the American experiment, they
redefined these terms to mean what they wanted them to mean. Democracy
and republicanism both came to mean representative government, and liberty
and freedom both came to mean liberty.

The Rube Goldberg electoral system that emerged from the Philadelphia
convention of 1787 was designed to check America's free democratic impulses
and ensure that the best people, not the most popular, would run things.
Accordingly, the Framers limited the franchise and relied heavily on indirect
representation, so that not just any boy could grow up to be president.

Yet the United States was in most respects fortunate in its founders. They
were an exceptionally thoughtful and principled group – more so than any
other political elite in the world at that time, and quite possibly since. They
took seriously progressive ideas about individual rights and limited, accountable government, and if they did not unreservedly trust ordinary people, they
did not fear or disdain them as aristocracies invariably do.

The men who wrote the Constitution were self-interested, but they did not
seize power for themselves or impose class rule.[49] A few grew rich as a result of
the new constitution, but many more, including Madison and Jefferson, died
deeply in debt. Their fate was simply an accepted risk of public service at the
time.[50]

Later generations improved the original Constitution in some ways, creating
new rights and opening the political system to racial minorities, women, and
other previously excluded groups. In other ways, however, succeeding generations failed to preserve or improve on what the Founders and Framers began.

Although de Tocqueville admired the United States in many respects, he
was pessimistic about the long-term prospects for democracy in America. He
predicted that the political freedoms that New Englanders enjoyed in 1821
would not last, and that popular participation and public virtue would fade, as
Americans grew more preoccupied with their own affairs and less interested in
public life and the common good.

Today, most Americans consider political participation to be a distasteful
chore, rather than a fundamental virtue of republican government. Voting rates
are in long-term decline, as more Americans disengage from public life. Taking

[49] Historian Charles Beard set forth a strong counterargument in his classic treatise, *An Economic
Analysis of the Constitution of the United States* (1913). Although Beard's book remains essential reading, much of his evidence and analysis was subsequently discredited, and Beard himself
eventually disavowed his own thesis.
[50] This is in sharp contrast to today's politicians, who routinely leave office far richer than when
they began their life of public service. Wealthy candidates often try to use this to their advantage,
claiming that because they are already rich they have little incentive to use public office for personal benefit. Yet even wealthy candidates, once in office, usually manage to advance their own
financial situation and supplement the fortunes of their families, friends, and supporters.

advantage of flagging public interest and oversight, elites and highly motivated fringe interest groups increasingly drive the political process, as government officials grow more detached from, and unresponsive to, the citizens they are supposed to serve.

The widening gulf between the people and their representatives has only accelerated popular alienation from government. As people lose their sense of efficacy, and stop believing that they have a personal stake in the system, rational patriotism fades, and people begin to see government not as an extension of themselves, or as an indispensable partner, but as an outsider and oppressor. Apathy, or the surly spirit of resistance and rebellion, replaces the optimistic, can-do attitude of a healthy democracy.

To the extent that this grim scenario plays out the way that de Tocqueville feared, the fault will lie not in our stars or our politicians, but in ourselves. American freedoms have not been lost through fraud, duress, coercion, or conspiracy. We, the people, have abandoned freedom in the pursuit of liberty and self-interest.

But it would be a mistake to underestimate America's resilience, or its enduring commitment to democratic government. On countless occasions over the last two centuries, America's enemies have gleefully anticipated her demise, only to be frustrated by the country's extraordinary ability to meet every challenge and bounce back stronger than before. In the end, it has always been America's enemies who find themselves consigned to the dustbin of history.

American democracy is admirable in many ways, but it is not the only sensible form of self-government. Other democracies, including some radically different from our own, are worthy of study and respect. We can learn from these alternative experiments in the people's government, and use their lessons to improve our own democracy, in our continuing quest to create a more perfect union.

Glossary and Biographies

I. GLOSSARY

affirmative action: A policy or practice to offer compensatory assistance or preferences to groups that have suffered from invidious discrimination. Assistance might include preferential university admissions or special hiring and promotion programs that favor members of previously disadvantaged groups.

apartheid: A system of state-enforced racial or ethnic segregation and political exclusion. Originally used to describe South Africa's former white-dominated government and society.

aristocracy: Rule by the few, based on the ruling class's claimed superior qualities and virtues. Literally, rule by the best. According to Aristotle, the benign form of rule by the few. (See oligarchy).

authoritarian: Rule by the few or the one; a government that is not accountable to the people and lacks effective limits on its power.

authority: A form of noncoercive power, based on a subjective, internalized acceptance that an order should be obeyed because it is the right thing to do.

city-state: A compact political system consisting of a sovereign metropolitan area (metropole) and adjacent associated agricultural lands and villages.

civil law: A legal system derived from the Roman legal tradition and the Napoleonic Code. The main source of law is a comprehensive scholarly legal code, supplemented by legislative enactments. Judges are usually considered to be civil servants or administrators, rather than lawmakers; their decisions are not a significant source of law, unlike common law judges. (See common law). In common law systems, the term civil law also refers to non-criminal cases, such as divorce, probate, or personal injury lawsuits.

civil service: The body of professional government administrators (also called civil servants or bureaucrats) who execute authoritative public policy decisions.

civil society: The collection of private individuals and groups who form a relatively stable, peaceful, noncoercive, and self-regulating community largely independent of the state. Civil society strengthens communities, creates civic-minded citizens, moderates antisocial behavior, and serves as a check on state power.

common law: A legal system derived from English law, where judge-made law and precedent serve as a main source of law, along with statutes and executive regulations. Unlike civil law systems, there is no formal, comprehensive, scholarly legal code. (See civil law.)

commonwealth: A political community, based upon a social contract or other form of popular consent, to promote the general welfare in the spirit of "all for one and one for all."

Congregationalism: A Protestant movement, begun in the late sixteenth century, characterized by a loose alliance of autonomous local religious denominations, each free to create its own governing laws and institutions. Most denominations adopted democratic rules for church governance, which they later transferred to govern secular politics, as well. Congregationalist societies were especially common in New England during the colonial period.

consociational democracy: A form of representative government that guarantees a specified level of official representation – usually proportional – for officially recognized groups. It is designed to promote political stability and social reconciliation in political communities troubled by factional conflict.

democratization, cyclical: An unstable republican system, characterized by alternating periods of volatile semi-democratic regimes and authoritarian rule.

democratization, dialectical: A violent transition from authoritarian to popular institutions and procedures. According to Huntington, this usually results in political instability and resurgent authoritarianism. Also called revolutionary democratization.

democratization, evolutionary: The gradual process of instilling republican habits, expectations, procedures, and institutions in a political society. Arguably the most effective way to institutionalize democracy. Also called linear democratization.

direct democracy: Popular government in which citizens habitually debate, discuss, and decide public policy issues themselves, rather than through representatives. Also called free democracy.

duty: What one owes to others or to the state.

enlightened self-interest: Individualism leavened with equal concern for the common good; the subjective understanding that individual good and the common good are mutually dependent concepts.

Enlightenment, The: A philosophical movement of the seventeenth and eighteenth centuries that promoted reason, science, and empirical evidence – rather than faith, superstition, and tradition – to understand the universe and improve the human condition.

equality, economic: A relatively flat distribution of material resources within a political community, to avoid extreme variations in wealth between the richest and poorest members.

equality, legal: A political system in which the course of justice does not depend on wealth, class, political connections, social status, or other extraneous factors.

equality, political: A society in which all eligible citizens have the same vote and voice in elections and public policy decisions.

equality, social: A society without hierarchical class, caste, or other status distinctions based on birth, wealth, or law.

faction: A group of any size, united by a common interest or passion, that is adverse to the interests or passions of others.

fascism: A form of corporatism; a political organization in which the state has absolute power, the collective is everything, and ordinary individuals count for little or nothing. Derives from the Roman magisterial symbol of individual wheat shafts bound together to form an unbreakable whole (*fasces*). Italian dictator Benito Mussolini articulated the three principles of fascism: "Everything in the state, nothing outside the state, nothing against the state."

federalism: A political system in which power is divided between the central authority and various semi-sovereign regional governments.

first-past-the-post system: An electoral landscape composed of single-member districts, in which candidates who receive the most votes win. Also called a winner-takes-all, or plurality voting system.

free democracy: A form of popular government based on broad, direct public participation in political decision–making. Also called direct democracy.

free market: A system for the exchange of goods and services that is open, fair, transparent, and competitive, where no one – including the government or coordinated private interests – has the power to control prices or manipulate supply and demand.

freedom: The right to participate in politics; the right to be an equal and active member of a political community.

general will: Consensual decisions made by the entire people assembled, based upon reasoned debate about what is best for the community as a whole.

guided democracy: A one-party state, where the ruling party has a political monopoly, but periodically seeks public affirmation through elections. Elections are usually noncompetitive, and only the dominant party's candidates appear on the ballot. The system can be considered democratic if the government treats elections as popular referenda on proposed officials and policies.

habeas corpus, writ of: A court order requiring the government official responsible for holding a person in custody to prove that the detention is legal. Literally, "you have the body," or "deliver the body," which is how the writ customarily begins. Also known as "the Great Writ," it is a fundamental judicial safeguard against illegal arrest and confinement.

illiberal democracy: A political system that has the appearance of a popular government without the substance. A pseudo-democracy, where formal state institutions, laws, and procedures are consistent with popular government, but ordinary citizens have no real say in governance and have few, if any, effective rights against the state. A faux democracy, where the government oppresses its people, rather than protecting and promoting individual rights and liberties.

initiative, political: A proposed constitutional amendment or law, put to a vote of the people by public petition.

instinctive patriotism: Loyalty to one's country based on affection for one's place of birth or residence. A form of irrational or infantile patriotism that is unthinking and unreflective. (See rational/reflective patriotism)

interest group: A collection of like-minded people who join together to pursue a common passion, cause, or concern. Also called a faction or voluntary association.

isonomy: A condition of self-rule or no rule, where fundamental rights of individuals and minority groups are guaranteed against the will of the government, majorities, and other adverse factions.

judicial review: A court's power to determine the constitutionality of any law, regulation, policy, or other government decision or action.

liberal democracy: A form of popular government, characterized by a fundamental commitment to individual liberty, with a limited and accountable representative government that promotes the rule of law and periodically seeks popular consent through regular open, free, and fair elections.

liberty: The right to be an autonomous individual; the right to think and act in accordance with one's own personal preferences, subject to reasonable constraints based on law and respect for the equal rights of others. The right to be left alone to live as one chooses, without undue restraint by the state or by others.

monarchy: A system of government in which sovereignty resides in one person, usually a king or queen. According to Aristotle, the benign form of rule by the one. (See tyranny).

natural rights: The idea that people have inherent freedoms and liberties that exist apart from and above positive law. Natural rights supersede conflicting human laws, because they are derived from a superior, immutable, and possibly infallible source – either divine law (Locke) or the laws of nature (Hobbes).

objectivism: The idea, first proposed by Ayn Rand, that radical selfishness is the only true virtue, and competing notions, such as government, community, concern for the common good, redistributive justice, negotiated compromise, and democracy are all morally corrupt.

oligarchy: Rule by the few; rule by a powerful and rapacious clique. According to Aristotle, the decadent form of rule by the few. (See aristocracy).

parliamentary system: A form of representative democracy, where executive ministers are drawn from, and must answer to, the legislature.

pluralism: A diverse society in which a multitude of factions maintain their distinct interests, passions, customs, and traditions, while peacefully coexisting with those who do not share their values or views.

political elitism: The idea that a small ruling class inevitably dominates all societies, including democracies. The ruling class takes an exceptional interest in public affairs, has superior organizational skills, and enjoys other advantages over ordinary citizens, who tend to be poor, uneducated, disorganized, and uninterested in politics.

political science: The systematic study of social and institutional power.

politics: How power is organized and used to allocate resources and regulate human activity.

positivism: The idea that state institutions and officials, following established and authoritative rulemaking procedures, are the ultimate source of all fundamental rights, duties, and laws in society. (See natural rights).

power: The ability to get someone to do something that they would not have done otherwise.

preferential voting: An electoral system in which voters rank candidates for each office in descending order. If no candidate wins a majority of first-place votes, the candidate with the fewest votes is eliminated, their voters' next preferences noted, and the votes re-tallied. This process is repeated until one candidate secures more than 50 percent of the vote. Also known as alternative voting, Bucklin voting, open list, range voting, and ranked voting. One variation, known as a Borda count, avoids multiple recounts by averaging each candidate's rankings by all voters during the first tally, to select the candidate with the largest overall number of points.

Progressivism: An American political movement during the first half of the twentieth century that sought to end the political dominance of corporations and empower ordinary citizens. Progressivism was especially influential in reform-minded states such as California, Minnesota, Vermont, and Wisconsin. Leading figures include Hiram Johnson and Robert M. La Follette at the state level, and Theodore Roosevelt, Franklin Roosevelt, and Lyndon Johnson at the federal level.

proportional representation (PR): An electoral system that allocates legislative seats according to the percentage of votes each political party receives. Electors typically vote for a party list, rather than for individual candidates.

proposition, voter: A proposed law or constitutional amendment that the government submits to the electorate for approval. Also called a plebiscite.

qualified democracy: A republican government in which a dominant faction, often an ethnic group or religious sect, enjoys official recognition, preferred status, special prerogatives, and unique rights and privileges denied to other groups.

rational patriotism: Loyalty to one's country based on enlightened self-interest – where self-interest and the common good align, and individuals feel fully invested in society. Also known as reflective patriotism. (See instinctive/irrational patriotism)

referendum: A public vote of confidence on a political leader, ruling party, law, policy, or constitutional question. The vote can either be binding or advisory.

Reformation, The: A sixteenth century protest and reform movement to end perceived abuses by the Roman Catholic Church, culminating in a radical reassessment of the relationship between the individual and God. The Reformation led to the establishment of separatist Protestant churches that rejected papal authority in spiritual and earthly matters.

representative democracy: A republican form of government, in which citizens periodically select political delegates, who hold and exercise the people's power in trust, to make important policy decisions on their behalf.

res publica: Literally, a public matter or a public thing. Originally associated with free or participatory democracy, it refers to the open public space where citizens assemble to discuss and decide public issues and matters of common concern.

right: What one is owed by the state or by others.

rights, group: Liberties and freedoms that belong to organizations, interests, factions, or other collective entities, rather than to individuals.

rights, individual: Liberties and freedoms that attach to discrete natural persons, rather than to groups or artificial entities.

rights, natural: See natural rights.

rights, negative: Liberties that guarantee individual autonomy; the right to be left alone to think and act without undue constraints by government or others.

rights, positive: Obligations or entitlements that the government and/or others owe to individuals or groups.

rule of law: A system in which properly enacted and generally applicable norms guide, regulate, limit, proscribe, and prescribe the actions of governments, groups, and individuals. Substantive and procedural norms must be readily accessible and understandable by ordinary people, and are interpreted and applied to individual cases by an independent and impartial judiciary, whether professional, lay, or mixed.

ruling elites: See political elitism.

secular state: A government based upon the strict separation of religion and government, where official laws, policies, and practices cannot tend to advance the cause of any or all religions, favor one religion over another, or advantage belief over nonbelief.

social anarchy: An egalitarian, classless, self-sufficient community without established leaders or followers, based on principles of individual liberty and mutual aid. Social anarchy emphasizes voluntary cooperation and communitarianism, which Peter Kropotkin called federalism. Other leading social anarchists include Mikhail Bakunin and P. J. Proudhon.

social contract: A foundational set of rules, adopted by mutual consent, to govern the manner of living together in a political community.

social democracy: A republican form of government that promotes economic equality among citizens.

sortition: Choosing political officials by random selection, such as by lottery.

sovereign: The ultimate source of state power or supreme authority.

state: An ordered, hierarchical society, with a geographical division that separates it from all other societies, where leaders are distinguished from ordinary citizens, and with a government that has a monopoly on the authoritative use of violence.

subsidiarity: Deciding political and policy issues at the most local levels practicable. A presumptive preference for decentralized authority and responsibility.

tyranny: Unchecked power; where all government power rests in the same set of hands, whether the one, few, or many, and regardless of the manner of selection.

tyranny of the majority: Unchecked rule by the many, where the rights and welfare of the minority are routinely ignored or violated.

tyranny of the minority: Unchecked rule by the few, where the rights and welfare of the many are routinely ignored or violated.

tyrant: A ruler who governs without effective restraint or limitation. According to Aristotle, the decadent form of rule by the one. (See monarchy).

utilitarianism: A nineteenth-century political theory, proposed by James Mill and Jeremy Bentham, that human beings are rational creatures, who act according to self-interest based on a cost-benefit analysis. Utilitarian theory holds that the best form of government is that which seeks the greatest good for the greatest number.

virtú: Machiavellian virtue. On an individual basis, a practical understanding of political power, combined with the ability and will to take, keep, and use power effectively. In a people, virtú is a broad popular awareness of political reality, combined with a common willingness to challenge authority if it does not serve their interests.

voluntary association: An interest group.

voting, indirect: Representative government once removed. Electors choose an intermediary body that in turn selects the authoritative decision maker(s). For example: American voters in presidential elections vote to select delegates to the Electoral College, who meet separately to elect the president.

voting, weighted: Elections in which some electors have multiple votes, or some votes count for more than others; any election not governed by the principle of one person, one vote.

II. BIOGRAPHIES

John Adams (1735–1826). American lawyer, revolutionary, political thinker, legislator, and president. Adams believed that every society has a natural aristocracy – a meritocracy composed of especially bright and talented people – who should be selected to rule in a limited and accountable government. Adams disparaged Britain's ruling class as an artificial aristocracy, based on heredity, class, and law, rather than merit. Despite the best efforts of his remarkable wife, Abigail, Adams refused to consider extending political rights to women.

Adams died on July 4, 1826, the same day as Thomas Jefferson. His last words were, "Jefferson lives!"

Anacharsis (c. late seventh to early sixth centuries BC). Scythian prince, traveler, and political sage. Anacharsis visited Athens c. 594 BC, where he became one of Solon's friends and advisors. One of a handful of foreigners ever granted political rights by the Athenians. The honor was extraordinary, because he was considered a barbarian, even though his mother was Greek. Anacharsis was reportedly executed upon his return to Scythia, because he had become Hellenized.

Hannah Arendt (Johanna Arendt)(1906–1975). German-American political theorist, professor, and journalist. While a student at the University of Marburg, she began an affair with German phenomenologist Martin Heidegger which ended when Arendt found out about Heidegger's Nazi connections. The Gestapo arrested Arendt in 1933, and upon her release she fled to Paris. When France fell, she was interned in a concentration camp in Gurs. She escaped and immigrated to America in 1941, using an illegal visa issued by Hiram Bingham, an American diplomat who provided unauthorized immigration documents to more than 2,500 Jews. Arendt became a naturalized American citizen in 1950. Her books and essays, notably *The Origins of Totalitarianism* (1951), *The Human Condition* (1958), *Eichmann in Jerusalem* (1963), and *On Revolution* (1968), made her one of the most important political thinkers of the twentieth century. Arendt taught at the University of California, Princeton, Northwestern, Chicago, Wesleyan, The New School, and Yale. There is an asteroid named for her, Hannaharendt, discovered in 1990.

Aristotle (384–322 BC). Athenian philosopher and political theorist. Arguably history's most influential political philosopher. Aristotle was one of Plato's star students, and later taught at Plato's Academy. He tutored the thirteen-year-old son of King Philip II of Macedon, who became Alexander the Great. Aristotle opposed Athenian democracy, preferring a timocracy in which the 6,000 richest male citizens would rule. During the European Dark Ages, when classical knowledge was lost to the West, philosophers such as Avicenna, Averroes, and Maimonides preserved Aristotle's works in the Islamic world, making it possible for Thomas Aquinas and others to "rediscover" Aristotle and other classical scholars in the thirteenth century.

Jeremy Bentham (1748–1832). British political theorist, economist, barrister, and social reformer. Graduated from Oxford at age sixteen, the youngest student at that time to have graduated from either Oxford or Cambridge. His work with James Mill led to utilitarianism, the most influential modern theory of human behavior and socioeconomic reform. Bentham requested that upon his death his head and skeleton be preserved and publicly displayed, fully clothed, along with Dapple, his favorite walking stick. He currently resides in a special case, known as the auto-icon, at University College, London. Bentham's head fell off some time ago, and became a favorite target for student pranksters. Bentham's torso now has a wax replica head, and his real head is stored separately.

Jean Bodin (1529–1596). French lawyer, political philosopher, and econo-mist. Bodin is best known for his views on sovereign power, which he believed to be indivisible and absolute. He is credited with coining the phrase, "political science."

Cincinnatus (Lucius Quinctius) (519–430 BC). Roman farmer, general, and politician during the early republican era. Cincinnatus was a nickname, meaning a boy with curly hair. When the Aequians attacked Rome, the Senate begged Cincinnatus to leave his farm and become a dictator, to save the repub-lic. He agreed, quickly raised an army, and forced the Aequians to surren-der. Rather than stay in power, Cincinnatus immediately disbanded his army, resigned his commission, and returned to his farm, having served as Rome's dictator for only sixteen days. Many years later, the Senate called Cincinnatus from his plow once more to save the republic, and again he quickly triumphed and immediately retired to his farm, this time for good. Cincinnatus, New York, and Cincinnati, Ohio, were named to honor Lucius Quinctius and the American Cincinnatus, George Washington.

Jose Figueres Ferrer (1906–1990). President of Costa Rica: 1948–1949, 1953–1958, and 1970–1974. Figueres first became president as the head of a provisional junta in 1948. During his first term, he abolished the national army, based on his belief that Latin American military leaders had systematically sab-otaged regional democratization efforts. Figueres credited H. G. Wells' classic book, *Outline of History*, for inspiring his decision.[1] As president, he promul-gated a new constitution, established the country's first professional civil ser-vice, and extended the franchise to women, racial minorities, and illiterates.

Thomas Hobbes (1588–1679). English political theorist. Hobbes contem-plated the state of nature during the English Civil War, as the country lurched violently between anarchy and tyranny, and did not like what he saw. Hobbes hypothesized that people are, by nature, radically and irredeemably selfish, and that life in a state of nature – that is, life without a government – is a war of all against all, where life is solitary, nasty, brutish, and short. Hobbes concluded that an all-powerful government – a Leviathan – is necessary to control the violent impulses of human nature.

Richard Hooker (1554–1600). British theologian and philosopher. His eight-book series, *Of the Laws of Ecclesiastical Polity*, helped to inspire liber-alism and liberal democracy. Hooker advocated reason, toleration, and limited authority in both church and civil governance. He also advanced the idea of social contract – a mutually agreed upon set of rules governing the manner of living together. Hooker's views profoundly influenced John Locke, who called him "the judicious Hooker."

---

[1] Wells wrote, "The future of mankind cannot include armed forces. Police, yes, because people are imperfect." Figueres read the book while he was a student at MIT. Joanne Omang, "Costa Rica's Ex-Leader Praises U.S. Policy on Salvadoran War," *Washington Post*, June 22, 1984.

Samuel Huntington (1927–2008). American political scientist. Huntington earned his PhD and began teaching at Harvard in 1950, at age twenty-three. Denied tenure nine years later, Harvard invited him back in 1963, where he taught until his death in 2008. Among Huntington's areas of expertise were democratization and international politics. He was nominated twice to the National Academy of Science, but was rejected both times due to opposition from leading mathematicians, who dismissed his work as pseudoscientific.

Thomas Jefferson (1743–1826). American revolutionary, political theorist, philosopher, inventor, farmer, diplomat, governor, president, and free democrat. Jefferson was the main author of the Declaration of Independence, and as president he more than doubled the size of the United States with the Louisiana Purchase, paying Napoleon $15 million, or three cents per acre. Jefferson founded the University of Virginia and helped to establish the Library of Congress.

At a White House dinner for Nobel Prize winners in 1962, President John Kennedy said, "...[T]his is the most extraordinary collection of talent, of human knowledge, that has ever been gathered together at the White House – with the possible exception of when Thomas Jefferson dined alone."

Peter Kropotkin (1842–1921). Russian anarchist, scientist, and geographer. Kropotkin was born a prince of the Riurik family, the tsarist dynasty prior to the Romanovs. Kropotkin renounced his royal title when he was twelve, becoming the anarchist formerly known as Prince. In 1876, he was arrested for his opposition to the tsarist regime, but escaped and went into exile for forty years. While traveling in Switzerland, he stumbled upon an anarchist watchmakers' guild in the Jura Mountains and became an immediate convert. He spent the rest of his life trying to prove that social anarchism is scientifically sound and sustainable.

Aung San Suu Kyi (1945–). Burmese politician and democratic activist. Suu Kyi led the nonviolent resistance movement to the brutal military regime of U Ne Win and his successors during the 1980s. In 1989, the ruling junta placed her under house arrest, and she spent the next fifteen years in state custody. Suu Kyi earned the Nobel Peace Prize in 1991.

Vladimir Ilyich Lenin (Vladimir Ilyich Ulyanov) (1870–1924). Russian political theorist, revolutionary, and politician. Lenin founded the Russian Communist Party, and was the first premier of the Soviet Union following the November Revolution of 1917. He radically modified Marxist theory to fit Russia's peculiar circumstances, and Marxism-Leninism quickly became the dominant theory of revolution throughout the developing world. Lenin claimed that an absolute dictatorship by Party elites (the Vanguard) is necessary during the revolutionary and transitional socialist phases, until the capitalist class is liquidated and a classless, stateless society established. After Lenin's death in 1924, Russian physiologist Ivan Pavlov leaked the news to the West that Lenin had not died of a stroke, as the Soviet state media insisted, but of advanced syphilis.

John Locke (1632–1704). English political theorist and godfather of liberal democracy. Locke's most notable political books are *Two Treatises on Government*, and *Letters Concerning Toleration*. Another work, *An Essay Concerning Human Understanding*, revolutionized Western understanding of the human mind. Locke's behavioral theories were eventually superseded by utilitarianism and modern psychology, but his political influence continues unabated, especially in the United States. Locke helped write the founding laws and constitution of the Carolina colony in 1669, and he served as secretary to the colony's lords proprietors until 1675.

Niccolo Machiavelli (1469–1527): Florentine political theorist and diplomat. In his classic essay, *The Prince*, Machiavelli offered practical advice on how to win, hold, and use power. In his masterwork, *The Discourses Upon the First Ten Books of Titus Livius*, he extolled the virtues of republican government and political participation. Scholars still argue about which of these two books reflects Machiavelli's core beliefs. (Hint: it is *The Discourses*). Machiavelli was the first political theorist to grasp the game-changing significance of a new and unprecedented political system that first appeared during his lifetime – the nation-state. Modern acolytes call themselves political realists, and are especially influential in international relations and diplomacy.

James Madison (1751–1836). American revolutionary, political theorist, and president. Madison assumed a leading role in writing both the Constitution and Bill of Rights, and is known as the Father of both. He wrote many of the most important essays in *The Federalist*, including Nos. 10 and 51, which discuss separation of powers, federalism, and the role of the judiciary in mediating disputes and protecting minority rights.

Madison was president during the War of 1812, when British troops sacked and burned Washington, DC. Critics blamed him for the debacle, and labeled the conflict "Mr. Madison's War." At his death in 1836, Madison was the last surviving Founder Father and Constitutional Convention delegate.

Nelson Mandela (Rolihlahla Mandela) (1818–2013). South African political activist, lawyer, journalist, and the first president of postapartheid South Africa. As the leader of the African National Congress (ANC), Mandela managed South Africa's peaceful transition from a white-minority-dominated apartheid state to an inclusive and pluralistic liberal democracy. He earned the Nobel Peace Prize in 1993, along with previous South African president, F. W. de Klerk. Mandela's birth name, Rolihlahla, means "troublemaker."

Karl Marx (1818–1883). German political theorist, philosopher, newspaper editor, and revolutionary. Marx saw human history as the story of class struggle, driven by dialectical materialist forces. In the four main phases of class society (slavery, feudalism, capitalism, socialism) a dominant class controls the means of production and exploits the underclass. In the final phase of human development – communism – all of the injustices and contradictions of class society are resolved, and society is reorganized as a classless, stateless community, where everyone gives according to ability and takes according to need. Marx's nickname was "the Moor," because of his dark complexion. He reportedly had an illegitimate son with Helene Demuth, the family housekeeper.

John Stuart Mill (1806–1873). Liberal theorist, economist, and early feminist. Mill's classic monograph, *On Liberty*, contemplated the virtues of responsible liberty and sought to balance liberty against legitimate state and community interests in self-defense and the common good. In *Representative Government*, Mill injected elements of direct democracy into liberalism, including universal adult suffrage and juries. Mill appreciated the educational benefits of political participation. He proposed, however, that educated citizens and property owners be allowed to vote more than once, to ensure that more intelligent and virtuous citizens have a greater say in political decisions.

Mill was involved in an eccentric love triangle with John and Harriet Taylor for nearly two decades, until Mr. Taylor died. Mrs. Taylor subsequently became Mill's muse, editor, and eventually, his wife. Mill maintained that Taylor was a transcendent genius, although his judgment was not universally shared. Mill bequeathed nearly half of his estate to advance women's education.

Mohammed Morsi (1951–). Egyptian Islamist politician and leader of the Egyptian Islamic Brotherhood. In 2012, Morsi became the country's first democratically elected president. He was overthrown in a military coup the following year. Two of Mr. Morsi's five children are American citizens, born while he was earning his PhD at the University of Southern California.

Gaetano Mosca (1858–1941). Italian political scientist and law professor. Mosca proposed the theory of political elitism – the idea that a small, organized political class dominates every society, including democracies. Mosca criticized liberal democracy, but thought that it had one advantage over other political systems: competing interests, rather than a monolithic ruling class, helped ensure a beneficial circulation of elites. Considered Italy's first modern political scientist, Mosca was frustrated by the lack of endowed chairs in political science at Italian universities, and by his failure to secure a lucrative fellowship that would have allowed him to study and teach abroad.

Robert Nozick (1938–2002). American philosopher and professor. During his undergraduate years at Columbia, Nozick was a socialist and a cofounder of the League for Industrial Democracy, a forerunner of Students for a Democratic Society. As a Harvard professor, Nozick renounced socialism and developed a systematic philosophy of libertarianism, based on a pure justice-as-fairness system. Reacting to John Rawls's social democratic theory of justice, Nozick advocated a minimal state, where government has only limited responsibilities to enforce contracts and protect individuals against force, theft, fraud, and coercion. Nozick's minimal state has no power to redistribute wealth to address social or economic inequalities, and no right to limit individual liberty for one's own good.

Pericles (495–429 BC). Athenian politician and statesman. Pericles was a leading demagogue, before antidemocratic propagandists turned the term into an epithet. He ushered in the golden age of Athenian democracy, and supervised the development of the Acropolis, including the Parthenon. Pericles was extraordinarily popular, and was elected chief strategos (military leader) almost every year until his death. His Funeral Oration was the most famous and articulate defense of free democracy in history. He died soon afterward, during the great plague of 429. Pericles's mistress, Aspasia, was an exceptionally intelligent and influential woman in a strictly patriarchal society. Pericles's son, also named Pericles, was executed for dereliction of duty after the battle of Arginusae in 406.

Plato (424–347 BC). Athenian philosopher and aristocrat. Plato was Socrates' student and Aristotle's teacher. All three men vigorously opposed Athenian democracy, and were either directly or indirectly involved in efforts to overthrow the government. One of the cruel ironies of history is that Plato, Aristotle, and other implacable foes of Athenian democracy wrote the only surviving first-hand accounts of Athenian politics during its golden age.

Ann Rand (Alisa Rosenbaum) (1905–1982). Born in Russia during the final years of tsarist rule, Rand grew up in a time of extreme turmoil, culminating with the Bolshevik revolution of 1917. Her family smuggled her out of Russia to live with relatives in America. Rand reacted to Bolshevik collectivism by adopting the view that radical, unalloyed, selfish egotism is the only true virtue. Rand called her philosophy objectivism. She opposed democracy on the ground that "the masses" are "imbeciles," "lice," "parasites," "savages," "refuse," and "imitations of living beings." She favored what she called a "democracy of superiors" – rule by the rich and powerful.

Rand encouraged her followers to smoke, because she thought it symbolized "man's victory over fire." She became addicted to amphetamines while writing *The Fountainhead*, and struggled to shake her addiction for more than thirty years. Rand died in 1982 from lung cancer.

John Rawls (1921–2002). American political philosopher and professor. Rawls was a star pitcher at Princeton as an undergraduate, and was offered a minor league farm contract. He served as an army private during WWII, and saw action in New Guinea and the Philippines, before joining the occupation of postwar Japan. In 1952, Rawls became a Fulbright Fellow at Oxford, where he was inspired by the work of H. L. A. Hart and Isaiah Berlin. Rawls is best known for developing his dual theory of justice, combining individual rights (the liberty principle) and socioeconomic equality (the difference principle).

Jean-Jacques Rousseau (1712–1778). Swiss philosopher and composer. Born in the Protestant city-state of Geneva, Rousseau left home at fifteen and wandered around Europe, before settling near the French city of Chambery, where he found himself in a lovers' triangle with his patroness, Francoise-Louise de Warens and her house steward. In 1742, Rousseau moved to Paris, where he fell in with, and then fell out with, French Enlightenment philosophers, including Diderot and Voltaire. Rousseau attacked the Enlightenment ideal of progress through reason and science. He warned that science is not the engine of progress, but the instrument of human destruction, and the arts were merely "the flowers that cover the chains that men bear." Rousseau urged men to reject modern civilization in favor of small, simple, free democracies. Rousseau's main political models were Sparta and the rural Swiss canton of Neuchatel, two societies that consciously ignored the complexities of progress and modernity. His most famous work, *The Social Contract*, set forth his theory of free democracy and the general will. Rousseau also composed seven operas and numerous other musical works.

While living in Paris, Rousseau began an affair with a seamstress, Therese Levassuer. They had five illegitimate children, and abandoned each of them at the local foundling's home. This did not stop Rousseau from later claiming to be an expert on child rearing and education. Rousseau and Levasseur eventually married, and she became the sole heir of the philosopher's estate. In Alaska, Rousseau Peak and nearby Mount Lavasseur (*sic*) are named for the couple.

Socrates (470–399 BC). Athenian philosopher. Socrates was Plato's teacher and mentor. He was a vocal critic of Athenian democracy, and his students conspired with Sparta and the domestic aristocracy to overthrow the Athenian government. Socrates was eventually arrested, tried, condemned, and executed for impiety and corrupting Athenian youth. Plato considered Socrates to be the only true philosopher in a city full of sophists, but Aristophanes portrayed him as an eccentric and corrupt sophist in his comedy, *The Clouds*.

Socrates consciously sought to leave no material trace of his existence after his death. He became immortal against his will, thanks to Plato and other admirers.

Solon (640–560 BC). Athenian leader and political reformer. Solon wrote a new Athenian constitution during a time of acute conflict between the aristocracy and upstart democrats. It established the rule of law, reformed Athenian class society, ended debt slavery, and instituted a variety of quasi-democratic reforms. After Athens swore to uphold his laws for at least ten years, Solon went into voluntary exile, so that he could not be accused of interfering with or benefitting from his reforms. Solon's constitution influenced Athenian politics through the democratic era. While in exile, Solon traveled to Egypt, Lydia, and Cyprus. When he returned to Athens, he found the city still in turmoil, and retreated to Cyprus, where he lived for the rest of his life.

Margaret Thatcher (1925–2013). British politician, barrister, and research chemist. Mrs. Thatcher was the daughter of an English greengrocer, who rose quickly through the ranks of the Conservative Party. While serving as Education Secretary (1970–1974), she abolished Britain's free milk program and became known as "Thatcher the milk snatcher." As Prime Minister, from 1979–1990, she became the formidable "Iron Lady." Thatcher believed in liberty, individual responsibility, and limited government. Her supporters maintain that she saved Britain from socialism, class conflict, and permanent economic malaise; her critics claim that she destroyed the British social contract, promoted individual greed and selfishness, and systematically favored the rich at the expense of the poor.

Alexis de Tocqueville (1805–1859). French political scientist, sociologist, and politician. De Tocqueville's classic work, *Democracy in America*, is arguably the most important study of democratic theory and practice in history. De Tocqueville wrote the book to teach France how democracy worked in the United States, so that the country it could democratize without repeating the violent excesses of the French Revolution. American jurist and statesman Joseph Story later accused de Tocqueville of stealing most of his ideas from Story's *Commentaries on the Constitution of the United States*, and from other contemporary American sources.

Bibliography

Acton, John Emerich Edward Dalberg, *Essays in the History of Liberty: Selected Writings of Lord Acton* (Liberty Classics 1985).

Albertoni, E. A., *Mosca and the Theory of Elitism* (Blackwell 1982).

Anderson, James, *Transnational Democracy: Political Spaces and Border Crossings* (Routledge 2002).

Archibugi, Daniele and David Held, *Re-Imagining Political Community: Studies in Cosmopolitan Democracy* (Simon & Schuster 2001).

Arendt, Hannah, *Eichmann in Jerusalem: A Report on the Banality of Evil* (Viking 1963).

On Revolution (Penguin 1963).

The Human Condition (Penguin 1958).

Aristophanes, *Aristophanes, Three Comedies* (Ann Arbor Paperbacks 1987).

Ayittey, George B. N., *Indigenous African Institutions* (Transnational Publishers 1991).

Bailyn, Bernard, *The Ideological Origins of the American Revolution* (Harvard University Press 1967).

Barber, Benjamin, *Strong Democracy* (University of California Press 1984).

Baum, Lyman Frank, *The Wonderful Wizard of Oz* (George M. Hill Company 1900).

Beard, Charles A., *An Economic Analysis of the Constitution of the United States* (Dover Publications 2004).

Benhabib, Seyla (ed.), *Democracy and Difference* (Princeton University Press 1996).

Berlin, Isaiah, *Four Essays on Liberty* (Oxford University Press 1990).

Berlinski, Claire, *There Is No Alternative: Why Margaret Thatcher Matters* (Basic Books 2008).

Bishop, Bill and Robert G. Cushing, *The Big Sort: Why the Clustering of Like-Minded America Is Tearing Us Apart* (Houghton Mifflin Harcourt 2008).

Bohman, James and William Rehg, *Deliberative Democracy: Essays on Reason and Politics* (MIT Press 1997).

Carlyle, Thomas, *Latter-Day Pamphlets* (Create Space 2013).

Chua, Amy, *World on Fire: How Exporting Free Market Democracy Breeds Ethnic Hatred and Global Instability* (Doubleday 2002).

Craig, John Herbert McCutcheon, *A History of Red Tape: An Account of the Origins and Development of the Civil Service* (Macdonald & Evans 1955).

Cray, Ed, *Chief Justice* (Simon & Schuster 1997).

Cronin, Thomas E., *Direct Democracy: The Politics of Initiative, Referendum, and Recall* (Harvard University Press 1989).

Dahl, Robert A., *On Democracy* (Yale University Press 2000).

  Democracy and Its Critics (Yale University Press 1989).

  A Preface to Democratic Theory (University of Chicago Press 1963).

  Who Governs? Democracy and Power in an American City (Yale University Press 1961).

Downs, Anthony, *An Economic Theory of Democracy* (Harper 1957).

Dunn, John, *Democracy: A History* (Atlantic Monthly Press 2006).

  Democracy: The Unfinished Journey (Oxford University Press 1994).

El Fadl, Khaled Abou, *Islam and the Challenge of Democracy* (Princeton University Press 2004).

Elshtain, Jean Bethke, *Democracy on Trial* (Anansi 1993).

Femia, Joseph V., *Marxism and Democracy* (Clarendon Press 1993).

Florini, Ann, *The Coming Democracy: New Rules for Running the World* (Island Press 2003).

Foner, Eric, *History of American Freedom* (Norton 1998).

Gillman, Howard, *The Votes That Counted: How the Court Decided the 2000 Presidential Election* (University of Chicago Press 2001).

Guinier, Lani, *The Tyranny of the Majority: Fundamental Fairness in Representative Democracy* (Free Press. 1994).

Gutmann, Amy, *Identity and Democracy* (Princeton University Press 2003).

Gutmann, Amy and Dennis Thompson, *Why Deliberative Democracy?* (Princeton University Press 2004).

Hamidani, MarYam G., Hazel Rose Markus, and Alyssa S. Fu, "In the Land of the Free, Interdependent Action Undermines Motivation," 24 *Psychological Science* 189 (2013).

Hansen, Bradley A., "The Fable of the Allegory: The Wizard of Oz in Economics," 33 *Journal of Economic Education* 254 (2002).

Hansen, Mogens Herman, *The Athenian Democracy in the Age of Demosthenes: Structure, Principles, and Ideology* (Blackwell 1991).

  The Athenian Assembly in the Age of Demosthenes (Blackwell 1987).

Hart, Michael and Antoni Negri, *Multitude: War and Democracy in the Age of Empire* (Penguin 2004).

Hayduk, Ron, *Democracy for All: Restoring Immigrant Voting Rights in the United States* (Routledge 2006).

Hendriks, Frank and Th. A. J. Toonen, *Polder Politics: The Re-invention of Consensus Democracy in the Netherlands* (Ashgate Press 2001).

Hooker, Richard, *The Works of Richard Hooker: Of the Laws of Ecclesiastical Polity and Other Works* (CreateSpace 2010).

Hume, David, *Essays, Moral, Political, and Literary* (Liberty Fund 1987).

Jay, Antony and Jonathan Lynn, *The Complete Yes Minister* (BBC Books 1989).

  The Complete Yes Prime Minister (BBC Books 1989).

Kann, Mark E., *Thinking about Politics: Two Political Sciences* (West 1980).

Kant, Immanuel, *Perpetual Peace: A Philosophical Sketch, 1795* (Classic Reprint 2012).

Kaufman, Herbert, *Red Tape: Its Origins, Uses, and Abuses* (Brookings Institution Press 1977).

Kidd, Thomas S., *God of Liberty: A Religious History of the American Revolution* (Basic Books 2012).

Klinghoffer, Judith Apter and Lois Elkis, "'The Petticoat Electors': Women's Suffrage in New Jersey, 1776–1807," 12 *Journal of the Early Republic* 159 (1992).

Levin, Michael *The Spectre of Democracy: The Rise of Modern Democracy as Seen by Its Critics* (Macmillan 1992).

Lijphart, Arend, *Patterns of Majoritarian and Consensus Government in Twenty-One Countries* (Yale University Press 1984).

  Democracy in Plural Societies: A Comparative Exploration (Yale University Press 1977).

Lindberg, Staffan, *Democracy and Elections in Africa* (The Johns Hopkins University Press 2006).

Littlefield, Henry, "The Wizard of Oz: Parable on Populism," 16 *American Quarterly* 47 (1964).

Locke, John, *Two Treatises of Government and A Letter Concerning Toleration* (Yale University Press 2003).

Locke, John and Mark Goldie, *Locke: Political Essays* (Cambridge University Press 1997).

Macpherson, C. B., *The Real World of Democracy* (Canadian Broadcasting Corporation 1965).

Madison, James, Alexander Hamilton, and John Jay, *The Federalist Papers* (Signet Classic 1961).

Magagna, Victor V., *Communities of Grain: Rural Rebellion in Comparative Perspective* (Cornell University Press 1991).

Manin, Bernard, *The Principles of Representative Government* (Cambridge University Press 1997).

Mansbridge, Jane J., *Beyond Adversary Democracy* (Basic Books 1980).

Markoff, John, *Waves of Democracy: Social Movements and Political Change* (Pine Forge Press 1996).

Matsusaka, John G., *For the Many or the Few: The Initiative, Public Policy, and American Democracy* (University of Chicago 2005).

May, Larry and Stacey Hoffman, *Collective Responsibility: Five Decades of Debate in Theoretical and Applied Ethics Savage* (Rowman & Littlefield 1991).

Meacham, Jon, *Thomas Jefferson: The Art of Power* (Deckle Edge 2012).

Meyer, Lisa S., "Taking the 'Complexity' Out of Complex Litigation: Preserving the Constitutional Right to a Civil Jury Trial," 28 *Valparaiso Law Review* 337 (1993).

Michels, Robert, *Political Parties, a Sociological Study of the Oligarchical Tendencies of Modern Democracy* (Free Press 1966).

Mill, John Stuart, *On Liberty and the Subjection of Women* (Penguin Classics 2007).

Moore, Jr., Barrington, *Social Origins of Dictatorship and Democracy: Lord and Peasant in the Making of the Modern World* (Beacon Press 1966).

Morstein-Marx, Robert, *Mass Oratory and Political Power in the Late Roman Republic* (Cambridge University Press 2004).

Mosca, Gaetano, *The Ruling Class* (McGraw-Hill, 1939).

Mouffe, Chantal, *The Democratic Paradox* (Verso 2000).

Mwakikagile, Godfrey, *Africa and the West* (Nova Science Publishers 2000).

Nisbett, Richard E., *The Geography of Thought: How Asians and Westerners Think Differently ... and Why* (Free Press 2003).

Nozick, Robert, *Anarchy, State, and Utopia* (Basic Books 1977).

Nye, Joseph S. and John D. Donahue, *Governance in a Globalizing World* (Brookings Institution Press, 2000).

Ossewaarde, M. R. R., *Tocqueville's Moral and Political Thought: New Liberalism* (Routledge Press 2004).

Owusu, Maxwell, "Democracy and Africa – a View from the Village," 30 *The Journal of Modern African Studies* 369 (1992).

Pareto, Vilfredo, *The Rise and Fall of Elites* (Transaction Publishers 1991).

Pateman, Carole, *Participation and Democratic Theory* (Cambridge: Cambridge University Press 1970).

Peltason, Jack W., *58 Lonely Men: Southern Federal Judges and School Desegregation* (University of Illinois Press 1971).

Phillips, Anne, *Feminism and Politics* (Oxford University Press 1998).

The Politics of Presence (Oxford University Press 1995).

Pitkin, Hanna Fenichel, *The Concept of Representation* (University of California Press 1967).

Pleij, Herman, *Hollands Welbehagen [The Wellbeing of Holland]* (Ooievaar 1998).

Plutarch, *Greek Lives* (Oxford World Classics 2009).

Putnam, Robert D., *Bowling Alone: The Collapse and Revival of American Community* (Simon & Schuster 2001).

"Bowling Alone: America's Declining Social Capital," 6 *Journal of Democracy* 65 (1995).

Reinicke, Wolfgang H., *Global Public Policy: Governing without Government?* (Brookings Institution Press 1998).

Rejai, Mostafa, *Democracy: The Contemporary Theories* (Atherton Press 1967).

Ritter, Gretchen, "Silver Slippers and a Golden Cap: L. Frank Baum's *The Wonderful Wizard of Oz* and Historical Memory in American Politics," 31 *Journal of American Studies* 171 (1997).

Sandel, Michael, *Democracy's Discontent: America in Search of a Public Philosophy* (Harvard University Press 1998).

Sartori, Giovanni, *Theory of Democracy Revisited* (Chatham House 1987).

Schreuder, Yda, "The Polder Model in Dutch Economic and Environmental Planning," 21 *Bulletin of Science, Technology & Society* 237 (2001).

Schumpeter, Joseph, *Capitalism, Socialism, and Democracy* (Allen and Unwin 1943).

Shapiro, Ian and Casiano Hacker-Cordon, *Democracy's Edges* (Cambridge University Press 1999).

Sinclair, R. K., *Democracy and Participation in Athens* (Cambridge University Press 1988).

Sklar, Richard L., "Democracy in Africa," 26 *African Studies Review* 11 (1983).

Slater, Philip, *The Pursuit of Loneliness* (Beacon Press 1990).

Stevenson, Randolph T. and Lynn Vavreck, "Does Campaign Length Matter? Testing for Cross-National Effects," 30 *British Journal of Political Science* 217 (2000).

Stiglitz, Joseph E., *The Price of Inequality: How Today's Divided Society Endangers Our Future* (W. W. Norton 2012).

Story, Joseph, *Commentaries on the Constitution of the United States* (3 vols., Hilliard, Gray and Company 1833).

Taylor, Charles, "The Dynamics of Democratic Exclusion," 9 *Journal of Democracy* 143 (1998).

Taylor, Lilly Ross, *Roman Voting Assemblies from the Hannibalic War to the Dictatorship of Caesar* (University of Michigan Press 1966).

Thucydides, *Thucydides: The War of the Peloponnesians and the Athenians* (Cambridge University Press 2013).

History of the Peloponnesian War (Penguin Classics 1954).

Tocqueville, Alexis de, *Democracy in America* (University of Chicago Press 2011).

Journey to America (Greenwood Press 1981).

Waldron, Jeremy, "Participation: The Right to Have Rights," 98 *Proceedings of the Aristotelian Society* 307 (1998).

Weber, Max, *Economy and Society* (2 vols., University of California Press 1978).

Williams, J. Michael, *Chieftaincy, the State, and Democracy* (Indiana University Press 2009).

"Leading from Behind: Democratic Consolidation and the Chieftaincy in South Africa," 42 *The Journal of Modern African Studies* 113 (2004).

Williams, Melissa, *Voice, Trust, and Memory: Marginalized Groups and the Failings of Liberal Representation* (Princeton University 1998).

Wills, Garry, *Explaining America: The Federalist* (Penguin 2001).

Yakobson, Alexander, *Elections and Electioneering in Rome: A Study in the Political System of the Late Republic* (F. Steiner 1999).

Young, Iris Marion, *Inclusion and Democracy* (Oxford University Press 2000).

Zakaria, Fareed, "The Rise of Illiberal Democracy," 76 *Foreign Affairs* 22 (1997).

Index